real world
micro

eleventh edition

edited by

Amy Offner,
Chris Tilly, and the
Dollars & Sense
Collective

REAL WORLD MICRO
ELEVENTH EDITION

ISBN: 1-878585-29-0

Published by:

Dollars and Sense
Economic Affairs Bureau, Inc.
740 Cambridge Street
Cambridge, MA 02141-1401

617-876-2434
617-876-0008
dollars@dollarsandsense.org
www.dollarsandsense.org

Real World Micro is edited by the *Dollars & Sense* Collective — publishers of *Dollars & Sense* magazine and *Real World Macro, Real World Globalization, Current Economic Issues, Real World Banking, Introduction to Political Economy, Unlevel Playing Fields,* and *The Environment in Crisis.*

The *Dollars & Sense* collective: Marc Breslow, Beth Burgess, Chuck Collins, Ellen Frank, Amy Gluckman, Erkut Gomulu, Maryalice Guilford, Darius Mehri, John Miller, Amy Offner, Laura Orlando, Alejandro Reuss, Adria Scharf, Chris Tilly, Rodney Ward, Adam Weiss, Thad Williamson, and Jeanne Winner.

Interns: Ben Boothby, Dori Peleg, Todd Tavares, James P. Wirth.

Cover Art and Design: Nick Thorkelson
Production: Sheila Walsh

Manufactured by Transcontinental Printing
Printed in Canada

CONTENTS

CHAPTER 6: LABOR MARKETS AND THE DISTRIBUTION OF INCOME

CHAPTER 7: MARKET FAILURE, GOVERNMENT POLICY, AND CORPORATE GOVERNANCE

CHAPTER 8: POLICY SPOTLIGHT: INDUSTRY SUBSIDIES AND INTERNATIONAL TRADE

INTRODUCTION

THE TWO ECONOMIES

It sometimes seems that the United States has not one, but two economies. The first economy exists in economics textbooks and in the minds of many elected officials. It is a free-market economy, a system of promise and plenty, a cornucopia of consumer goods. In this economy, people are free and roughly equal, and each individual carefully looks after him- or herself, making uncoerced choices to advance their own economic interests. Government is but an afterthought in this world, since almost everything people need can be provided by the free market, itself guided by the reassuring "invisible hand."

The second economy is described in the writings of progressives, environmentalists, union supporters, and consumer advocates—as well as honest business writers who recognize that real-world markets do not always conform to textbook models. This second economy features vast disparities of income, wealth, and power. It is an economy where employers have power over employees, where large firms have the power to shape markets, and where large corporate lobbies have the power to shape public policies. In this second economy, government sometimes adopts policies that ameliorate the abuses of capitalism, and other times does just the opposite, but it is always an active and essential participant in economic life.

If you are reading this introduction, you are probably a student in an introductory college course in microeconomics. Your textbook will introduce you to the first economy, the harmonious world of free markets. *Real World Micro* will introduce you to the second.

WHY "REAL WORLD" MICRO?

A standard economics textbook is full of powerful concepts. It is also, by its nature, a limited window on the economy. What is taught in most introductory economics courses today is in fact just one strand of economic thought—neoclassical economics. Fifty years ago, many more strands were part of the introductory economics curriculum, and the contraction of the field has imposed limits on the study of economics that can confuse and frustrate students. This is particularly true in the study of microeconomics, which looks at markets for individual goods or services.

Real World Micro is designed as a supplement to a standard neoclassical textbook. Its articles provide vivid, real-world illustrations of economic concepts. But beyond that, our mission is to address two major sources of confusion in the study of economics at the introductory level.

The first source of confusion is the striking simplification of the world found in orthodox microeconomics. Standard textbooks describe stylized economic interactions that bear scant resemblance to the messy realities of buying, selling, producing, and consuming that we see around us. There is nothing wrong with simplifying. In fact, every social science *must* develop simplified models—precisely because reality is so complex, we must look at it a little bit at a time in order to understand it. Still, much mainstream economic analysis calls to mind the story of the tipsy party-goer whose friend finds him on his hands and knees under a streetlight. "What are you doing?" asks the friend. "I dropped my car keys across the street, and I'm looking for them," the man replies. "But if you lost them across the street, how come you're looking over here?" "Well, the light's better here." In the interest of greater clarity, economics often imposes similar limits on its areas of inquiry.

As the title *Real World Micro* implies, one of our goals is to rub mainstream microeconomic theory up against reality—to direct attention to the areas not illuminated by the streetlight, and particularly to examine how inequality, power, and environmental imbalance change the picture. The idea is not to prove the standard theory "wrong," but to challenge you to think about *where* the theory is more and less useful, and *why* markets may not act as expected.

This focus on real-world counterpoints to economic theory connects to the second issue we aim to clarify. Most economics texts uncritically present key assumptions and propositions that form the core of standard economic theory. They offer much less exploration of a set of related questions: What are alternative propositions about the economy? Under what circumstances will these alternatives more accurately describe the economy? What difference do such propositions make? Our approach is not to spell out an alternative theory in detail, but to raise questions and present real-life examples that bring these questions to life. For example, textbooks carefully lay out "consumer sovereignty"—the notion that consumers' wishes ultimately determine what the economy will produce. But can we reconcile consumer sovereignty with an economy one of whose main products—in industries such as soft drinks, autos, and music—is consumer desire itself? We think it is valuable to see ideas like consumer sovereignty as debatable propositions—which requires hearing other views in the debate.

In short, our goal in this book is to use real-world examples from today's economy to raise questions, stimulate debate, and dare you to think critically about the models in your textbook.

WHAT'S IN THIS BOOK

Real World Micro is organized to follow the outline of a standard economics text. We have specifically keyed our table of contents to David Colander's *Economics* (5th edition) and its *Microeconomics* "split," but since the topics covered by all major texts are similar, this reader is a good fit with other textbooks as well. Each chapter leads off with a brief introduction, including study questions for the entire chapter, and then provides several short articles from *Dollars & Sense* magazine that illustrate the chapter's key concepts—42 articles in all. In many cases, the articles have been updated or otherwise edited to heighten their relevance.

Here is a quick walk through the chapters.

Chapter 1, Markets: Ideology and Reality, starts off the volume by taking a hard look at the strengths and weaknesses of markets, with special attention to weaknesses that standard textbooks tend to underemphasize.

Chapter 2, Supply and Demand, presents real-world examples of supply, demand, and taxation in action. *Dollars & Sense* authors question the conventional wisdom on topics such as rent control and tax fairness.

Chapter 3, Consumers, raises provocative questions about utility theory and individual consumer choice. What happens when marketers shape buyers' tastes? What happens when important information is hidden from consumers? Does consumer society threaten environmental sustainability?

Chapter 4, Firms, Production, and Profit Maximization, illustrates how business strategies often squeeze workers to boost profits—and challenges students to think about other ways of organizing work.

Chapter 5, Market Structure and Monopoly, spotlights monopoly power, just one example of the unequal power relationships that pervade our economic system. The chapter critiques monopoly power in pharmaceutical and agribusiness companies, but also questions whether small business dominance would be an improvement.

Chapter 6, Labor Markets and Income Distribution, examines problems of workforce discrimination and inequality, and discusses policy solutions.

Chapter 7, Market Failure, debates when and how public policy should address both particular and systemic failures of markets, with particular attention to environmental issues.

Chapter 8, Policy Spotlight: Industry Subsidies and International Trade, continues the discussion of public policy, offering alternative views on these two controversial and timely topics.

KEY TO COLANDER

In each chapter introduction, we provide a key that links our text to David Colander's *Economics*, 5th edition. The chapters in that book's microeconomics "split," *Microeconomics*, 5th edition, are numbered identically, so these keys should work with either version of Colander's book. Professors and students using other textbooks should, of course, feel free to ignore these keys. Here is the summary key for the entire table of contents.

Chapter 1 – Colander chapters 1-3
Chapter 2 – Colander chapters 4-7
Chapter 3 – Colander chapter 8
Chapter 4 – Colander chapters 9-11
Chapter 5 – Colander chapters 12-15
Chapter 6 – Colander chapters 16-17
Chapter 7 – Colander chapters 18 and 20
Chapter 8 – Colander chapters 19 and 21

CHAPTER 1
Markets: Ideology and Reality

INTRODUCTION

Economics is all about tradeoffs. The concept of opportunity cost reminds us that in order to make a purchase, or even to make use of a resource that you control (such as your time), you must give up other possible purchases, other possible uses. Markets broaden the range of possible tradeoffs by facilitating exchange between people who do not know each other, and in many cases never meet at all—think of buying a pair of athletic shoes in Atlanta from a company based in Los Angeles that manufactures shoes in Malaysia and has stockholders all over the world. As the idea of gains from trade suggests, markets allow many exchanges that make both parties better off.

But markets have severe limitations as well. The articles in this chapter probe some of them. Markets ration goods to those most able to pay (Frank, article 1.1). As Nobel prize-winning economist Amartya Sen points out, in extreme circumstances such as famine, the ordinary functioning of the market ensures that poor people starve even though food is available—at a price (Reuss, article 1.2). More generally, if we rely on markets to distribute goods that we think of as basic needs or even rights—health care, housing, education, and so on—lower-income people will get "rationed out," receiving fewer or poorer-quality goods (Gluckman, article 1.4). What's more, markets are built around *private* decisions to produce or consume. When society needs to make some basic investment that will benefit *the public* (such as vaccinations, a mass transit system, or the infrastructure of the Internet), markets often fall down on the job (Baxandall, article 1.3).

KEY TO COLANDER

This chapter is designed to be used with Chapters 1-3.

Most of these articles are keyed to ideas in Chapter 3, "The Evolving U.S. Economy in Perspective."

They also anticipate some of the arguments put forward in Chapter 5 under the heading, "The Roles of Government."

DISCUSSION QUESTIONS

1) (General) What things should *not* be for sale? Beyond everyday goods and services, think about human bodies, votes, small countries, and other things that might be bought and sold. How do you draw the line between what should be for sale and what should not be?

2) (General) Advocates of unregulated markets often argue that deregulating markets doesn't just promote mutually beneficial exchanges, but also fundamentally expands freedom. Explain the logic of their argument, the logic of the opposing view, and evaluate the two points of view.

3) (General) If not markets, what? What are other ways to organize economic activity? Which are best equipped to solve the problems raised in this chapter?

4) (Frank) Ellen Frank claims that markets erode democracy. Explain her perspective. Do you agree? Do *all* markets undermine democracy?

5) (Reuss) Amartya Sen leaves open the possibility that "hard-headed investment calculations" explain why many more boys than girls survive to adulthood in poor countries. Explain and evaluate his reasoning. What would it take to prevent this from happening?

6) (Baxandall) Many argue that open markets are needed to unleash the potential of information technology. Phineas Baxandall says that just the opposite is true. Explain the two opposing viewpoints. Where do you come down in this debate?

7) (Gluckman) Boosters of educational management organizations (EMOs) say that privatization, by bringing competition to education, will result in innovation and improved efficiency. Amy Gluckman counters that for the most part this has not happened, and that EMOs have resorted to socially destructive ways to cut costs. Explain. If Gluckman is correct that EMOs have not increased efficiency, why do you think they are spreading?

February 1999

THE IDEOLOGY OF THE FREE MARKET

BY ELLEN FRANK

When the County Commissioner for Lake County, Florida, proposed last year that the fire department be turned over to a private, for-profit company, he unleashed a torrent of opposition and the idea was dropped. Throughout the United States, similar proposals to "privatize" public schools, education, and health services face strong resistance from taxpayers and state workers. Yet the overall trend in U.S. public policy for at least 20 years has been toward greater reliance on market forces and the profit motive to provide what used to be considered public goods and services.

In liberal Massachusetts, substantial portions of the public bus system are now run by private businesses; in New York City, private security forces patrol sections of Manhattan. Nationwide, some 15% of hospital beds are now owned and operated by for-profit corporations. Privately run prisons, trash disposal companies, social service providers are growing in importance everywhere.

"The era of big government," President Clinton announced a few years ago, "is over." In its place we have the market. But can the market deliver?

MARKET MYTHS

Markets, boosters contend, foster individual freedom. Consumers in market economies are free to express their individuality, assert their unique identity, by buying the precise things they want. For Americans raised on 28 choices of breakfast cereal, one-size-fits-all, big-government fire departments and health-care programs just won't do. Competition, so the story goes, will lead to more and better choices. Why? Because firms can only make money by producing what consumers are willing to pay for.

Governments and non-profit institutions might be less greedy, more humane in their motives, but they are under no particular pressure to cater to consumer demand. The profit motive is the consumer's best friend, forcing firms, as the textbooks say, to allocate resources efficiently, producing only the goods consumers desire.

MARKET REALITIES

The problem with this rosy view of things is that all voices are not equal in the market place. Upper-income consumers, with cash to spare, can bid up prices and walk away with the lion's share of society's output. For poorer folks, the vaunted "rationing" function of prices often means being priced out of the market, unable to afford the goods they want and need.

There is no question that market economies deliver goods in abundance. Wherever capitalism has been given free reign, streets are choked with automobiles and shops overflow with goods. When the former Soviet countries embraced capitalist markets several years ago, for example, commentators noted the extraordinary increase in goods available for sale. Formerly barren store shelves suddenly burst with local and imported goods of every manner and description. Unfortunately, though, few people in Russia could afford to buy any of it. The markets operated mainly for the benefit of a small and wealthy elite.

MARKET INEQUITIES

Evidence abounds that markets, unless tempered by active government interventions, open up vast chasms of social and economic inequality, generating unprecedented affluence but also astounding poverty. The United Nations in its most recent report on human development found that, as markets expanded throughout the world, the richest one fifth of the world's population consumed 86% of the world's output, while the poorest fifth received just over 1%. The richest 225 people in the world today have assets equal to the annual income of the poorest 2.5 billion people.

In the United States, where faith in markets amounts to a state religion, such issues are rarely broached. Staggering levels of inequality are everywhere to be seen, yet rarely discussed. In a country where exclusion on the basis of race or gender is widely regarded as intolerable, Americans routinely accept exclusion on the basis of income. Imagine if every up-scale suburb were to post signs at their borders saying, "Minimum Annual Income of $1,000,000 Required for Residence." Americans might be shocked by the candor, but not by the sentiment.

In America, the wealthy are distrusted, but not despised, and Bill Gates, whose personal wealth (now some $40 billion) equals the total wealth of the poorest 106 million Americans, is feted in the press, a kind of cultural icon.

MARKETS AND FREEDOM

Advocates of free markets don't apologize for these tremendous inequities. The freedom to choose, they contend, isn't only about breakfast cereals and fashion statements. Individuals in market economies must compete for the rewards the market doles out. People can choose to be rich, or not to be; to work hard or to take it easy; to succeed or to fail. In a market economy, people get what they deserve, or so the myth goes.

But this myth ignores the very serious inequities in power that flow, inevitably, from inequities in income. High incomes lead to wealth and wealth to the exercise of power, the ability to control others, to command their labor and constrain their freedom, including their freedom to buy and sell. This is why it is illegal, in most countries, to sell your organs for transplant, though there is no lack of willing buyers and sellers. It is legal to sell your blood for transfusion or (in some places) your body for sex, and studies of the markets for blood and for prostitutes come to the same finding: when human bodies are exchanged for money, the poor lose control of their bodies.

MARKETS AND DEMOCRACY

The freedom promised by markets is, for this reason, incompatible with democratic ideals of free, self-governing citizens. In democratic countries, governments provide basic goods and services and restrict market transactions not because doing so is "efficient," but because the freedom from want and exploitation is a precondition for meaningful citizenship. For example, 43 million Americans currently lack even minimal health care coverage; as the health care system shifts into for-profit mode, these people are at risk of falling too ill to compete in the marketplace or even to participate freely in governance.

If education were to become a buy-and-sell proposition, as some conservatives advocate, large numbers of citizens (and prospective citizens) will go uneducated and unable, therefore, to exercise their rights or protect their freedoms.

Economic inequities are not the only injury markets cause to democratic practice. The insatiable quest for gain that propels behavior in the marketplace disrupts the ecology of the earth and uproots communities. All over the world, clear-cutting, deforestation, strip-mining, toxic-dumping, and other environmentally damaging excesses of unrestrained markets have torn apart stable, self-governing towns and villages, turning secure citizens out on the open road; the hobos and homeless of our modern era.

The competitiveness engendered by markets is also at odds with democratic ideals. Psychologist Alfie Kohn has shown, for example, that people in competitive situations are more likely to cheat and to express feelings of distrust. Yet a spirit of trust and cooperation is essential to successful governance.

In opposing the private takeover of their fire department, the citizens of Lake County, Florida, seem to have understood a basic truth about limitations of markets. It may well be that private, for-profit firms can fight fires or patrol the streets more cheaply than the government can, but a trusted government can fight fires and patrol streets more democratically.

ARTICLE 1.2

January/February 1999

NOBEL PRIZE WINNER TWEAKS FREE MARKETEERS

BY ALEJANDRO REUSS

Last October, Amartya Sen, a leading authority on hunger and an unrelenting advocate for the most deprived, won the rare accolade of the Nobel Prize for Economics. Still rarer was his "honor" of being denounced the day after winning by the free-marketeers on the op-ed page of *The Wall Street Journal*.

Journal editorialist Robert L. Pollock accused Sen of having "done little but give voice to the muddleheaded views of ... establishment leftists." Sen is in fact one of the most wide-ranging and questioning economists in the field, whose thoughts are as likely to turn to philosophical investigations of equality as to the measurement of economic well-being.

Born in Bengal, India, in 1933, Sen witnessed the Bengal famine of 1943 in his youth. This experience not only shaped his urgent concern with hunger, but also his "entitlement" approach to the study of famine. This approach starts with the insight that having food available in a country or region does not mean everyone living there is "entitled" to it. In market economies, people are entitled to food according to their ability to produce it for themselves or to pay or swap for it.

If some group loses its entitlement to food, whether there is a decline in the available supply or not, a famine can occur. This may seem obvious, yet before — and after — Sen, famine studies have remained fixated on the drop in food available instead of whether specific social groups are entitled to it.

Sen's analysis illuminates the causes not only of the Bengal famine — in which the booming wartime economy priced rural workers, with their low, stagnant incomes, out of the food market — but also of the Irish famine of 1848 and sub-Saharan famines of the 1980s, when food was exported from famine areas to areas where it could fetch a higher price.

> IN MARKET ECONOMIES, IF SOME GROUP LOSES ITS ENTITLEMENT TO FOOD, WHETHER THERE IS A DECLINE IN THE AVAILABLE SUPPLY OR NOT, A FAMINE CAN OCCUR.

Sen's analysis points to relief measures different from the typical "get food to the famine areas" approach. After all, there may be enough food present. Rather, for Sen, the issue is to restore the starving groups' entitlement to food. Cash relief or public works programs, therefore, may be the most effective responses to the danger of famine. Such policies can kick the market into reverse, causing the private food trade to bring food to those in danger, rather than take it away.

It is typical of Sen's work that he acknowledges the positive role that both state action and private markets can play in averting famine, and warns against one-sided ideological prescriptions (whether "indiscriminate liberalism" or "paralysing control") that can hurt famine victims further.

Sen also reveals how distinctions among poor people mark some as vulnerable during famines. While he credits Marx for understanding the economic insecurity of wage workers in general, famine, he says, often strikes subgroups of caste or gender. The same principle holds within families. Looking at family income or resources alone can obscure the deprivation of some household members compared to others.

In *Hunger and Public Action*, Sen (with Jean Drèze) notes that in the early stages of famine, young children are usually protected, the elderly are frequently neglected, and adult men are usually prioritized over adult women.

Even during normal, nonfamine, times in much of the world, women and girls suffer much higher death rates than boys and men, despite the fact that, physiologically, females are hardier than males. Females should have lower rates of death given similar access to food and medical care.

In Europe, North America, and to a lesser extent sub-Saharan Africa, the female-to-male ratio is about what you'd expect, with more women than men. China and Southern Asia are another story, say Sen and Drèze. To have a ratio in China similar to that in sub-Saharan Africa, one would have to add 44 million women. That is, there are 44 million "missing women" due to the relative deprivation (and resulting higher rates of death) of women and especially girls compared to men and boys. In India, the "missing women" number about 37 million. Worldwide, the number exceeds 100 million.

Sen argues that there are fewer missing females where women enjoy independence and greater control of resources such as land, or better access to outside employment. He leaves open the question of whether families make "hard-headed investment calculations" favoring boys over girls to take advantage of boys' higher future earning potential. His attitude is, however, markedly different from that of free-market economists who complacently accept the circumstances under which these sorts of "rationally maximizing" calculations are made.

Instead, Sen emphasizes that no famine has ever raged in a country with an oppositional press and functioning electoral system, since hell-raising by newspapers and oppositional political groups at the first signs of starvation forces governments into action. While it's not enough to end all hunger or gender inequity, Sen, with Drèze, finds hope in civic action: "Ultimately," they write, "public action will be determined by what the public is ready to do, what sacrifices it is ready to make, what things it is determined to demand, and what it refuses to tolerate."

March/April 2002

DOES THE 'NEW ECONOMY' TILT TO THE RIGHT?

BY PHINEAS BAXANDALL

Back in the 1950s, the Soviet Union proclaimed that computerization heralded the triumph of centralized economic planning over decentralized markets. Computers would allow planners to process unprecedented amounts of information and accurately forecast and fine-tune the economy. Success with computerization at individual plants and regional ministries only made Soviet officials more confident of its potential for the economy as a whole. Across the sea, U.S. officials fretted that the Soviets were right, that the Soviet economy was catching up to the West, and that computerization would show the world that markets were obsolete.

The Soviet vision of a computer-planned future may seem silly today, but it puts in perspective the recent free-market hype about the so-called "New Economy." Free-marketeers, no less than Soviet bureaucrats, tend to project their own fondest wishes onto technology itself. "Governments of the Industrial World, you weary giants of flesh and steel," cyberlibertarian John Perry Barlow demands, "on behalf of the future, I ask you of the past to leave us alone." The main effect of the "New Economy" has been to convince people that information technology and computer networks somehow make government regulation obsolete—more or less the Soviet dream in reverse.

Today, the bloom is off the rose of the "New Economy." With high-tech stock prices plummeting after March 2000 (the NASDAQ index lost over half its value within a year), few people still believe that a computer and an online stock account guarantee overnight riches. Dot-com millionaires no longer represent the glorious future, and chastened "New Economy" boosters have had to accept that the business cycle is not just an iron-age relic. Nonetheless, even in today's recession, we still hear that government regulation is an "Old Economy" dinosaur.

Three largely unexamined myths perpetuate this nonsense. First, the belief that information inherently resists regulation. Second, that the networked economy favors spontaneous markets over slow-footed government bureaucracies. And third, that new technologies have globalized the economy beyond the influence of national governments. There is a grain of truth in each, but none of it leads to the conclusion that public regulation is either impossible or undesirable.

Myth #1: Information must be governed by "free markets" because "information must be free."

Free-market enthusiasts have missed the most novel thing about information goods as a commodity—that after the research and development is done, the cost of producing each unit is very low. Think of software giants. It costs just a few cents to burn each copy of WindowsXP or Excel onto a CD. For digitalized property such as databases, electronic music files (such as the "MP3s" exchanged on Napster), or password-protected information, there is virtually no cost for an additional copy. In economics lingo, the "marginal cost" of these goods is zero or close to zero.

Mainstream "neoclassical" economics argues that the most efficient price for a product is equal to its marginal cost. If the price is lower, people who do not value the product as much as its cost will buy it. If the price is higher, people who value the product more than its cost will forego it. Either way, there will be a "net welfare loss" to society. The neoclassical argument that competitive markets are efficient depends on the view that they push prices to this efficient level. But "zero marginal cost" goods turn these arguments on their head. In the words of Berkeley economist Brad DeLong, the "assumptions ... of the invisible hand fray when transported into tomorrow's information economy."

Take the analogy of paying for a bridge. The bridge is expensive to build, but once it is constructed there is virtually no additional cost for an additional individual to use it. If people are charged more than this miniscule cost, there will be a net welfare loss (since some people who would benefit from using the bridge will be prevented from using it by the artificial cost of the toll). Even mainstream economists are forced to conclude that a private toll is a less efficient way to pay for a bridge than a general tax. The same is true for information goods like digital music files. Once you pay the members of the band and the sound engineers, for example, pretty much all the costs of producing a Metallica song are accounted for, whether you create one digital sound file or millions. Therefore, charging people to download the file would cause a net welfare loss. "Even though economic theory is severely biased toward markets," concludes economist Michael Perelman, "according to the criteria of economics, information should not be treated as private property."

Following this logic, the Canadian government levies a small tax on recording media, such as blank CDs and tapes, and uses the revenue to fund Canadian artists who lose sales as a result of people recording their work for free. Germany and other European countries have explored attaching a fee to the sale of computers and other devices that can be used to copy recorded music. The revenue from this fee would then be distributed to recording companies to compensate them for royalties lost due to unauthorized copying of their copyrighted music. As economist Dean Baker of the Economic Policy Institute argues, this approach has great advantages over prosecuting information "pirates" or adding elaborate mechanisms to disrupt copying: "While there are problems with the system devised by Germany, it should lead to vast economic gains compared to the systems being developed in the United States. The inefficiency associated with the traditional copyright is enormous in the Internet age."

> THE MORE INTERNATIONAL FINANCE SYSTEMS ARE DIGITAL AND NETWORKED, THE MORE VIABLE REGULATION WILL BECOME.

The Internet itself did not result from "free markets" but centralized planning. In the early years of the Cold War, the U.S. Defense Department sought to establish communications networks that might survive a nuclear war. At the time, only the military and large universities had powerful computers, which researchers across the country wanted to use. Networking prevented them from sitting idle. In order to enable different computers to talk to each other, the Defense Department funded the development of communications standards called TCP/IP, adopting them in 1980.

The Defense Department then released the standards for free to the general public. Nobody has to pay to use these technical protocols to send email or post or view web pages. The U.S. government even pushed for the widespread adoption of the freely available TCP/IP standards, instead of alternate versions developed by private European companies that refused to share their inventions. The Web has grown so quickly and become such a rich and varied source of information largely because these open standards make it accessible to anyone with a computer and a modem.

Even outside of government, some of the fastest-growing parts of the "New Economy" have flourished by making technologies freely available. The most important email transport software (Sendmail), the most important Internet server software (Apache), the most widely used programming language on the Web (Perl), the domain-name service for the entire Internet (BIND), and the fastest-growing computer operating system (Linux) are all examples of public domain (or "open-source") software.

Linux is the best known of these "open-source" products. Linus Torvalds, a Finnish computer-science student, invented the new computer operating system in 1991, based on the existing strengths of the UNIX system. But instead of applying for a patent, he posted the code on the Internet for other programmers to add to and improve. Many programmers were interested in the Linux project because UNIX had just been taken over by private firms like IBM. These companies kept their underlying code secret and designed their programs to lock users into their products. Programmers were also worried about the growing dominance of Microsoft's clumsy operating systems. By 1998, over 10,000 software developers from 31 different countries had contributed improvements or helped develop new versions of Linux. By the year 2000, the program boasted about 16 million users and a quarter of the market share. Major high-tech firms, like Intel, Oracle, Dell, Hewlett-Packard, IBM, and Compaq, have all made major commitments to use Linux or cater to Linux users.

A conventional argument for private ownership is that owners have greater incentive to produce things. People are more willing to cultivate a garden on a piece of ground they can fence off, more willing to improve a house when they own it, and more willing to work hard in a business if they share in the profits. But intellectual products can be shared with others without diminishing their value. In fact, computer programs and other information technology are often more valuable when many other people also have them. Many users, for example, do not buy Microsoft Word because they think it is the best word-processing program, but because they know others use the program and will be able to read their files. Likewise, Linux and similar "open-source" projects work so well because they have large numbers of users who identify glitches and devise improvements. They can expect that future versions of the operating system will include not only their contributions but also those of thousands of other contributors. Online communities of programmers voluntarily contribute their efforts to building better software because the product remains in the public domain.

Allowing others to reproduce a computer program does not take anything away from the owner. It merely refuses to help the owner get rich from artificially enforced scarcity. As *Wired* magazine puts it, "The central economic distinction between information and physical property is that information can be transferred without leaving the possession of the original owner. If I sell you my horse, I can't ride him after that. If I sell you what I know, we both know it." This feature of information goods might make redistribution from property owners to the public more politically appealing in the "New Economy" than in the "Old

Economy." Seizing somebody's land or factory to help the poor deprives the old owners of what was theirs. Not so with computer software or digital audio files.

Myth #2: The "networked" economy favors spontaneous and flexible markets over slow-footed regulators.

To many free-marketeers, the Internet is like heaven on earth. It seems to exhibit all the ideal qualities of markets: decentralized, instantaneous, unregulated. The wild growth of online trading (at sites like E*Trade and Ameritrade) and auction sites (like eBay) seems to prove some kind of affinity between "free markets" and the digital age. A recent article in the *Wall Street Journal* urges us to "think of the Internet as an economic-freedom metaphor for our time. The Internet empowers ordinary people and disempowers government."

While it is true that the 1990s saw a rollback in government regulation at the same time as a rapid growth of information technology, the new technology did not cause the tilt towards "free-market" capitalism. Businesses have certainly implemented new technologies in ways that make certain kinds of regulation more difficult. And politicians have often used the "New Economy" as a pretense for opposing social programs or regulatory policies. But these are ultimately political issues. New information technologies did not require the deregulation associated with the "New Economy," and a changing political tide could reverse the ways those technologies have been implemented.

As with all markets, the results of electronic production and commerce depend on what rules govern businesses: what businesses can own, what privileges and responsibilities come with ownership, what kinds of contracts are legally binding, how they will be taxed, etc. This institutional "architecture" of markets is especially important in information technologies.

Unlike traditional markets, whose rules have evolved over hundreds of years, the online architecture is new enough that we can see how it results from specific policies of governments and corporations. Such thinking challenges the notion that market outcomes are "spontaneous" at all.

People in power can use architecture to control the behavior of others, designing environments to encourage certain kinds of actions while discouraging others. If a local government wants to discourage motorists from driving fast down a street, one way is to legislate a speed limit and have police chase down cars that drive too fast. But another way is through the architecture of a speed bump, which changes behavior more automatically, without obvious laws or games of cat and mouse. Architecture can also be used to change behavior in more insidious ways. In the wake of late-1960s campus protests, for example, universities redesigned campuses with fewer open common areas, in order to discourage student demonstrations.

Just as the architecture of buildings manipulates the laws of physics to human ends, so does the architecture of cyberspace constrain online interactions to serve the ends of those who design or control it. America Online (AOL), for example, limits the number of people who can join one of its chat rooms to 23. The AOL rule can't even be broken in protest because the prohibition is enforced automatically by the software code itself. Attempts to be the 24th participant in the conversation are just met with an error message.

As Internet traffic moves increasingly from phone lines into the control of cable-TV companies, these companies will try to exert even greater control over the traffic they carry. Already some cable companies have tried to prevent Internet users from using "streaming video," which competes with the companies' own pay-per-view channels. Internet companies like Yahoo, which provide "portals" for reaching other websites, already steer people towards businesses that pay to have "banner" ads linking to their sites or to get top billing when people use a search engine. The logical next step is for media conglomerates to use their cable companies to make it faster and easier to reach their product content, to view trailers for their movies, and perhaps to charge users extra for any time spent out of their universe of "infotainment." The trend gives more power to large media conglomerates. The majority of Internet traffic has already been gobbled up by corporations like AOL Time Warner (which owns CNN.com) and Disney (which owns ESPN.com).

Stanford law professor Lawrence Lessig points out, however, that "the changes that make [Internet] commerce possible are also changes that will make regulation easy." For instance, business continues to struggle with how to authenticate who is logging on, and if they really are who they say. E-business has long favored a system of digital certificates that could authenticate a user's identity when surfing the web. Such a system could pose serious dangers—to reduce users' privacy or even threaten their civil liberties. But it could also mean greater abilities to implement public regulations. For example, states do not currently charge state sales tax on purchases made over the Internet. Digital certificates could allow states (or even cities) to charge taxes for online purchases to the certificate holder.

> THE ARCHITECTURE OF CYBERSPACE CONSTRAINS ONLINE INTERACTIONS TO SERVE THE ENDS OF THOSE WHO DESIGN OR CONTROL IT.

Myth #3: As a result of the information revolution, the global economy can no longer be influenced by government.

New information technologies are often seen as having made governments impotent to influence anything on the Net, since web sites can relocate outside the legal jurisdiction of governments that wish to regulate them. The state of Missouri can make it illegal to host a gambling or pornography site from a computer within the state, but it can't stop people from logging onto such a site launched from another state or country. The Amazon.com site based in Germany may comply with that country's laws by refusing to carry Nazi literature, but cyber-Nazis in Germany can order Hitler's *Mein Kampf* from Amazon.com sites hosted in the United States or other countries.

But electronic finance is different. When a bank wires money, it relies on a centralized infrastructure guaranteed by governments to make sure that money is subtracted from one account and added to another. A system of mutual recognition and settlement between powerful institutions like central banks confirms that the person transferring the money actually has those funds and is not simultaneously promising them to banks all over the world. Globalized money will, for this reason, never fully conform to the libertarian fantasy. The same infrastructure that makes it possible to send money electronically across borders also makes it technically possible to restrict and tax these transfers.

> POLITICIANS HAVE OFTEN USED THE "NEW ECONOMY" AS A PRETENSE FOR OPPOSING SOCIAL PROGRAMS OR REGULATORY POLICIES. BUT THESE ARE ULTIMATELY POLITICAL ISSUES.

Governments have done just that for over a century. It has been possible to wire funds more or less instantaneously since the invention of the telegraph. Even today, most capital transfers are communicated through faxes or telex machines and authenticated with pen-and-ink signatures. Today's system of capital transfers, however, has become centralized through national central banks. This system already assigns a unique identifying number to each capital transfer. Far from making regulation unfeasible, the more these finance systems are digital and networked, the more viable regulation will become.

A system of capital controls would make it possible to stop international money laundering, which the IMF estimates drains away 2-5% of the world's income, and to squelch corruption—especially in poorer countries where warlords or kleptocrats steal essential investment funds. A tiny transaction fee of the kind charged by the Securities and Exchange Commission (SEC) in the United States could discourage market volatility caused by trigger-happy investors seeking tiny profit margins on huge currency transactions. More ambitiously, a levy of one penny on every million dollars in international financial transfers would not discourage any productive investment, but would raise more money than the U.N. estimates is required to provide for basic health, nutrition, education, and water sanitation to the 1.3 billion people on the planet who live without. (See Thad Williamson, "The Headline Your Newspaper Ignores: Global Economic Inequality.")

Creating an international architecture of capital controls would not be easy. The big U.S. banks might be particularly resistant to capital controls. U.S. banks receive large quantities of international money partially due to the United States' weak laws on disclosure and taxation of foreign funds. Foreign investors, unlike U.S. citizens or residents, pay no tax on interest or capital gains and do not have to disclose the sources of their earnings to the IRS.

Just as the Great Depression made the federal government establish the agencies that regulate domestic finance (the SEC, the Federal Deposit Insurance Corporation, etc.), the September 11 destruction has brought more attention to the need for regulation of international finance. Some commentators have called for greater international scrutiny of secretive Saudi banks, the likely conduits of terrorist funds. Legislation signed into law in October 2001 bars U.S. banks, which often do business with overseas "paper" corporations, from dealing with a foreign bank unless the latter has a physical existence somewhere with at least one employee. The Treasury Department can now require banks to monitor accounts formally held by overseas banks, especially to determine who is the real owner of the account.

So far, it is not clear that these few, halting steps will lead to real change, but new wisdom has a way of gaining momentum as new practices become more common. Once a capital control system got under way, banks might find it to be in their interests to comply with regulations on international transactions, or face exclusion from the centralized payment systems that make this lucrative business possible. Who knows? They might even reassure their stockholders that, after all, information technology makes it inevitable.

Whatever the future of the Internet may bring, the way markets will operate in cyberspace will not result from some inexorable logic of technology itself. The logic of the Net will depend on the architecture built there—and who has the power to build it.

January/February 2003

MOVE OVER HMOs, THE EMOs ARE COMING

BY AMY GLUCKMAN

Do you love your HMO?

A new crop of entrepreneurs thinks so, or at least that, just as U.S. health care has been remade in the image of the HMO, public education should be remade in the image of its equivalent: the education management organization, or EMO.

Here's the view from the conservative *National Review*:

"Analysts compare education today to the health-care industry twenty years ago. Until the 1970s, health care was inefficiently managed and dominated by the public sector and non-profit entities that had little direct competition and little incentive for innovation. Costs rose markedly without corresponding improvements in the quality of care. Doctors and boards of directors of non-profit hospitals were the 'gatekeepers' in those days, much as local school boards and unionized teachers have a lock on service delivery in education. Then along came HMOs, and a multibillion-dollar industry was born."

You'd expect the article to go on and describe how the HMO era has seen the quality of health care improve and costs fall. This claim is absent, probably because it would have had zero credibility even among *National Review*'s market-loving readers.

Of course, for-profit businesses are nothing new in public education. For years, public schools have been buying products such as textbooks and services such as transportation from private contractors. But these vendors have been confined to particular niches within the overall school program. There is also nothing new about private schools, but these have generally been non-profits.

What's new is that for-profit companies are now in the business of running entire public schools. Edison Schools is the only EMO that has received much publicity, but there are a number of others. These companies run public schools under contracts: primarily charter schools, but also regular district schools in some cities. Although the contract specifics can vary, EMOs are typically paid by either the district (to run district schools) or the state government or other chartering authority (to run charter schools) according to a formula based on the per-pupil spending in nearby school districts. The regular district schools that EMOs win contracts to run are often "failing" schools in large urban centers. The majority of EMO-managed schools, though, are charter schools; many of these are in suburban locations with easier-to-serve populations. In Florida, developers have actually teamed up with EMOs to build charter schools within new, high-end subdivisions—a novel amenity for wealthy homebuyers.

For the past several years, EMOs have garnered lots of excitement in the business world. Lehman Brothers held a conference in 1996 to highlight investment opportunities in the for-profit education sector; the firm's conference report stated, "The education industry may replace health care as the focus industry." Investors see a market that is both huge—over $600 billion annually—*and*, perhaps, on the verge of significant privatization. As Henry Levin, director of the Center for the Study of Privatization in Education at Columbia University, notes, until recently education has been "the largest government sector untouched by privatization."

This $600 billion market covers everything from day care to college, from textbooks to test-prep classes to corporate training seminars. EMOs are in fact a very small slice of the ed market pie, and the hype about them in the business world is far exceeding actual profits. To date, the major EMO firms have made almost no profits managing schools, and some have experienced large losses.

But EMOs are significant in ways that go beyond either their size or their profits. Unlike companies that sell textbooks or food services to schools, EMOs represent an attempt to reshape entire schools (and potentially entire school systems) in line with the profit motive and with market concepts like "branding." But as the EMOs are discovering, there is no way to make a profit managing K-12 schools that does not involve moving funds out of instruction in one way or another. This cost-cutting comes at the expense of students and teachers, whether in the EMO-managed schools themselves or in the regular district schools that are "left behind." And privatizing school management is likely to change the very nature and meaning of public education in the United States. If public elementary and high schools get turned into profit centers for corporations, an erosion of democratic control over public education is inevitable, replaced by, at best, a consumer model where the parents of children in a particular school—and, of course, the investors—are the only ones with any say.

EMO BASICS

EMOs currently run over 300 public schools across the country and serve about 125,000 students. Edison is the largest EMO, with about 75,000 students in its 130 schools. Chancellor Beacon Academies is another large player, running both public charter schools and private day schools. The company currently enrolls about 19,000 preK-12 students in eight states and the District of Columbia. Some companies are focused primarily in a single state: White Hat Management runs 20 schools in Ohio, and National Heritage Academies runs 24 schools in Michigan. Both of these companies are beginning to expand into other states, however. Education Alternatives, Inc., the nation's largest EMO in the mid-1990s, folded in 2000.

> EDISON SCHOOLS' HEAD CHRISTOPHER WHITTLE URGED INVESTORS TO THINK OF EDISON AS AN EDUCATION VERSION OF HOME DEPOT, MCDONALDS, OR WAL-MART.

Charter schools "provide a fertile ground for companies waiting to penetrate the K-12 education market," in the words of one industry-group report. Charter schools are public schools that are "chartered" and paid for by state education departments or local school boards (and free to students) but are independent of many policies and regulations governing traditional public schools. Some states' charter-school laws permit for-profits to apply for charters directly; in other states, charters are supposed to be granted only to non-profit organizations. EMOs have made headway in both situations. In Florida, for example, where only non-profits are legally entitled to run a charter school, for-profit firms have created non-profit boards made up of their own people, who then turn around and hire the EMO to run the school. In some states, such as Michigan, most of the charter schools are managed by for-profit firms. In others, EMOs play a much smaller role. Nationally, about a quarter of charter-school students attend charters run by EMOs. The trend is unmistakable, though; each year EMOs are running an increasing share of charter schools, squeezing out the non-profit, community-based parent and teacher groups many education reform advocates had in mind when the charter-school idea was first gaining ground a decade ago.

In addition to charters, EMOs have also won contracts to run regular district schools in some districts. This fall, the city of Philadelphia contracted with three different EMOs to run a total of 30 elementary schools in the city. Philadelphia's schools were placed under state receivership in 2001; against significant community opposition, trustees made the decision to privatize the management of these schools. (The district gave over the management of twelve additional schools to non-profits, including Temple University and the University of Pennsylvania.)

EMOs do not have a promising track record in running regular district schools. The largest of such experiments to date involve Baltimore and Hartford. In 1992, the Baltimore school district hired Education Alternatives, Inc. (EAI) to manage nine of its schools. After a long series of disputes, Baltimore terminated the contract in November 1995. During EAI's tenure in Baltimore, the federal government found the company in violation of special-education laws and forced it to adopt an extensive corrective action plan. Local reporters uncovered instance after instance of EAI publicizing significant student achievement gains in the schools it ran, only to have the data turn out to be inaccurate; the company blamed these episodes on clerical errors. In the EAI schools, the ratio of certified teachers to students actually fell, as did the average experience level of the teachers. In spite of EAI's troubles in Baltimore, the Hartford school district hired the company to provide district-wide management services in 1995; less than a year later, Hartford also terminated its EAI contract.

It is too soon to tell how Philadelphia's experiment with handing some of its schools over to EMOs will turn out. Children, parents, and teachers have had mixed reactions so far; meanwhile, investors are wondering whether these companies will ever make any money on the deal.

WHAT'S THE THEORY?

Investors are putting money into the field of public school management on the basis that EMOs will be able to make a profit at it—that spending the same amount per pupil as a regular public school, they will be able to attract "customers" by offering a superior education and still have dollars left over to provide a return to investors. So far, the rewards to investors have been meager. Edison, for example, has lost $261 million since its founding; its stock dropped from $36 a share in early 2001 to around $1.00, where it has hovered since last spring.

For students, parents, teachers, and anyone who cares about public education, however, the real question is not whether investors will get their money back. It's what policies the EMOs will adopt in their attempt to turn a profit, and who will get hurt by those policies. EMOs claim they can provide innovative approaches to education—novel curricula, superior methods of instruction, better ways of hiring and training teachers—that the public schools have not been able to offer. EMO advocates also claim that public schools waste a lot of money on administration and bureaucracy, and that better (read: private) management can recapture these funds and funnel them into both improving instruction and rewarding investors. On the other hand, maybe the EMOs are trying to become profitable merely by cutting costs, e.g. by providing fewer services or cutting teachers' salaries.

WHAT DOES THE EVIDENCE SUGGEST SO FAR?

Innovation in curriculum and instruction does not appear to be the EMOs' strong suit. Many of them are selecting off-the-shelf curricula that are available to (and used by any number of) ordinary public schools. Edison schools, for example, often employ a widely used reading program called *Success for All* and an increasingly popular math curriculum, the University of Chicago's *Everyday Math*. Only for social studies does Edison use what it describes as a "project-based, proprietary curriculum." Several other firms use E.D. Hirsch's *Core Knowledge* curriculum, a widely used program that purports to list the facts and stories that all American children should learn in each grade.

In terms of innovations in instructional methods, there is likewise not much evidence that EMOs have any particularly effective tricks up their sleeves. They tend to hire inexperienced teachers; this in turn may explain why many have adopted direct instruction and other "teacher-proof" modes of instruction where teachers are trained to deliver tightly pre-scripted lessons. Some EMOs bring more computers into their schools and market their use of instructional technology as a selling point. In many cases, however, students appear to be using software that drills them in basic skills, not learning about computers themselves or their more advanced applications.

There are certainly some exceptions. A few EMOs, such as Mosaica, have created innovative curricula that engage students in doing in-depth projects. And according to many observers, including Rutgers education policy professor Katrina Bulkley, some EMOs deserve credit for implementing existing curricula in a more coherent way than often happens in regular public schools—aligning curriculum with instructional method, assessment, and professional development in ways that can make a big difference. The idea that reforms work much better when they're implemented in a coherent way is not a new one, though; many regular public schools are also engaged in what's often referred to as "whole school reform."

Ultimately, concludes Iowa State University professor Christopher Lubienski, EMOs are producing standardization more than innovation. In a study of whether competition and choice foster innovation in education, Lubienski concluded that "interventions by public bureaucracies have often succeeded in encouraging classroom innovations, while market mechanisms appear to contribute to standardization. ... While competitive environments often serve as catalysts for innovative practices, competition and choice can also lead toward emulation and standardization—trends that are missed in simplistic portrayals of markets."

The companies that Edison Schools head Christopher Whittle chose to compare his project to are telling. In 1996, according to *Education Week*, Whittle "urged investors to think of Edison as an education version of Home Depot, McDonald's, or Wal-Mart—companies that have become leaders in their industries through innovation. 'We hope you think of us in that group,' Mr. Whittle said."

Many EMOs argue that their curricular and instructional choices should be judged only on bottom-line results—student achievement. Here, researchers widely agree that the jury is still out. An October, 2002, review by the General Accounting Office (GAO) looked at five studies of student achievement in charter schools run by three major EMOs. The GAO concluded that most of the studies do not allow valid comparisons to be made between students in EMO-run schools and comparable students in other public schools. The one study that the GAO considered rigorous enough found no difference in student achievement. Another careful study was conducted in 2002 by the Dallas school district to assess the effectiveness of seven district schools managed under contract by Edison. The study's conclusion: While the Edison students made test score gains, these were less than or equal to the gains made by comparable students in regular district schools. These results are in sharp contrast to EMO marketing materials, which typically claim that their programs produce huge academic gains.

COST SAVINGS: CUT FAT, OR TEACHERS?

Apparently swayed by an ideology that claims private enterprises are always more efficient, EMOs and their investors assumed that they would find plenty of fat to cut in public school budgets, and that they would benefit from economies of scale as the companies and their schools grew. In general, neither assumption has turned out to be true.

There is probably not a school principal in the United States who would say that his or her school site budget contains any fat, and the EMOs don't seem to have found much either. Instead, they have tried to save money largely by cutting direct instructional expenses, even though the initial promise of these firms was that they would shift money *into* instruction. Schooling is a labor-intensive activity; personnel costs are by far the largest expense. EMOs save on these costs by hiring inexperienced teachers. The teachers EAI hired in Baltimore, for example, averaged less than five years of experience, compared to 14.5 years on average for Baltimore public school teachers. (EAI also replaced seasoned classroom paraprofessionals with inexperienced interns, hired through a temp agency and paid just over the minimum wage with no benefits!) Teachers don't stay young and inexperienced, though, so how this strategy will play out over time is unclear. EMO-run schools may have a hard time retaining teachers if they do not offer seniority pay comparable to area school districts. It's possible that many firms have simply built a permanent high rate of teacher turnover into their business plans. Indeed, teacher turnover in charter schools is already high, according to a July, 2002, report by the American Federation of Teachers (AFT).

The issue of teacher pay in EMO-run and other charter schools will be played out in a largely non-union environment. Although a comprehensive figure is not available, National Education Association senior policy analyst Heidi Steffens confirms that the rate of unionization in charter schools is very low. Even in states whose charter laws give charter-school teachers collective bargaining rights, each school must often be organized as a separate unit; this is very hard to do. (When EMOs run regular district schools, they typically do have to operate under any existing union contract.)

When public-education critics acknowledge that individual school budgets are generally lean, they often point to oversized bureaucracies at the district level as the real problem. But contracting with EMOs to manage individual charter or district schools doesn't help; it just adds an additional layer of management since school department administrators must still be in place to oversee the contracts and manage a variety of district-wide services.

LOCAL REPORTERS UNCOVERED INSTANCE AFTER INSTANCE OF EAI PUBLICIZING SIGNIFICANT STUDENT ACHIEVEMENT GAINS IN ITS SCHOOLS, ONLY TO HAVE THE DATA TURN OUT TO BE INACCURATE.

It's easy to imagine that, in a few years, this may become an argument EMOs make to take over entire districts and not just individual schools. Some industry insiders already talk about this as a long-term goal. In a November 2000 story headlined "For-Profits Brand New School Systems," the *Education Industry Report (EIR)* describes a firm called Knowledge Universe (KU) that owns both hundreds of preschools and a minority stake in Nobel Learning Communities, an EMO that operates around 160 K-12 schools. "KU could stitch together an alternative to public schools," the story concludes. "Parents might select a KU-branded education solution, watching their child proceed from a Knowledge Learning preschool facility to a school run by Nobel." Other EMOs are pressing to take over larger and larger shares of existing school districts. In 1997 the *EIR* quoted Samuel Flam, consultant and author of *Public Schools/Private Enterprise*: "It's too early in the time line for an EMO to take over an entire school district. … As [successful experiences with privatizing part of a district] become engrained in our psyche, at some point the privatization of the entire operation will have an easier time."

AVOIDING "EXPENSIVE" STUDENTS

EMOs have also cut costs by finding ways to serve "less expensive" students. Few charter schools, whether EMO or non-profit, serve students with moderate to severe disabilities. For example, Massachusetts' charter school law states that charters are not required to admit the most severely disabled children. In 1997, a Springfield, Mass., charter school managed by Sabis, Inc., wanted to send two moderate special needs students back to the local district. School administrators said no; the next day, Sabis informed the district that it had re-evaluated these two students and that under their new special education plans, they now fell into the severely disabled category of children that charter schools are not required to serve.

Other charter schools have "counselled out" children with special needs, advising their parents that they would be better served in the regular district schools. One study of charter schools in Massachusetts found that EMO-run charter schools have engaged in this practice more frequently than non-profit charters. Perhaps as a result, nationwide, "charter schools run by private management companies serve an even smaller proportion of special education students than other charter schools and dramatically fewer than their host school districts serve," according to the AFT's charter school report. And like private and parochial schools, charter schools can expel "troublesome" students without providing them with an alternative placement; regular public schools do not have this luxury.

A few EMOs do focus specifically on serving high-risk students who are likely to need extra services. But if charter schools, especially those run by EMOs, serve a disproportionately low number of "expensive" students overall, then they are siphoning funds away from the regular public schools that are left to serve a needier student population. This is particularly true in states where the charter-school funding formula is based on a per-pupil average that includes all students; under such formulas, charter schools are being paid to serve special-education and other "expensive" students but are not doing so.

Even the fact that most charter schools are elementary schools, not high schools, represents a way of focusing on less expensive students. High schools are more expensive to run on a per-student basis, but in many states the reimbursement rate for charter schools is based on a districtwide per-student average that includes both elementary schools and high schools. So in those states, EMOs can get an extra slice of the budget by focusing on the elementary-school market.

ECONOMIES OF SCALE?

For-profit firms have also hoped that they'd be able to benefit from economies of scale—as the overall size of the firms and the size of the schools they ran grew, and as they adopted a standardized, "branded" educational approach across schools. According to Columbia's Levin, however, this hope was not based on any careful analysis of how schools work and has largely proven incorrect. In terms of the size of individual schools, industry spokespeople are clear that they are not interested in running small schools, and in fact, EMO-run charter schools are larger on average than non-profit charter schools. Unfortunately, though, from the standpoint of the ultimate goal of improving educational quality, there is a growing body of evidence that small schools work better.

Implementing a standard educational model across schools is another way EMOs have hoped to achieve cost savings. If they do so, for example, they can buy textbooks and other materials in bulk. So it is not a surprise that, as we've seen, EMO-run schools in general are moving toward standardization more than toward innovation or experimentation. Unfortunately, this trend is contrary to the whole spirit of education reform in general and of charter schools in particular—at least in the eyes of many progressive ed reform advocates. Many still speak of charter schools in "let a hundred flowers bloom" terms, as laboratories for the development and dissemination of innovative educational practices that address the specific needs of different communities. While this remains the vision of many of the small, non-profit charter schools, it does not seem to be what most of the EMOs have in mind.

In the end, according to Columbia's Levin, EMOs may find that managing public schools is just not that profitable. He notes that for-profits have never moved into the independent-school market, even though these schools charge tuition that is typically two to three times what public schools can spend per student. In the future, he predicts, EMOs may shift their efforts away from whole-school management and toward making money on "peripherals": proprietary curriculum materials, consulting, e-learning, and web services.

CITIZENS OR CONSUMERS?

Those who are concerned about the future of public education as a democratic institution can only hope that for-profits ultimately opt out of the school management business. For the effect of privatizing the management of entire schools is to substitute consumer choice for the democratic control over public schools that communities have traditionally exercised through school boards and elected officials. EMO advocates frequently point out that their efforts are held to a high standard: that if they don't do a good job educating children, then parents will vote with their feet. That's true, but it places parents—not even parents in general, but only the parents of students in a particular school—as the sole stakeholders in public education. Consider National Heritage Academies, an EMO that markets its charter schools to evangelical Christian families. Parents and civil-liberties groups have had to take this company to court to force it to stop practices such as holding mandatory staff development sessions that were essentially revival meetings, sponsoring an on-site moms' prayer group, and building special partnerships with a private Christian school and a Baptist church. It's likely that a majority of the parents who enroll their children in National Heritage's schools are happy to find these evangelical Christian touches in a tuition-free "public" school, but that doesn't mean that such schools are in the public interest or that taxpayer dollars should be funding them.

And depending on the specific contractual arrangements between a charter school and an EMO that manages it, even local parental control can be severely limited. One reason that EMOs are managing an increasing number of charter schools is that they typically have access to the startup funds needed to build, buy, or renovate a facility. Most states' charter laws do not provide money for such capital expenditures, which represent the greatest obstacle to non-profit community groups wishing to start a charter school. But, as Rutgers's Bulkley notes, if the EMO owns the school building, it's very difficult for even an independent-minded charter school board to terminate the relationship.

Of course, contracting with for-profit firms to run public schools raises all of the same issues that have led progressives to fight privatization in general: union busting, the substitution of low-wage for high-wage jobs, the transfer of taxpayer dollars into private profits. With the Bush administration's recent announcement of a plan to contract out hundreds of thousands of federal jobs, it is clear that privatization is proceeding apace. Perhaps in the arena of the public schools, however, privatization may be scrutinized and slowed—either because public education is too underfunded to yield private profits or because parents, teachers, students, and Americans in general decide that public schools under democratic control are worth saving.

Resources: Henry M. Levin, "Potential of For-Profit Schools for Educational Reform," Occasional Paper No. 47, National Center for the Study of Privatization in Education (NCSPE), Teachers College, Columbia University, June 2002; American Federation of Teachers, "Do Charter Schools Measure Up? The Charter School Experiment After 10 Years," July, 2002; Nancy J. Zollers and Arum Ramanathan, "For-Profit Charter Schools and Students with Disabilities," *Phi Delta Kappan*, December 1998; Christopher Lubienski, "The Relationship of Competition and Choice to Innovation in Education Markets," NCSPE Occasional Paper No. 26; Eduventures.com, Inc., *Education Industry Report* and *The Education Economy*, various issues; U.S. General Accounting Office, "Insufficient Research to Determine Effectiveness of Selected Private Education Companies," October 2002.

CHAPTER 2
Supply and Demand

INTRODUCTION

Textbooks tell us that supply and demand work like a well-oiled machine. The Law of Supply tells us that as the price of an item goes up, businesses will supply more of that good or service. The Law of Demand adds that as the price rises, consumers will choose to buy less of the item. Only one equilibrium price can bring businesses' and consumers' intentions into balance. Away from this equilibrium point, surpluses or shortages tend to drive the price back toward the equilibrium. Of course, government actions such as taxation or setting a price ceiling or floor can move the economy away from its market equilibrium, creating what economists call a deadweight loss.

Our authors raise vexing issues about the mechanism of supply and demand. Marc Breslow argues that supply and demand do not always produce the best outcomes for society, noting that shortages lead to skyrocketing prices (Breslow, article 2.1). But he also suggests that government should *use* the Law of Demand, increasing taxes on fuel to drive down fuel consumption (Breslow, article 2.2). Ellen Frank questions the textbook idea that rent controls (and other price ceilings) lead to permanent shortages. She maintains that rent control helps to equalize power between landlords and tenants and to assure a supply of affordable housing (Frank, article 2.3). In a different article, Frank offers a spirited defense of using the tax system to shift income from rich to poor (Frank, article 2.4). Taken together, these articles make a strong case for using the powers of government to *modify* supply and demand in the interest of fairness.

KEY TO COLANDER

This chapter is designed to be used with Chapters 4-7.

Breslow (article 2.1) and Frank (article 2.3) take up issues found in Chapters 4 (supply and demand), 5 (using supply and demand, price ceilings), and 6 (elasticity).

Breslow (article 2.2) and Frank (article 2.4) address topics from Chapters 6 (elasticity, incidence of a tax) and 7 (taxation).

DISCUSSION QUESTIONS

1) (General) A number of the articles portray situations in which suppliers (landlords, energy companies) hold disproportionate power over buyers. Can you think of situations in which buyers have disproportionate power over suppliers? (Hint: Large corporations can be buyers as well as suppliers.)

2) (General) The authors of these articles call for a larger government role in regulating supply and demand. What are some possible results of expanded government involvement, positive and negative? On balance, do you agree that government should play a larger role?

3) (Breslow article 2.1) One way of summarizing Marc Breslow's article is, "The Law of Demand guarantees that there will sometimes be price-gouging." Explain what this means. Do you agree?

4) (Breslow article 2.1) Breslow says that shortages have different effects on prices in the short run and the long run. Explain the difference. How is this difference related to the concepts of elasticity of demand and elasticity of supply?

5) (Breslow article 2.2) Breslow argues that gas prices should be higher than they are, in order to take into account the full cost—including the environmental cost—of gasoline use. If Breslow is right, why are suppliers selling gas for less than its full cost?

6) (Breslow article 2.2) If a gas tax is levied, how should the proceeds of the tax be used? (Breslow offers one suggestion.) What principles of taxation are guiding your answer?

7) (Frank article 2.3) Ellen Frank states that because modern rent control laws are "soft," they do not lead to housing shortages. Explain. Do you agree with her reasoning?

8) (Frank article 2.4) Should the tax system be used to redistribute money from rich to poor? Why or why not? And if so, how should we decide the right amount to redistribute?

October 2000

PRICE GOUGING: IT'S JUST SUPPLY AND DEMAND

BY MARC BRESLOW

- May 2000: Growing demand, along with supply cutbacks by OPEC, lead to soaring gasoline prices around the United States, especially in the upper Midwest, where they reach $2 a gallon, almost twice the levels of a year earlier.
- September 2000: Both presidential candidates, George W. Bush and Al Gore, offer plans to prevent dramatic increases in the price of heating oil during the coming winter, due to expected supply shortages.
- 1999 and 2000: red-hot high-tech economies in the San Francisco Bay and Boston areas draw in more professional workers, and raise the demand for housing. Vacancy rates dwindle to near zero, and prices for both rentals and house purchases rise out of sight. Moderate- and low-income renters are evicted for non-payment and forced to move into smaller quarters or out of these metropolitan areas.

Critics of the oil industry charge that the companies are conspiring to raise prices during shortages, ripping off consumers and gaining huge profits through illegal behavior. The industries respond that there is no conspiracy, prices are rising due to the simple functioning of supply and demand in the market. The media debate the question: can evidence be found of a conspiracy? Or are rising prices simply due to increased costs as supplies are short? Politicians ask whether companies are guilty of illegal activity, and demand that investigations be opened.

What's going on? In reality, critics of the industries are missing the point of how a capitalist "free market" operates during times of shortages. The industry spokespersons are more on target in their explanations — but that doesn't mean what the companies are doing is okay. In fact, they *are* profiting at the expense of everyone who is forced to pay outrageous prices.

Both the media and public officials want to know whether rising costs of operation are causing the high prices, and therefore the companies are justified. Why?

Because simple textbook economics says that in a competitive market we should get charged according to costs, with companies only making a "normal" profit. But a careful reading of the texts shows that this is only in the "long run" when new supplies can come into the market. In the short run, when a shortage develops, "supply and demand" can force prices up to unbelievable levels, especially for any product or service that is really a necessity. It doesn't have any relationship to the cost of supplying the item, nor does it take a conspiracy. The industry spokespeople are right that market pressures are the cause.

What confuses consumers is why a relatively small shortage can cause such a huge price jump, as it did for gasoline and electricity. Why, if OPEC reduces world oil supplies by only 1% or 2%, can the price of gasoline rise by perhaps 50%? Why shouldn't prices rise by the 1% or 2%? The answer lies in a common-sense understanding of what happens during a shortage. Everyone who owns a car, and still needs to get to work, drop the kids off at child care, and buy groceries, still needs to drive. In the short run, you can't sell your car for a more energy-efficient one, nor move someplace where public transit is more available, nor find a new day care center closer to home. Even if there are subways or buses available where you live, tight work and family time schedules probably make it difficult for you to leave the car at home.

So, as prices rise, everyone continues trying to buy as much gasoline as they did before (in technical terms, the "short run price elasticity of demand" is very low). But there is 2% less gas available, so not everyone can get as much as they want. Prices will continue rising until some people drop out of the market, cutting back on their purchases because they simply can't afford to pay the higher prices. For something as essential to modern life as gasoline, this can take quite a price jump. If the price goes from $1.20 to $1.30 will you buy less? How about $1.50? Or $1.80? You can see the problem. Prices can easily rise by 50% before demand falls by the 2% needed for supply and demand to equalize.

Note that this situation has nothing to do with the costs of supplying gasoline, nor do oil companies in the United States have to conspire together to raise prices. All they have to do is let consumers bid for the available gasoline. Nothing illegal has taken place — OPEC is acting as a cartel, "conspiring," but the United States has no legal power over other countries. Profits can go up enormously, and they may be shared between OPEC, oil companies such as Exxon/Mobil and Royal Dutch Shell, and firms lower on the supply chain such as wholesalers and retail gas stations.

Housing is perhaps the worst of these situations, as no one should be forced to leave their home. But the "invisible hand" of the market will raise prices, and allocate housing, according to who has the greatest purchasing power, not who needs the housing. A highly-skilled computer programmer, moving into San Francisco from elsewhere, will get an apartment that some lesser-paid worker, maybe a public school teacher or a bus driver, has been living in, perhaps for many years.

In all these cases, the market has done what it does well — allocate sales to those who can afford to buy, without regard to need; and allocate profits to those who have a product in short supply, without regard to costs of production. The human costs to people of moderate- and low-incomes, who are priced out of the market, can be severe. But they can be prevented — by price controls that prevent price-gouging due to shortages. Such controls have been used many times in the United States — for rent in high-demand cities, for oil and gas during the "crises" of the 1970's, and for most products during World War II. Maybe it's time we made them a staple of sensible economic policy.

Resources: "In Gas Prices, Misery and Mystery," Pam Belluck, *The New York Times*, 6/14/2000; "Federal action sought to cut power prices from May," Peter J. Howe, *The Boston Globe*, 8/24/2000; "Industry Blames Chemical Additives for High Gas Prices," Matthew L. Wald, *The New York Times*, 6/26/2000.

ARTICLE 2.2   *May/June 2000, revised June 2003*

WANT A COOL PLANET? RAISE GAS PRICES!

BY MARC BRESLOW

So gasoline prices have risen above $1.50 a gallon and threaten to go even higher. To hear many commentators and politicians talk, this is a tragedy rivaling the bubonic plague of the Middle Ages. How dare OPEC threaten Americans' god-given right to cheap gas! Why, after all, did we fight two Gulf Wars, if not to keep gas as cheap as bottled water?

No matter that even at $1.50 a gallon, gas is still not much more expensive, adjusted for inflation, than it was in the early 1970's, or that it is half the price that people pay in Britain, France, Germany, and Japan. It's still time to dip into the strategic oil reserve, cut the federal gas tax, and lift restrictions on oil drilling in environmentally-sensitive areas of Alaska.

I beg to differ. It's hard to think of another issue in which U.S. attitudes are more wrong-headed. The rest of the world knows that, because of global warming and because oil is eventually going to run out (unless we allow drilling to destroy every last bit of pristine environment anywhere), we have to reduce our burning of fossil fuels, including oil. Only the United States, under the political domination of the oil and auto companies, refuses to recognize reality.

Higher gas prices are one of the best things that could happen to this country. If we are lucky, they will start a trend toward smaller cars and away from SUVs. In the long run SUVs threaten to destroy the global environment. In the short run, they threaten to kill all of us foolish — or cash poor — enough to continue driving normal cars. Federal regulators have found that in a collision between an SUV and a car, car occupants are three times as likely to be killed as if they were hit by another car.

Just recently automakers have finally acknowledged this fact, and say they will redesign future SUV models with lower frames to make them less of a threat. But wouldn't it make more sense to just get rid of most of them? Doubling gas prices would be the surest way of making that happen.

Won't that hurt the U.S. economy? Well, yes. Unfortunately, once you have built an economy on wasting energy, rebuilding it in an energy-efficient manner will involve substantial costs. And that is a reason to make the transition gradual — perhaps raising gas prices 20 cents a year for the next ten years would be a reasonable schedule. By that time most people would be ready to get rid of their old gas guzzlers anyway. Not only could they downsize, but they could buy one of the new "hybrids," combination gas/electric vehicles (the engine charges the batteries) that Honda and Toyota are releasing this year. Just changing from SUVs (which get 15 or so miles to the gallon) to these hybrids (which get 60 or more), would go a long way toward meeting the United States' commitment to reduce carbon dioxide emissions in response to global warming.

What about the effects of higher fuel prices on moderate- and low-income people, who may be driving regular cars but still can't afford gas at $2 or $3 a gallon? There is an answer here. Rather than let the Kuwaiti royal family get the benefits of oil scarcity, we should do what Europe and Japan do — tax the hell out of oil (and coal and natural gas, which also create carbon dioxide when burned). Then we should redistribute the tax revenues in a progressive manner, so that low-income people come out even or ahead.

Peter Barnes, creator of the Sky Trust Initiative, has perhaps the best proposal for how to do this. He suggests that rather than letting the federal government use the oil-tax revenue on anything it wants — which could be something horribly regressive like further cuts in income or capital-gains taxes — the money should go into a trust fund. Then it should be handed back to every U.S. resident on an equal per-capita basis. This method would mean low-income households getting back more than they pay for higher fuel costs — so we help the environment and economic equity at the same time. Not to mention sticking it to Exxon.

Resources: Earth Day 2000, which is focusing on energy: www.earthday.net; the Sky Trust Initiative, *www.skytrust.cfed. org*; the Union of Concerned Scientists, *www.ucsusa.org*; the Sierra Club, including its program on Transportation and Sprawl: *www.sierraclub.org*.

March/April 2003

DOES RENT CONTROL HURT TENANTS?

BY ELLEN FRANK

Dear Dr. Dollar,

What are the merits of the argument that rent control hurts tenants by limiting the incentives to create and maintain rental housing?

—Sarah Marxer, San Francisco, CA

The standard story of rent control, laid out in dozens of introductory economics textbooks, goes like this. In the housing market, landlords are willing to supply more rental units when prices are high, and tenants are willing to rent more units when prices are low. In an unregulated market, competition should result in a market-clearing price at which the number of apartments landlords are willing and able to provide just equals the number tenants are willing and able to rent. Thus, when prices are allowed to rise to their correct level, shortages disappear. Rent controls, in this story, disrupt the market mechanism by capping rents at too low a level. Artificially low rents discourage construction and maintenance, resulting in fewer available apartments than would exist without the controls. At the same time, low rents keep tenants in the area, searching for apartments that don't exist. The result: permanent housing shortages in rent-controlled markets.

What's wrong with this story? Just about everything.

First, the story ignores the unequal power that landlords and tenants exercise in an unregulated market. Boston College professor Richard Arnott notes that tenants are, for a number of reasons, averse to moving. This gives landlords inordinate pricing power even in a market where housing is not in short supply—and in areas where vacancy rates are low, land is scarce, and "snob zoning" commonplace, landlords can charge truly exorbitant prices. In Boston, rent controls were eliminated in 1997, and average apartment rents have since climbed nearly 100%. The city's spiraling rents show that without controls, landlords can—and do—gouge tenants.

Second, rent control opponents misrepresent the structure of controls. As practiced in the real world, rent control does not place fixed caps on rent. New York City enacted an actual rent freeze after World War II, and a small number of apartments still fall under this "old-law" rent control. But most rent-controlled apartments in New York and all controlled apartments in other U.S. cities fall under what Arnott calls "second generation" or "soft" controls, which simply restrict annual rent increases. Soft rent controls guarantee landlords a "fair return" on their properties and require that owners maintain their buildings. They allow landlords to pass along maintenance costs, and many allow improvement costs to be recouped on an accelerated schedule, making building upkeep quite lucrative.

Consequently, controlled apartments are not unprofitable. And as Occidental College professor and housing specialist Peter Dreier points out, landlords won't walk away as long as they are making a decent return. Residential landlords are not very mobile: they have a long-term interest in their properties, and only abandon them when *market* rents fall below even controlled levels as a result of poverty, crime, or economic depression. Rent controls themselves do not foster abandonment or poor maintenance.

Third, all second-generation rent control laws—enacted chiefly in the 1970s—exempted newly constructed buildings from controls. Thus, the argument that controls discourage new construction simply makes no sense. As for the oft-heard complaint that developers fear that rent controls, once enacted, will be extended to new buildings, the 1980s and 1990s construction booms in New York, Boston, San Francisco, and Los Angeles—all cities with controls—indicate that developers aren't all that worried. There is plenty of housing and construction in cities with and without rent controls.

Nevertheless, even in many cities with rent controls, there is a shortage of *affordable* apartments. Market housing costs have been rising faster than wages for at least two decades. That some apartments in New York and San Francisco are still affordable to low- and middle-income families is due primarily to rent control.

Indeed, limited as they might be, rent controls deliver real benefits. They prevent price-gouging and ration scarce apartments to existing tenants. The money tenants save in rent can be spent in the neighborhood economy, benefiting local businesses. Meanwhile, more secure tenants create neighborhoods that are stable, safe, and economically diverse. And rent controls are essential if tenants are to have credible legal protection against slumlords: the legal right to complain about lack of heat or faulty plumbing is meaningless if landlords can retaliate by raising rents.

There are many problems with the U.S. housing market. High prices, low incomes, and lack of public housing or subsidies for affordable housing all contribute to homelessness and housing insecurity in major American cities. Rent control is not the cause of these problems, nor is it the whole solution. But along with higher wages and expanded public housing, it is part of the solution. As Dreier puts it, "Until the federal government renews its responsibility to help poor and working-class people fill the gap between what they can afford and what housing costs to build and operate, rent control can at least help to keep a roof over their heads."

Resources: Richard Arnott, "Time for Revisionism on Rent Control?" *Journal of Economic Perspectives*, Winter 1995. Dreier and Pitcoff, "I'm a Tenant and I Vote," *Shelterforce*, July/August 1997. *Shelterforce* website: <http://www.nhi.org/>.

September/October 2002

DON'T THE RICH PAY A LOT OF TAXES?

BY ELLEN FRANK

Dear Dr. Dollar:

The Heritage Foundation, a conservative think tank, has a website that purports to present evidence that the wealthiest group of Americans historically pay more taxes than middle- or low-income folks. Their sources include the U.S. Treasury Department, the Office of Management and Budget, and the Census Bureau. The wealthiest 1% paid over a third of taxes, while those in the lower 50% paid only 4% of income taxes in 1999. How do those of us who criticize the tax system as inherently unfair to middle- and lower-income folks respond to this apparently progressive tax system?

—*Bruce Boccardy, Allston, Massachusetts*

The most comprehensive source of information on "tax incidence"—who actually pays how much in taxes—is the Congressional Budget Office (CBO), which compiles data from the Internal Revenue Service every couple of years. The CBO's most recent report, entitled *Effective Tax Rates*, was released in October 2001 and is available online at <www.cbo.gov>. (The effective tax rate is the percentage of income actually paid in taxes—as opposed to the tax bracket—after deductions and exemptions and loopholes and all the rest.)

The CBO divides families into five "quintiles"—from the lowest earning one-fifth of taxpayers (incomes ranging from $0 to $13,000 in 1997) to the highest paid fifth (incomes of $50,800 and up)—and further breaks down the top fifth into the top 10%, 5%, and 1%.

As the table shows, the top income groups do in fact pay income taxes at a greater rate than they earn. The poorest quintile gets 4% of income but pays -2% of federal income taxes—negative because most qualify for the Earned Income Tax Credit. The top fifth garners 53% of income but shells out 80% of the income tax. And the richest 1% of taxpayers (average income of $1,016,000) receives about 16% of income but pays one-third of federal income taxes. After those taxes are collected, the wealthiest income groups end up with a slightly smaller share of the economic pie than they started out with, while the poorer groups end up with slightly more. So the folks at Heritage are not wrong. The federal income tax is indisputably progressive; it is intended to redistribute income, and that is what it does.

But the redistributive impact is mild—and it's milder still since last year's tax reform. The top quintile starts out with slightly more than half of all pre-tax income generated by the U.S. economy, and ends up with just under half of all after-tax income. The poorest fifth begins the game with just 4% of income and ends up with less than 5%. The folks at Heritage, of course, oppose government redistribution schemes on principle. But redistributing income is the whole point of a progressive tax, and advocates of progressive taxation should not shy away from defending this. If one believes that Ken Lay deserved no less than the $100 million he collected from Enron last year, while the burger-flippers and office cleaners of America deserve no more than the $6.50 an hour they collect, then a progressive tax would seem immoral. But if one believes that incomes are determined by race, gender, connections, power, luck and (occasionally) fraud, then redistribution through the tax system is a moral imperative.

The Heritage study also conveniently overlooks the impact of levies other than the federal income tax. Social Security taxes, excise levies, tariffs, and other duties are regressive—their effective rates decline as income goes up. When these other federal taxes are added in, the tax burden on lower-income groups increases significantly. Social Security taxes take an especially large bite out of low-income workers' paychecks; the bite is even larger when we include payroll taxes paid by the employer. (Labor economists believe that the employer share of the Social Security tax functions, in practice, as a levy on wages, since employers reduce wages to compensate for the tax instead of paying for it out of profits). Further, because state and local governments collect regressive sales, excise, and property taxes, the lower four quintiles pay a larger share of their income in state and local taxes than the top quintile. If we were to add all of these taxes together, we would almost certainly find that the U.S. tax system, as a whole, is not progressive at all.

DISTRIBUTION OF INCOME AND TAXES BY INCOME GROUPS, 1997

Income Group	1	2	3	4	5	6
Lowest 20%	$11,400	4.0%	−2.0%	4.8%	0.9%	12.4%
Second 20%	$28,600	9.0%	1.1%	10.1%	5.2%	10.3%
Third 20%	$45,500	13.9%	6.4%	14.9%	10.4%	9.4%
Fourth 20%	$65,600	20.2%	14.5%	20.8%	18.1%	8.6%
Top 20%	$167,500	53.2%	80.0%	49.7%	65.4%	7.0%
Top 10%	$240,700	38.7%	65.4%	35.3%	50.4%	n.a.
Top 5%	$355,800	28.9%	53.8%	25.8%	39.4%	n.a.
Top 1%	$1,016,000	15.8%	33.6%	13.7%	23.1%	5.8%

1 = Average Household Income; 2 = Share of Pre-Tax Income; 3 = Share of Federal Income Taxes; 4 = Share of After-Tax Income; 5 = Share of All Federal Taxes; 6 = Effective State and Local Tax Rate (1995)

Sources: Congressional Budget Office, *Effective Tax Rates, 1979-1997*; Citizens for Tax Justice, *Who Pays? A Distributional Analysis of the Tax Systems in All 50 States*, 1995 (last column).

CHAPTER 3

Consumers

INTRODUCTION

In the theory of consumer choice, the "two economies" described in the Introduction—the textbook economy and the economy portrayed by critics of the status quo—come into sharp contrast. In the textbook model of consumer choice, rational individuals seek to maximize their well-being by choosing the right mix of goods to consume—a decision that includes how they spend their time. They decide for themselves how much they would enjoy various things, and make their choices based on full information about the options. More of any good is almost always better, but diminishing marginal utility says that each unit of a good brings less enjoyment than the one before. The theory looks at one individual at a time, and tells us that there is no accurate way to compare utilities across individuals.

But critics launch a variety of challenges to this simplified model. The first two articles in this chapter contend that the idea of consumer sovereignty—that consumer wishes determine what gets produced—does not fit the facts. The advertising that saturates our daily lives constantly *creates* new wants, including "needs" such as the need to be rich or good-looking that are unattainable for many (Kiron, article 3.1). In many transactions, consumers are less than fully informed about what they are getting or even the price they are paying. Predatory lending, in which unscrupulous lenders saddle borrowers with hidden fees and high interest rates, is an extreme example (Bradley and Skillern, Leffall, article 3.2). Alan Durning puts forward an even more radical critique, arguing that more is often *worse*, not better—that the accumulation of material goods in affluent societies threatens the environment, widens global inequalities, and hollows out our lives (Durning, article 3.3). Finally, Phineas Baxandall writes that if we break consumer theory's rules and compare utility across individuals, we arrive at an argument for reducing economic inequality (Baxandall, article 3.4).

KEY TO COLANDER

This entire chapter is keyed to Chapter 8, "The Logic of Individual Choice."

Colander raises some of the same issues in his section entitled "Applying Economists' Theory of Choice to the Real World."

DISCUSSION QUESTIONS

1) (Kiron) Standard consumer theory still applies if advertising is simply a way to inform consumers. But David Kiron insists that advertising shapes our tastes and desires. Think of some of the purchases, that you have made in the last six months. For which purchases was advertising primarily a source of information, and for which was it more of a taste-shaper?

2) (Kiron, Bradley and Skillern, Leffall) Mainstream economic theory depicts consumers as autonomous individuals making careful choices based on the preferences they themselves have developed. Kiron, Bradley and Skillern, and Leffall describe consumers as manipulated by crafty advertisers and dishonest businesses. In what areas of consumer choice is each picture more accurate? Which do you think is more accurate overall?

3) (Bradley and Skillern) Bradley and Skillern allege that predatory lenders often target African American and Hispanic borrowers. Why would they do this? More generally, why would businesses discriminate (by race, gender, or other categories) in what consumers they seek out and are willing to sell to?

4) (Durning) Alan Durning says that it's wrong for people in rich countries to consume so much when others in the world live in poverty. His viewpoint could be summarized as, "Live simply, so that others may simply live." Do you agree with this outlook?

5) (Durning) One conclusion from Durning's argument is that rather than seeking pleasure by consuming material goods, we should seek enjoyment through family, friends, and community. How could you use standard utility theory to describe this kind of choice? (Hint: can family, friends, and community be "goods"?) What are some possible problems in using the theory in this way?

6) (Baxandall) Phineas Baxandall states that because of diminishing marginal utility, a dollar is worth more to a poor person than a rich one, so we should increase overall utility by shifting resources from rich to poor. Some conservatives might respond, "Many of the rich are better off precisely *because* they value a dollar more—because they were willing to work harder, sacrifice, save, and invest." Which viewpoint do you believe is more persuasive?

7) (Baxandall) Suppose we decided that everybody should have the *same* amount of money and other resources. What might be some benefits of this? What might be some problems, from the viewpoint of utility theory? From the viewpoint of other economic goals?

September 1997

MARKETING POWER

BY DAVID KIRON

On any given day, 18 billion display ads appear in magazines and daily newspapers across the United States. In consumer cultures like the United States, the urge to buy is sanctioned, reinforced, and exaggerated in ways so numerous, so enticing, so subtle, that ignoring them is not an easy option. The sales message is perhaps nowhere more vivid and insistent than on television. And with credit more widely available, buying is easy, its consequences distant. The cumulative impact on the psyche of all this urging and buying is never fixed as dissatisfaction recurs with each reminder that the goods we have are not good enough.

And the reminders are everywhere; the long tentacles of marketing now intrude upon nearly every aspect of modern life. From the perspective of economics, this is all for the best. Economic theory assumes that advertising is simply a benign provision of information that consumers use when they make decisions in the marketplace. But the reality is that marketers seldom offer consumers product information with which to make informed decisions. Instead marketers go for the consumer's jugular, targeting their beliefs, emotions, and desires. Manufacturers spend millions to place their products in movies, not to inform consumers, but to link their products with entertainment mega-hits. Nike pays sports stars like Michael Jordan and Tiger Woods to associate their success with its brand name in the hope that consumer fascination with celebrities will carry to the Nike label. Marketers also take aim at the most basic of consumer desires, such as those for identity, status, and self-esteem, but offer little hope of satisfying them. Most consumers will never achieve the hard bodies displayed in ads for gym memberships, or the ruggedness of the Marlboro man, or the success enjoyed by shoe-promoting sports stars.

Advertising and the mass media together foster consumer culture. It is nearly impossible to avoid commercial messages in populated areas; whether one goes to the movies, enters a classroom, takes a bus, visits a museum, or opens a can of soup — the message to buy will be there as well. Advertising and media have become the essence of commercialism, the driving force behind the consumerist mentality.

DOES COMMERCIALISM PROMOTE THE PUBLIC GOOD?

Economic competition and the winner-takes-all structure of many markets prompted per capita advertising expenditures (in the United States) to quadruple between 1935 and 1994. But it is far from clear that the volume and nature of contemporary advertising is desirable from a consumer standpoint. Enormous amounts of money are spent on ads, rather than enhancing the quality of products. In 1994, ad expenditures (in all different media, including newspapers, magazines, television, and billboards) in the United States totalled $148 billion — equal to what the nation spent on higher education in 1990.

When advertising, television, and credit cards were first introduced, consumers were led to believe that each would further the public good. In the mid-1920s, commercial sponsorship of entire radio programs was widely accepted as a public service and marketers argued that the radio medium should not be debased by advertisements for specific products. In 1940 David Sarnoff, president of the Radio Corporation of America (RCA, then owner of NBC, the National Broadcasting Company), predicted that mass distribution of commercial television would unify the nation and enhance the individual. In the late 1950s, Bank of America promoted credit cards as a service that would permit upstanding middle-class citizens to achieve the American Dream.

Today, however, instead of facilitating cultural goals such as national unity, commercial media tend to dominate consumer culture. Consider the role of television viewing in the United States, where more homes have televisions than indoor plumbing or telephones. The typical adult spends more time watching television than doing anything else besides working and sleeping — turning on the set for an average of four hours a day. Robert Putnam, a professor of political science at Harvard University, recently discovered a significant correlation between the abrupt arrival of television, when household ownership of televisions exploded from 9% in 1950 to 90% in 1959, and the beginning of a

> COMMERCIAL IMAGES HELP CREATE CONSUMPTION STANDARDS THAT EVERYONE MUST ACHIEVE IN ORDER TO GAIN RESPECT.

dramatic decline in civic participation, as measured by membership trends in organizations such as Parent Teacher Associations (PTAs) and bowling leagues.

From the perspective of economic theory, televisions simply provide a service to consumers, no differently than other appliances. Mark Fowler, a chairman of the Federal Communications Commission during the Reagan administration, once described televisions as toasters with pictures.

This point of view, however, is contradicted by survey evidence which shows that watching television affects the way consumers see the world. Adults who watch more than an average amount of television tend to exaggerate the wealth of others, to hold disproportionately conventional views on politics and society, and to suffer a mean-world syndrome which combines feelings of insecurity with a belief that violence is the solution to life's problems.

Although economists assume that consumers are willing to pay for what they want and that they are knowledgeable participants in the market, it may be impossible to be fully informed about the range of services provided by television. Many innovations in media technologies, such as VCRs, cable and the Internet, have led to new, unforeseen uses of televisions and enhanced the home as an entertainment center. However, these developments have also brought hidden costs to consumers. Once free from advertising, most home video rentals, cable programming, and many Internet websites carry unwanted commercial messages. Moreover, commercials are confusing to children. Young children (up to six years old) cannot understand that they are watching a sales message and cannot determine when a program stops and when a commercial begins.

DO MARKETS OFFER WHAT CONSUMERS WANT?

Consumer demand theory implies that economic activity does not shape consumer preferences. But as John Kenneth Galbraith argued long ago, advertising in wealthy countries creates tastes and desires for goods that contribute little to human well-being. Galbraith was one of the first economists to point out that producers not only manufacture goods that satisfy desires, but they also (indirectly) *create* desires for those goods.

Today, however, leading critics of advertising emphasize a different problem from the one Galbraith emphasized — some wants, even if they are not created by economic activity, may be impossible to satisfy through the market. Everyone wants to be beautiful, yet few consumers will ever attain the promise of beauty suggested by the painfully thin models displayed in many fashion ads.

Living in a culture where image is everything means that consumers are constantly bombarded with information about the things they need in order to be socially acceptable and successful. The confusion that results hits

some more than others. For instance, the ideal beauty image promoted by many thin female models in various media has contributed to higher rates of anorexia among white as compared to black women.

Ideal images of feminine beauty affect women differently across nations as well. White American women tend to follow current trends in U.S. media, which gratuitously promote the appeal of the busty female, by having cosmetic surgery to enlarge their breasts. But in France the media emphasizes other aspects of the female form. Not surprisingly, French women who want to change the appearance of their breasts tend to have breast reduction surgery. One of the most damaging effects of commercialism is its impact on the poor. Commercial images help create consumption standards that everyone must achieve in order to gain respect, leaving many poor persons unable to afford the badges of respectable membership in consumer culture. The true life tales of school children being beaten or killed for their new leather jackets or name-brand sneakers are powerful reminders of the influence of markets on consumer identities among the young and the poor.

A TAX ON DESIRE

The availability of credit makes possible much of today's high consumption levels, which are more than twice the levels of forty years ago. According to the authors of *Marketing Madness: A Survival Guide for a Consumer Society,* "The average cardholder carries eight to ten credit cards, owes about $2,500, and pays about $450 in interest annually." Some credit companies even reward taking on debt by awarding discounts and prizes on unpaid balances. In 1992, Americans spent $27 billion in finance charges alone. Instead of simply paying for the things they want, consumers pay for wanting what they want: a veritable tax on desire.

Until the late 1950s, the ability to acquire consumer debt was determined primarily by bank fiat. Consumers had to prove that they were good risks in face-to-face confrontations with loan officers, and were forced to wait for banks to process their applications each time they wanted a loan. After World War II, sporadic efforts were made to introduce credit cards, which would allow consumers to have more control over the lending process. The first major initiative, a fiasco, was undertaken in 1958 by the Bank of America in Fresno, California, before the bank was technically equipped to monitor credit use and avoid abuses. The success of the credit card as an institution awaited successful adaptation of technological innovations such as the computer to the specific requirements of credit card banking.

Between 1958 and 1970, 100 million credit cards were dispersed across the United States. With its mass distribution, the feel of the card and the spontaneity of credit transactions soon became commonplace. Yet as consumption per person has more than doubled (after correcting for inflation), so has the number of personal bankruptcies, which tripled between 1985 and 1994. Greater accessibility to credit is certainly a factor in this trend. It is easy to confuse the availability of credit with greater purchasing power; flexibility in payback schedules offers the illusion of immediate ownership. Credit card abuse is so pervasive that in San Francisco chapters of Debtors Anonymous hold 45 meetings a week.

In traditional economic models, rational consumers take on debt in order to purchase items that have a long lifetime, such as homes, autos, and appliances, and to balance fluctuations in their incomes. However, these models do not explain what really happens in the economy. They cannot explain why many people do not foresee or simply ignore the consequences of finance charges on unpaid balances. In 1992 Americans charged over $400 billion, while close to 900,000 people went bankrupt. It is hard to believe that rational planning would lead to so many bankruptcies. Like advertising, credit promises fulfillment but often delivers heartbreak.

The economic model of consumer behavior implies that an ideal life is one that is all consumption and no work. This alone should give us pause. And if we also take into account that emphasizing consumption as the primary route to happiness draws our attention from the economy's effects on the environment, we should pause

a moment longer. But silence should not be our response to the seeming inevitability of consumer culture.

Alternatives exist for both consumers and producers. On the consumer side, some individuals are opting for less work and less consumption to have more time with their families; others are living more simply, more conscientiously; others are living in co-operatives with their friends and consuming less as a collective. On the producer side, the work week can be shortened, job security can be increased, and corporations can become more socially responsible in their dealings with the environment. However, none of these changes will fundamentally alter consumer culture, unless we also realize that commercialism creates the illusion that we can buy our happiness in the marketplace.

Resources: Marketing Madness: A Survival Guide for a Consumer Society, Michael Jacobson and Laurie Ann Mazur, 1994; *A Piece of the Action: How the Middle Class Joined the Money Class*, Joseph Nocera, 1994; *The Consumer Society*, Neva Goodwin, Frank Ackerman, and David Kiron, 1997.

Editor's Note: Published with permission from *The Consumer Society* edited by Neva R. Goodwin, Frank Ackerman, and David Kiron ©Island Press, 1997. Published by Island Press, Washington, DC and Covelo, CA. For more information, contact Island Press directly at 1-800-828-1302, info@ islandpress.org, or <www.islandpress.org>.

ARTICLE 3.2   *January/February 2000, updated May 2003*

PREDATORY LENDING

BANKS TRICK POOR INTO EXPENSIVE LOANS

BY JEANETTE BRADLEY AND PETER SKILLERN

Laid off after 29 years of working for a local telephone company in North Carolina, "Roberta Green" was struggling. Although she had a part-time job driving a school bus, she was not earning enough to pay her bills. When she received a call from a man who said he could help her come up with some cash, it seemed like a godsend. The man said he worked for a home improvement company

and that he could find her a loan that would both pay for some remodeling on her house and leave enough cash left over to pay her bills.

Unfortunately for Green, the salesman actually worked as a mortgage broker for American Mortgage, and he was not peddling home improvement, but a refinancing of her existing home mortgage at a high interest rate. He invited Green to his office, where he chatted with her while he filled out a mortgage application for her. While he indeed gave her a "good faith estimate" — a form required by regulators that lists the proposed interest rate and fees on a loan — the loan he wrote up was not a home equity loan for the $6,000 she needed to pay off bills. It was a loan for $76,500 that refinanced her entire mortgage at a higher interest rate.

A couple of weeks later Green signed the loan papers and walked out with a check for $1,900. The signing went by so fast, Green didn't catch all that was written on the pages. But she trusted the broker and the lawyer in the room, and felt she had a pretty good grasp on what she was signing.

What Green didn't realize was that her loan terms had changed since she received that good faith estimate. The broker had added $6,500 in fees to her loan, and changed the loan from a fixed-rate to a more expensive adjustable-rate mortgage. Green was a victim of predatory lending.

Predatory lending is any unfair credit practice that harms the borrower or supports a credit system that promotes inequality and poverty. One of the most common predatory practices is placing borrowers into higher interest rate loans than their credit risk would call for. Although they may be eligible for a loan in the so-called "prime" market, they are channeled into more expensive and fee-padded loans in the "subprime" market supposedly just for credit risks. The result: financial services companies end up padding their profit margins by draining away the equity borrowers have built in their homes over the years. Unfortunately, unless a company discriminates against members of a minority group, the elderly, or others protected by law, predatory lending is legal in all states except North Carolina.

Predatory lending is becoming more of a problem as the home mortgage market undergoes rapid change. Banks — the sector of financial services that control the lower interest "prime" market — are issuing a declining share of home mortgages, and the subprime market is booming. The line between consumer finance — including credit cards and small home improvement loans — and home mortgages is blurring as homeowners borrow against their houses to consolidate their debt.

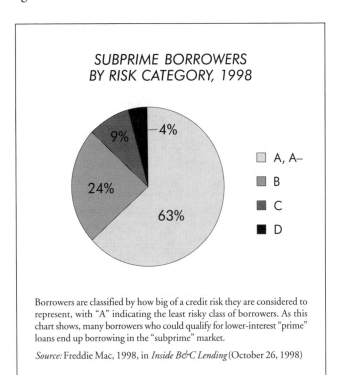

SUBPRIME BORROWERS BY RISK CATEGORY, 1998

- 4%
- 9%
- 24%
- 63%

- ☐ A, A–
- ▨ B
- ▨ C
- ■ D

Borrowers are classified by how big of a credit risk they are considered to represent, with "A" indicating the least risky class of borrowers. As this chart shows, many borrowers who could qualify for lower-interest "prime" loans end up borrowing in the "subprime" market.

Source: Freddie Mac, 1998, in *Inside B&C Lending* (October 26, 1998)

And companies are increasingly using computers to determine credit risk, but in ways that make predatory lending even easier. Credit scoring is a process in which information about a borrower's income, credit history, and job history is fed into a computer program that calculates the borrower's risk of default on the loan. Theoretically, the higher the score a borrower receives, the better credit risk she is, and the lower the interest rate she should receive. Under law, credit scoring should be race-blind, and should insure that similarly situated white and minority borrowers receive similar mortgage rates. However, individual lenders charge wildly different rates for the same score. Mortgage brokers and loan "originators" on the staffs of banks or mortgage companies are often paid incentive commissions for placing borrowers into rates higher than the risk-based price that the underwriting guidelines call for.

Those most hurt by the growing subprime market are black and Hispanic borrowers like Green, who is African American.

According to a 2001 study by the Association of Community Organizers for Reform Now (ACORN), minority borrowers are denied conventional loans far more often than whites. A November 2002 report by the same organization showed that subprime purchase loans to African Americans rose 686% between 1995 and 2001. Not all subprime lending is predatory; higher credit risks are normally charged higher interest on loans. But the growth in subprime lending to minorities, when coupled with the decrease in conventional prime lending, leads to concerns that minority borrowers with good credit are being shut out of conventional markets, and channeled instead into more expensive, subprime loans.

Good subprime lending to borrowers with risky credit can be profitable without engaging in any predatory practices. However, studies by Freddie Mac and Standard & Poor's indicate that 63% of subprime borrowers would have qualified for conventional "A" or "A-" quality loans (see chart).

MORTGAGE BROKERS:
THE WILD, WILD WEST OF CAPITALISM

Mortgage brokers originate over 50% of subprime loans. Some make money in the same way that prime-rate brokers do: they charge the customer a fee for finding a loan. Most make their money from what is known as a "yield-spread premium," a kick-back from the lender in exchange for placing the borrower into a higher-interest loan than what she would normally qualify for. The higher the fees and interest rates a mortgage broker packs into a loan, the greater their compensation.

Predatory lenders often aggressively market to moderate-income and minority communities, through mail, phone, TV, and even door-to-door sales. Their advertisements promise lower monthly payments as a way out of debt. What they don't tell potential borrowers is that they will be paying more and longer. Worse yet, they will

ROBERTA GREEN'S LOAN

Value of home	$81,000
Loan amount	$76,500
Payoff of existing mortgage	$53,000
Credit Insurance (not on Good Faith Estimate)	$3,000
Origination fee	$7,500
Broker fee (not on Good Faith Estimate)	$3,500
Paid debts	$5,690
Cash to borrower	$1,907
Equity left in house	$1,903

be entering a system that promotes a cycle of debt that has been compared to sharecropping, an economic system that is unequal and unfair.

Mortgage brokers often claim they have no responsibility to find borrowers a good loan. They operate on the unregulated fringes of the financial world, in an environment that has been called "the wild, wild west of capitalism." In many states, brokers need only register with the state without taking a licensing exam or any proof of training. Cosmetologists have higher licensing standards than do mortgage brokers in North Carolina. A mortgage broker that violates lending laws can simply close shop and open under a different name.

The mortgage broker who took advantage of Green's trust in him — and her fear that she wouldn't be able to get a loan from a bank — got a $3,500 fee from the mortgage company, which was taken out of Green's home equity. Green received a loan charging 10% interest, packed with inflated fees, including a loan origination fee of $7,500, 10% of the cost of the loan. Over 30 years, Green will pay $40,000 more in interest than she would have if she had gotten a loan at 8%.

CREDIT LIFE INSURANCE COMPANIES

The mortgage broker also tried to sell Green credit life insurance, another common financial service that is generally only sold on subprime loans. If Green should die, the credit life insurance policy would pay off some of the principal left on the loan. Green decided not to buy the insurance because it was too expensive, but the mortgage broker slipped the credit insurance papers into the stack of closing documents and Green signed anyway.

For the credit insurance she did not want, Green paid $3,000 financed over the 30 years of

THE FIGHT FOR PREDATORY LENDING REFORM

In the past year, New York, Los Angeles, and Oakland city councils all passed anti-predatory lending legislation.

New York's ordinance would ban the city from doing business with predatory lenders or companies that purchase predatory loans. Association of Community Organizers for Reform Now (ACORN) members packed City Hall in Manhattan at each stage of the process and successfully promoted the bill over the fervent opposition of major lenders. ACORN's New York branch estimates that the ordinance would save homeowners between $75 million and $100 million. The law was scheduled to take effect in February 2003, but mayor Michael Bloomberg filed a lawsuit in an attempt to repeal the measure.

Los Angeles' proposed ordinance was passed by a unanimous vote by city council in November 2002. And Oakland's ordinance is the toughest in the country.

In addition, there are state-level bills on the table in New Jersey, Massachusetts, and New Mexico—where in November the group protested at a local branch of Wells Fargo, with victims talking about the damage caused by the predatory loans they received from the lender. Most of these bills would ban prepayment penalties, put caps on points, and establish Annual Percentage Rate (APR) thresholds.

In the wake of these state and local efforts, Sen. Paul Sarbanes (D-Maryland), the chair of the Senate Banking Committee in the 107th U.S. Congress, proposed a bill with provisions to ban certain practices characteristic in subprime lending, such as prepayment penalties, credit insurance bundling, financing of fees, and balloon payments (large, lump-sum payments scheduled at the end of a series of smaller payments).

But while ACORN's David Swanson praises these recent small victories, he is concerned about what might happen if a Republican-controlled Congress and White House decide to reverse the progress that has been made.

"I'd hate think that this will all go for naught. That's why we're urging people to get involved in whatever way they can. We can't let the work be in vain," Swanson adds.

—Jabulani Leffall

Adapted from "A Matter of Life and Debt" (*Dollars & Sense*, March/April 2003). The article was produced under the George Washington Williams Fellowship for Journalists of Color, a project sponsored by the Independent Press Association.

the loan. This means that Green will be paying for 30 years on a life insurance product that is only good for five. She will end up paying $10,000 for this life insurance over 30 years.

Financial service companies often offer credit insurance that is financed over time to lower the monthly payments on the premium. This increases the cost of the policy, adding on high interest rates and financing fees to the premium. Also, the financing usually takes equity from the home to pay the insurance premium.

Lenders do not offer a range of competitive insurance products to choose from because they often own or affiliate with a credit insurance company whose product they offer. This insurance is more expensive than other types of insurance, while providing lower benefits. And borrowers often don't realize they bought the insurance, or how much it will cost them.

THE SECONDARY MARKET: WHAT IS THE RESPONSIBILITY OF INVESTORS?

Now Green is trapped into a high-rate loan because the penalties charged if she prepays the loan using a cheaper loan are so large she cannot afford to do it. Lenders typically add such penalties to subprime loans to keep borrowers from refinancing their loans. Without prepayment penalties, subprime loans are more difficult to sell on the secondary market.

Financial institutions raise more cash to make more

HIGH FINANCE PIRATES

Predatory lenders have been called "pirates" by their victims, but these "pirates" are not from some underworld of organized crime. They have links to the most respected institutions in the world, whose billboards celebrate the American dream. Two of the largest high finance firms with predatory lending links are Citigroup, Inc. and Household, Inc.—better known to their opponents as "Citigrope" and "Chokehold."

"CITIGROPE"

New York-based Citigroup is the world's second largest financial services concern and is America's largest consumer finance firm. Its 2001 revenue was $112 billion with profits of $14 billion. Citigroup's chief executive, Sanford Weill, is revered on Wall Street.

But in the past few years, Weill and Citigroup have drawn criticism for the actions of CitiFinancial, the firm's subprime consumer-lending arm—specifically, for CitiFinancial's 2000 acquisition of notorious predatory lender Associates First Capital.

In 2001, the Federal Trade Commission (FTC) alleged that Associates had violated the Federal Trade Commission Act through what it called "deceptive marketing practices that induced consumers to refinance existing debts into home loans with high interest rates, costs, and fees, and to purchase high-cost credit insurance." The FTC also said the company violated the Truth in Lending Act, the Fair Credit Reporting Act, and the Equal Credit Opportunity Act, and used unfair tactics in collecting consumers' payments on its loans.

Jodie Bernstein, then the director of the FTC's Bureau of Consumer Protection, stated in a press release:

"(Associates) hid essential information from consumers, misrepresented loan terms, flipped loans, and packed optional fees to raise the costs of the loans. What had made the alleged practices more egregious is that they primarily victimized consumers who were the most vulnerable—hard working homeowners who had to borrow to meet emergency needs and often had no other access to capital."

To shield itself from liability and attacks from the press, Citigroup launched a website called "Tell Citibank." The homepage says: "Associates Customer: Are you a customer of Associates First Capital? If so, you already may be a victim of predatory lending."

Despite Citigroup's newly deployed campaign for the little guy, it once again found itself the object of protest late last year. According to the California Reinvestment Committee (CRC), Citigroup hides behind its subsidiary CitiFinancial, which CRC contends still charges high points and fees on subprime loans, imposes prepayment penalties that trap borrowers into high cost loans, and sets arbitration provisions denying borrowers access to legal recourse.

The CRC further contends that CitiFinancial lends subprime monies to African-American and Latino borrowers, while low-cost lenders are three to four times as likely to deny African Americans as they are white applicants.

"It's the bait and switch," says Donnette Heard, treasurer for the Los Angeles-based Multicultural Real Estate Alliance For Urban Change. "If the big bank denies you, they send you to their subprime lenders who will then contact you. They keep your business and deal with you on their terms."

"CHOKEHOLD"

According to Internet business portal Hoovers, Household has "made lending to the little people profitable." With a company slogan that says: "Helping everyday people everyday," it is the second largest consumer finance company behind Citigroup. Yet for the past several years, consumer advocacy groups and attorneys general from scores of states have dragged Household through the courts for duping the low-income borrowers into high-interest hell.

In 2002, British Bank HSBC bought Household in a $14 billion deal. With 50 million customers at 1,400 retail branches, Household will lift the earnings before taxes of HSBC's North American operation to more than 30% of the conglomerate's total profits.

This deal, much like Citigroup's acquisition of Associates, is not without controversy. The Bronx, N.Y.-based Inner City Press (ICP), which in the past attacked big banks such as Citigroup, opposes the HSBC-Household deal. ICP revealed data showing that HSBC, even before the acquisition was announced, denied African-American loan applications 2.7 times more frequently than whites' applications. Groups like the ICP believe HSBC will willingly participate in the bait and switch, using Household and its units to trap consumers.

Both Citigroup and Household declined to comment for this article. Company spokespeople did, however, point to the large settlements made to predatory lending plaintiffs.

In the fall of 2002, Citigroup put up almost $250 million and Household about $484 million. The combined settlement money represents the largest sum in American history paid to settle a consumer lending complaint.

But considering that since 1995, predatory lending institutions have raked in almost $100 billion, the $734 million is, in layman's terms, chump change.

In the case of Household, regulators and attorneys general from 20 states had accused it of violating state laws by misrepresenting loan terms and failing to disclose material information. Household said it would record a $330 million charge in the third quarter as a result of the settlement and that its earnings for 2003 would miss Wall Street expectations.

Since the settlement, Citigroup and Household have issued "best practices guidelines" that they say can further prevent future exploitation of borrowers with low incomes or weak credit histories.

Despite Citigroup's and Household's mea culpa, the companies still differ in where they draw the line on abusive practice. And neither will concede that a good number of their predatory loans were issued based on race.

—Jabulani Leffall

Adapted from "A Matter of Life and Debt" (*Dollars & Sense*, March/April 2003). The article was produced under the George Washington Williams Fellowship for Journalists of Color, a project sponsored by the Independent Press Association.

loans by selling the loans they already made to the secondary market. Secondary market companies then "bundle" these loans together and sell them to insurance companies, pension plans, mutual funds, and other investors much as prime mortgages are bundled and resold by Freddie Mac, an entity created by the federal government for this purpose.

Green's loan may be sold on the secondary market. Because her loan has a higher rate of return than a prime-rate loan, the lender will be able to charge more for it and make more money. The law forbidding discrimination in the making of loans also applies to companies that buy discriminatory loans on the secondary market.

THE BOTTOM LINE: WHAT HAPPENS TO THE BORROWER

Before this loan, Green had built up $23,000 of equity in her home. After the loan, she had less than $2,000 left. More than half of her home equity was lost to fees.

Green will also end up paying more over the long term. Her monthly mortgage payments jumped from $500 a month to $740 a month. Her increased debt service and loss of wealth means that she will be even more vulnerable to economic shocks in the future, and more likely to lose her home through foreclosure.

Those who profited from Green's loss of wealth are the loan broker ($3,500), the lender ($13,900), the credit insurance company ($3,000), and the secondary market, which will make an extra $40,000 on Green's loan.

WHY IS PREDATORY LENDING A CRA ISSUE?

The Community Reinvestment Act (CRA) of 1976 allows community groups to hold banks accountable for their lending to minority and low wealth neighborhoods. CRA-regulated banks are subject to a high level of federal regulatory oversight and accountability for their lending practices.

Some banks covered by CRA own subsidiaries that target the subprime market. For example, Bank of America is the largest subprime lender in the country. Wells Fargo owns three subprime lenders: Norwest, Fidelity Financial and Community Credit Co. Some own credit insurance companies. Yet federal regulators do not investigate whether these subsidiaries comply with consumer laws. Independent finance companies that are not banks do not have regular consumer compliance reviews. Thus a two-tier system has evolved, consisting of regulated and unregulated lending.

WHY IS PREDATORY LENDING A FAIR HOUSING ISSUE?

Predatory lenders who discriminate get some scrutiny under the Fair Housing Act of 1968. The law requires equal treatment in terms and conditions of housing opportunities and credit regardless of race, religion, color, national origin, family status, or disability. This applies to loan originators as well as the secondary market.

The Equal Credit Opportunity Act of 1972 requires equal treatment in loan terms and availability of credit for all of these categories, as well as age, sex, and marital status. Lenders would be in violation of these acts if they: target African American, Hispanic or elderly households to buy higher priced and unequal loan products; treat loans of protected classes differently than those of comparably credit-worthy whites; or have policies and practices that have a disproportionate effect on the protected classes.

Examples of fair lending violations include giving a black borrower a higher-cost loan than a white borrower with a comparable credit rating, or buying such a loan on the secondary market. Systematic discrimination that creates a separate and unequal credit system that traps borrowers into higher cost loans is also a fair lending violation. But other victims of predatory lending are not protected under law in most states.

VISIONS FOR THE FUTURE

Ensuring that what happened to Green does not happen to others will require a combination of legislation, litigation, and education. Consumers need to know they can negotiate interest rates and not just take what is offered. They also need to know the warning signs of a predatory loan. Financial institutions also need to be held accountable for predatory practices. To prevent predatory lending we must:

• Strengthen consumer protection lending laws at the national level. (North Carolina's anti-predatory lending law should be used as a national model. It discourages loans charging interest 5 percentage points above the prime lending rate; bans up-front financing of credit life insurance; caps fees at 4% of the loan amount; limits refinancing; and requires credit counseling for subprime borrowers.)

• Require that mortgage brokers be licensed. Mortgage brokers are responsible for the creation of a huge percentage of all home mortgage loans but have virtually no professional legal standards for operation.

• Require that government regulators evaluate credit-scoring systems and standardized pricing guidelines. Credit scoring does not ensure fair pricing based on risk unless regulators oversee the pricing policies and practices of financing institutions.

• Hold subprime lenders and the secondary market accountable. The government must start evaluating whether subprime lenders and the secondary market are complying with consumer and fair lending laws.

Resources: Randall M. Scheessele, *1998 HMDA Highlights,* Department of Housing and Urban Development, Office of Policy Development and Research (September 1999); "Consumer Groups Seek 1999 Meeting with B&C Lenders," *Inside B&C Lending* (October 26, 1998); "Subprime Product Mix, Strategies Changed During a Turbulent 1998," *Inside B&C Lending* (December 21, 1998).

June 1991

ENOUGH IS ENOUGH

WHY MORE IS NOT NECESSARILY BETTER THAN LESS

BY ALAN DURNING

"Our enormously productive economy...demands that we make consumption our way of life, that we convert the buying and use of goods into rituals, that we seek our spiritual satisfaction, our ego satisfaction, in consumption... We need things consumed, burned up, worn out, replaced, and discarded at an ever increasing rate."

Victor Lebow, U.S. retailing analyst, 1955

Across the country, Americans have responded to Victor Lebow's call, and around the globe, those who could afford it have followed. And many can: Worldwide, on average, a person today is four-and-a-half times richer than were his or her great-grandparents at the turn of the last century.

Needless to say, that new global wealth is not evenly spread among the earth's people. One billion live in unprecedented luxury; one billion live in destitution. Overconsumption by the world's fortunate is an environmental problem unmatched in severity by anything except perhaps population growth. Surging exploitation of resources threatens to exhaust or unalterably disfigure forests, soils, water, air, and climate. High consumption may be a mixed blessing in human terms, too. Many in the industrial lands have a sense that, hoodwinked by a consumerist culture, they have been fruitlessly attempting to satisfy social, psychological, and spiritual needs with material things.

Of course, the opposite of overconsumption—poverty—is no solution to either environmental or human problems. It is infinitely worse for people and bad for the natural world. Dispossessed peasants slash and burn their way into Latin American rain forests, and hungry nomads turn their herds out onto fragile African range land, reducing it to desert. If environmental destruction results when people have either too little or too much, we are left to wonder how much is enough. What level of consumption can the earth support? When does having more cease to add appreciably to human satisfaction?

THE CONSUMING SOCIETY

Consumption is the hallmark of our era. The headlong advance of technology, rising earnings, and cheaper material goods have lifted consumption to levels never dreamed of a century ago. In the United States, the world's premier consuming society, people today on average own twice as many cars, drive two-and-a-half times as far, and travel 25 times further by air than did their parents in 1950. Air conditioning spread from 15% of households in 1960 to 64% in 1987, and color televisions from 1% to 93%. Microwave ovens and video cassette recorders reached almost two-thirds of American homes during the 1980s alone.

Japan and Western Europe have displayed parallel trends. Per person, the Japanese today consume more than four times as much aluminum, almost five times as much energy, and 25 times as much steel as they did in 1950. They also own four times as many cars and eat nearly twice as much meat. Like the Japanese, Western Europeans' consumption levels are only one notch below Americans'.

The late 1980s saw some poor societies begin the transition to consuming ways. In China, the sudden surge in spending on consumer durables shows up clearly in data from the State Statistical Bureau: Between 1982 and 1987, color televisions spread from 1% to 35% of urban Chinese homes, washing machines quadrupled from 16% to 67%, and refrigerators expanded their reach from 1% to 20%.

Few would begrudge anyone the simple advantages of cold food storage or mechanized clothes washing. The point, rather, is that even the oldest non-Western nations are emulating the high-consumption lifestyle. Long before all the world's people could achieve the American dream, however, we would lay waste the planet.

The industrial world's one billion meat eaters, car drivers, and throwaway consumers are responsible for the lion's share of the damage humans have caused common global resources. Over the past century, the economies of the wealthiest fifth of humanity have pumped out two-thirds of the greenhouse gases threatening the earth's climate, and each year their energy use releases three-fourths of the sulfur and nitrogen oxides causing acid rain. Their industries generate most of the world's hazardous chemical wastes, and their air conditioners, aerosol sprays, and factories release almost 90% of the chlorofluorocarbons destroying the earth's protective ozone layer. Clearly, even one billion profligate consumers is too much for the earth.

Beyond the environmental costs of acquisitiveness, some perplexing findings of social scientists throw doubt on the wisdom of high consumption as a personal and national goal: Rich societies have had little success in turning consumption into fulfillment. Regular surveys by the National Opinion Research Center of the University of Chicago reveal, for example, that no more Americans report they are "very happy" now than in 1957.

Likewise, a landmark study by sociologist Richard Easterlin in 1974 revealed that Nigerians, Filipinos, Panamanians, Yugoslavians, Japanese, Israelis, and West Germans all ranked themselves near the middle of a happiness scale. Confounding any attempt to correlate affluence and happiness, poor Cubans and rich Americans were both found to be considerably happier than the norm.

If the effectiveness of consumption in providing personal fulfillment is questionable, perhaps environmental concerns can help us redefine our goals.

IN SEARCH OF SUFFICIENCY

By examining current consumption patterns, we receive some guidance on what the earth can sustain. For three of the most ecologically important types of consumption—transportation, diet, and use of raw materials—the world's people are distributed unevenly over a vast range. Those at the bottom clearly fall below the "too little" line, while those at the top, in the cars-meat-and-disposables class, clearly consume too much.

Approximately one billion people do their traveling, aside from the occasional donkey or bus ride, on foot. Unable to get to jobs easily, attend school, or bring their complaints before government offices, they are severely hindered by the lack of transportation options.

Another three billion people travel by bus and bicycle. Kilometer for kilometer, bikes are cheaper than any other vehicle, costing less than $100 new in most of the Third World and requiring no fuel.

The world's automobile class is relatively small: Only 8% of humans, about 400 million people, own cars. The automobile makes itself indispensable: Cities sprawl, public transit atrophies, shopping centers multiply,

> AMERICANS TOSS AWAY 180 MILLION RAZORS ANNUALLY, ENOUGH PAPER AND PLASTIC PLATES AND CUPS TO FEED THE WORLD A PICNIC SIX TIMES A YEAR, AND ENOUGH ALUMINUM CANS TO MAKE 6,000 DC-10 AIRPLANES.

workplaces scatter.

The global food consumption ladder has three rungs. According to the latest World Bank estimates, the world's 630 million poorest people are unable to provide themselves with a healthy diet. On the next rung, the 3.4 billion grain eaters of the world's middle class get enough calories and plenty of plant-based protein, giving them the world's healthiest basic diet.

The top of the ladder is populated by the meat eaters, those who obtain close to 40% of their calories from fat. These 1.25 billion people eat three times as much fat per person as the remaining four billion, mostly because they eat so much red meat. The meat class pays the price of its diet in high death rates from the so-called diseases of affluence—heart disease, stroke, and certain types of cancer.

The earth also pays for the high-fat diet. Indirectly, the meat-eating quarter of humanity consumes nearly 40% of the world's grain—grain that fattens the livestock they eat. Meat production is behind a substantial share of the environmental strains induced by agriculture, from soil erosion to overpumping of underground water.

In consumption of raw materials, such as steel, cotton, or wood, the same pattern emerges. A large group lacks many of the benefits provided by modest use of nonrenewable resources—particularly durables like radios, refrigerators, water pipes, tools, and carts with lightweight wheels and ball bearings. More than two billion people live in countries where per capita consumption of steel, the most basic modern material, falls below 50 kilograms a year.

Roughly 1.5 billion live in the middle class of materials use. Providing each of them with durable goods every year uses between 50 and 150 kilograms of steel. At the top of the heap is the industrial world or the throwaway class. A typical resident of the industrialized fourth of the world uses 15 times as much paper, 10 times as much steel, and 12 times as much fuel as a Third World resident.

In the throwaway economy, packaging becomes an end in itself, disposables proliferate, and durability suffers. Americans toss away 180 million razors annually, enough paper and plastic plates and cups to feed the world a picnic six times a year, and enough aluminum cans to make 6,000 DC-10 airplanes. Similarly, the Japanese use 30 million "disposable" single-roll cameras each year, and the British dump 2.5 billion diapers.

THE CULTIVATION OF NEEDS

What prompts us to consume so much? "The avarice of mankind is insatiable," wrote Aristotle 23 centuries ago. As each of our desires is satisfied, a new one appears in its place. All of economic theory is based on that observation.

What distinguishes modern consuming habits, some would say, is simply that we are much richer than our ancestors, and consequently have more ruinous effects on nature. While a great deal of truth lies in that view, five distinctly modern factors play a role in cultivating particularly voracious appetites: the influence of social pressures in mass societies, advertising, the shopping culture, various government policies, and the expansion of the mass market into households and local communities.

In advanced industrial nations, daily interactions with the economy lack the face-to-face character prevailing in surviving local communities. Traditional virtues such as integrity, honesty, and skill are too hard to measure to serve as yardsticks of social worth. By default, they are gradually supplanted by a simple, single indicator—money. As one Wall Street banker put it bluntly to the *New York Times,* "Net worth equals self-worth."

Beyond social pressures, the affluent live completely enveloped in pro-consumption advertising messages. The sales pitch is everywhere. One analyst estimates that the typical American is exposed to 50 to 100 advertisements each morning before nine o'clock. Along with their weekly 22-hour diet of television, American teenagers are typically exposed to three to four hours of TV advertisements a week, adding up to at least 100,000 ads between birth and high school graduation.

Advertising has been one of the fastest-growing industries during the past half-century. In the United States, ad expenditures rose from $198 per capita in 1950 to $498 in 1989. Worldwide, over the same period, per person advertising expenditures grew from $15 to $46. In developing countries, the increases have been astonishing. Advertising billings in India jumped fivefold in the 1980s; newly industrialized South Korea's advertising industry grew 3540% annually in the late 1980s.

Government policies also play a role in promoting consumption and in worsening its ecological impact. The British tax code, for example, encourages businesses to buy thousands of large company cars for employee use. Most governments in North and South America subsidize beef production on a massive scale.

Finally, the sweeping advance of the commercial mass market into realms once dominated by family members and local enterprise has made consumption far more wasteful than in the past. More and more, flush with cash but pressed for time, households opt for the questionable "conveniences" of prepared, packaged foods, miracle cleaning products, and disposable everything—from napkins to shower curtains. All these things cost the earth dearly.

Like the household, the community economy has atrophied—or been dismembered—under the blind force of the money economy. Shopping malls, superhighways, and strips have replaced corner stores, local restaurants, and neighborhood theaters—the very places that help create a sense of common identity and community. Traditional Japanese vegetable stands and fish shops are giving way to supermarkets and convenience stores, and styrofoam and plastic film have replaced yesterday's newspaper as fish wrap.

All these things nurture the acquisitive desires that everyone has. Can we, as individuals and as citizens, act to confront these forces?

THE CULTURE OF PERMANENCE

The basic value of a sustainable society, the ecological equivalent of the Golden Rule, is simple: Each generation should meet its own needs without jeopardizing the prospects of future generations to meet theirs.

For individuals, the decision to live a life of sufficiency—to find their own answer to the question "how much is enough?"—is to begin a highly personal process. Social researcher Duane Elgin estimated in 1981—perhaps optimistically—that 10 million adult Americans were experimenting "wholeheartedly" with voluntary simplicity. India, the Netherlands, Norway, Western Germany, and the United Kingdom all have small segments of their populations who adhere to a non-consuming philosophy. Motivated by the desire to live justly in an unjust world, to walk gently on the earth, and to avoid distraction, clutter, and pretense, their goal is not ascetic self-denial but personal fulfillment. They do not think consuming more is likely to provide it.

Realistically, voluntary simplicity is unlikely to gain ground rapidly against the onslaught of consumerist values. And, ultimately, personal restraint will do little if not wedded to bold political and social steps against the forces promoting consumption. Commercial television, for example, will need fundamental reorientation in a culture of permanence. As religious historian Robert Bellah put it, "That happiness is to be attained through limitless material acquisition is denied by every religion and philosophy known to humankind, but is preached incessantly by every American television set."

Direct incentives for overconsumption are also essential targets for reform. If goods' prices reflected something closer to the environmental cost of their production, through revised subsidies and tax systems, the market itself would guide consumers toward less damaging forms of consumption. Disposables and packaging would rise in price relative to durable, less-packaged goods; local unprocessed food would fall in price relative to prepared products trucked from far away.

The net effect might be lower overall consumption as people's effective purchasing power declined. As currently constituted, unfortunately, economies penalize the poor when aggregate consumption contracts: Unemployment skyrockets and inequalities grow. Thus arises one of the greatest challenges for sustainable economics in rich societies—finding ways to ensure basic employment opportunities for all without constantly stoking the fires of economic growth.

DIMINISHING MARGINAL UTILITY AND THE UTILITY OF DIMINISHING INEQUALITY

BY PHINEAS BAXANDALL

If you have no chairs in your house then getting a first chair will be tremendously useful to you. A second chair would also be a huge help, though the difference it makes is probably smaller than the first chair. If you got more and more chairs, the pleasure obtained from each additional one would grow smaller and smaller. If you were to receive a tenth chair, its contribution to your well-being would be minimal. This fundamental principle of modern economics, taught in Econ 101 courses throughout the land, is called the Law of Diminishing Marginal Utility. It is an intuitive concept used to explain, among other things, why a firm may need to decrease the price of their product in order to boost sales.

But economists rarely consider that this economic "law" has serious implications for evaluating inequality of income and wealth. Economics courses briefly discuss "utility" in terms of goods, then move along to discuss benefits or costs exclusively in terms of dollars. Since pleasure, like pain, is experienced subjectively, an economist would be hard pressed to say whether the marginal utility of your second chair is greater than the additional usefulness from your second lamp. But if you paid $100 for the chair and $60 for the lamp, then, any introductory economics text would declare that you must value the chair more highly than the lamp. Since the goal of economic policy should be to maximize social welfare — the utility that people in the aggregate obtain from consuming goods and services — economists use dollar values as a stand-in for utility and compare dollar amounts when making comparisons about well-being or the results of different policy options.

The problem is that the marginal utility of a dollar is almost certainly greater for some people than for others. An additional dollar would make a bigger difference in the life of a poor person than it would for a wealthy person. To someone with no money, a few extra dollars can mean the difference between hunger and a meal or between sleeping in the snow or renting a room. That same few extra dollars in the hands of a millionaire represents the difference between a sirloin and filet mignon. By counting well-being in the shorthand of dollars, economists conclude that nothing is gained by

> AN ADDITIONAL DOLLAR WOULD MAKE A BIGGER DIFFERENCE IN THE LIFE OF A POOR PERSON THAN IT WOULD FOR A WEALTHY PERSON.

shifting money from a millionaire to poorer folks. Since no extra well-being or usefulness is created, redistributing income, economists say, is not "pareto optimal"; the poor are made better off, but only by making the rich worse off.

Economists recognize no difference between a situation where one million dollars is divided relatively equally among ten people and a situation where one person receives $900,000 while the remaining nine people get $11,000 each. By contrast, it seems obvious that ten chairs are much more usefully divided equally among ten people than if one person sat on nine chairs while the remaining nine people shared a single chair.

In recent decades, as inequality has increased in America, it makes less and less sense to always use dollars as a stand-in for what we really care about, actual utility or well-being. For instance, in the 1960s the average chief executive officer (CEO) heading a large corporation made about 45 times as much as their average worker. By the end of the 1990s a typical CEO made 475 times as much as their average employee. Major corporations argue it is worth paying these astronomical salaries in order to recruit CEOs who inspire confidence among investors. The question is whether society benefits when a few corporate executives receive millions while ordinary workers see pay increases of only a few dollars. Is social well-being enhanced when the very rich can build 10,000 square foot second homes, but the typical worker gets only enough for an extra tank of gas?

Some economists counter that the rich worked hard for their wealth and enjoy their summer homes every bit as much as the rest of us would all enjoy an extra night at the movies. Others contend that inequality has its own "utility" as a spur for people to work hard and innovate. But going back to the economic principle of diminishing marginal utility reminds us that real needs and satisfactions can be most usefully met by sharing resources more equally.

Resources: Executive Excess 2000: Seventh Annual CEO Compensation Survey, Institute for Policy Studies and United for a Fair Economy, August 2000.

CHAPTER 4

Firms, Production, and Profit Maximization

INTRODUCTION

How do producers make decisions? Textbooks describe a process that is rational, benign, and downright sensible. There is one best—that is, least costly and most profitable—way to produce any given amount of goods or services. Given a particular scale of operations, there is one most profitable amount to produce. Businesses adjust their total output and the mix of inputs at the margin until they achieve these most profitable outcomes. They pay the going wage for labor, just as they pay the going price for any input. And when businesses have achieved the lowest possible costs, market competition ensures that they pass on savings to consumers.

This chapter describes a reality that is more complicated, and in some ways uglier than the textbook model. Annette Bernhardt opens the discussion by suggesting that there may not be "one best way" for retail businesses, but two—a "high road" based on high levels of service, skilled and decently-paid employees, and higher prices, and a "low road" that offers low prices, no frills, and a low-paid, high-turnover workforce (Bernhardt, article 4.1). Alejandro Reuss notes that just as predatory lenders make profits at consumers' expense, businesses such as Wal-Mart boost profits by cheating workers. In fact, Reuss's main question is why allegations of illegal wage underpayment at Wal-Mart have generated so little public outrage (Reuss, article 4.2). Barbara Goldoftas describes how poultry processors have sped up their (dis-)assembly lines, extracting more work under unsafe conditions that can injure workers for life (Goldoftas, article 4.3). Cynthia Peters and Robin Hahnel offer another challenge to "one best way" logic, but instead of proposing a different organization within capitalism, they argue for an entirely new organization of work and society. They take as models alternative businesses where workers collectively control production and redistribute tasks to break down social hierarchies. Transforming work to make it more fulfilling and dignified need not hurt efficiency, they conclude—and even if it did, the tradeoff might be worth it (Peters and Hahnel, article 4.4).

All of these articles argue that the purchase and utilization of labor raises social and moral questions different from those involved in other decisions about production.

They suggest that businesses' pursuit of profit may have unacceptable costs to workers. What's more, they maintain that production can be organized in a variety of different ways, with very different implications for workers' well-being.

DISCUSSION QUESTIONS

1) (General) Do you agree that the use and purchase of labor raises different issues than other inputs for production? Why or why not?

2) (Bernhardt, Peters and Hahnel) Annette Bernhardt, Cynthia Peters, and Robin Hahnel argue that there is more than one "best" way to organize production, both within and outside capitalism. Do you agree? If other ways of organizing production are equally good, why are certain ways dominant, at least in particular industries?

3) (Bernhardt, Peters and Hahnel) Bernhardt and Peters and Hahnel say that we should change the rules of the competitive game to steer businesses toward better treatment of workers. Peters and Hahnel point out that current-day capitalism already has some such rules (such as those forbidding slavery), so it makes sense to think through what rules would best meet our goals as a society. What rule changes does each of these articles propose? What do you think of these proposals? Would other rule changes work better? Or do you think we should leave the rules as they are?

4) (Bernhardt) Bernhardt describes Wal-Mart's "just-in-time" competitive strategy. Explain how this approach changes the mix of fixed and variable costs, and the advantages this change offers Wal-Mart.

5) (Bernhardt, Reuss) Both Bernhardt and Alejandro Reuss tell about Wal-Mart's "fierce" drive to minimize costs. Where does aggressive cost-cutting cross the line? Would you draw the line at law-breaking, or are there some legal business practices—in addition to illegal ones—that you consider unacceptable?

6) (Goldoftas) Worker injuries seem to represent a cost that is not reflected in a firm's balance sheet. Or is it? How might economic processes result in higher wages for workers who risk injury? (Think back to supply and demand analysis, and what happens when suppli-

ers' costs go up.) Then, setting aside the theory, how much do you think this kind of process actually affects workers' wages?

7) (Peters and Hahnel) Production cost analysis tells us that businesses achieve higher productivity and lower costs through division of labor and worker specialization. But Peters and Hahnel warn that division of labor has usually meant creating a social hierarchy in which some people have pleasant, interesting jobs while others have dumbed-down, boring ones. Peters and Hahnel disagree that dividing up work requires extensive specialization and the creation of jobs that are intrinsically dull. They instead call for "balanced job complexes" that circulate workers through different kinds of work. Interestingly, they say the evidence is that work organized in this way is no less productive. How can this be? (Hint: Think about other advantages that may outweigh the lost advantages of division of labor.)

KEY TO COLANDER

These articles are designed to fit with Chapters 9-11, though they also anticipate some topics in Chapter 14, "Real World Competition and Technology," Chapter 15, "Antitrust Policy and Regulation," and Chapter 16, "Work and the Labor Market." For the most part, they do not link up to particular portions of Colander's analysis, but rather raise questions that go unasked in standard economic theory.

Question 4.3 (about the rules of the competitive game) connects especially to Chapter 11, "Perfect Competition."

Question 4.4 (about fixed and variable costs) and Question 4.7 (about division of labor) relate particularly to Chapter 9, "Production and Cost Analysis I."

Colander touches on Peters and Hahnel's argument about workplace democracy in a short box entitled "Democracy in the Workplace" that appears in Chapter 16.

September/October 2000

THE WAL-MART TRAP

BY ANNETTE BERNHARDT

For every woman shattering the glass ceiling, there are many more trapped in low-wage jobs and working conditions that don't look very different from those at the start of the women's movement. Since 1973, the gender gap in wages has almost been cut in half, but women still earn significantly less than men, are still segregated in traditionally female occupations, and are less likely to have health and pension coverage—despite total parity in education. The problem is especially severe at the bottom of the wage hierarchy. In 1997, 18% of white men earned poverty-level wages, compared to 32% of white women, 43% of black women, and 53% of Hispanic women.

So where are all the low-wage jobs coming from? And why haven't they gone away in the "postindustrial" economy? Most of them are service jobs, and most continue to be the territory of women and people of color: hotel room cleaners, nursing assistants, data-entry clerks, hamburger flippers, secretaries, childcare workers, cashiers, tellers, call-center operators. These jobs are not coming from dinosaur firms that somehow haven't yet caught on to the new "high-tech" credo. More and more, low-wage jobs are being created by efficient, technologically sophisticated firms. The new "high-tech, low-skill" business strategy is typified by the retail industry, and particularly by the business model of retail giant Wal-Mart. And because this model is so profitable, it will continue to dominate the working lives of many Americans, especially women.

SEGMENTATION IN THE RETAIL INDUSTRY

In the private sector, one in five Americans (21%) currently holds a retail job. Among the occupations with the largest projected job growth to 2006, cashiers and salespeople rank first and fifth, respectively. Yet retail wages for non-managerial workers averaged only $9.08 an hour in 1999. In 1997, nearly a third (31.7%) of the workers living in poverty worked in retail, compared to 15.8% of the overall population.

While jobs in this industry have never been good, retail wages have actually fallen as a percent of the national average, from 74% in 1973 to 68% in 1999. This deterioration in job quality has been driven by a splitting of the consumer market over the past two decades. On the one hand, there are now specialized department stores, upscale grocers, and home improvement and auto repair centers offering personalized, in-depth service. On the other hand are the mass discounters, outlet stores, and uncountable fast-food franchises offering no-frills service and cheap products. Here, wages and job quality rank at the bottom.

Bloomingdale's and Stern's department stores, both owned by Federated holding company, illustrate this split. Bloomingdale's serves high-income customers. Only 20% of its workers are part-time, turnover is low, wages are above average for Federated stores, and a significant amount of money is spent on recruiting polished workers with good "people skills"—mostly young white women attending college. By contrast, Stern's is a mass-market operation. It focuses not on service but rather on centralizing and streamlining operations with new technology and fewer people. Wages are significantly lower, about 60% of the jobs are part-time, and turnover is high. Employees tend to come from working-class backgrounds.

This market and job segmentation has emerged in such industries as healthcare, banking, telecommunications, insurance, and airlines. But retail is unique, because it is dominated by the low-wage strategy. And this strategy has been defined, almost single-handedly, by one company.

THE ASCENT OF WAL-MART

The "Wal-Mart model" is the leading retail strategy (perhaps the leading business strategy in any sector) to emerge since the 1970s. This model features a super-efficient production process in which each operation—buying products from manufacturers, distributing them to the retail stores, and selling them to customers—is linked to the next in a continuous "just-in-time" chain. Starting with the premise that its stores would compete with "everyday low prices," Wal-Mart has attacked this coordination problem on several fronts.

At the core of its strategy lies technology. Wal-Mart pioneered the use of inventory-managing technology, and in recent years has invested some $600 million in its information system. When scanning barcodes, cash registers instantaneously record and track every item sold, producing an up-to-the minute computerized inventory record. This information is then linked directly to both the warehouse distribution centers and the manufacturers that supply them, automating the whole restocking process.

Wal-Mart's integration of the entire supplier-distribution chain may seem straightforward, but it is in fact extraordinarily difficult to achieve. As of June 2000, the company was selling thousands of products in its 2,988

U.S. stores, staffed by 885,000 workers. These stores were supplied by 51 distribution centers and served more than 100 million customers weekly. The "just-in-time" flow depends on tighter relationships with suppliers, another Wal-Mart innovation. The company has increasingly focused on a small core of suppliers, pressuring them for bigger discounts, help in delivery and stocking, product testing and development, and even total dedication to supplying only Wal-Mart.

Technology is only a conduit for Wal-Mart's single-minded business strategy of total market dominance. Until recently, the company has wisely stuck to non-urban areas where retail competition is weak. When it enters a new region, Wal-Mart places one or two initial stores according to a grid. It then successively adds more stores, breaking the grid into smaller and smaller pieces, until the region is saturated and mom-and-pop stores have been driven out of business. This strategy has not gone unnoticed: in America's heartland, communities are increasingly protesting the arrival of new Wal-Mart stores.

CONTRARY TO HEAVY COMPANY PUBLICITY, SUCH AS TELEVISION COMMERCIALS FEATURING HAPPY WAL-MART "SALES ASSOCIATES," MOST JOBS AT WAL-MART ARE NOT GOOD JOBS.

PEOPLE UNDER THE WAL-MART MODEL

Contrary to heavy company publicity, such as television commercials featuring happy Wal-Mart "sales associates," most jobs at Wal-Mart are not good jobs. Sales associates basically ring up sales, stock and neaten shelves, and handle lay-aways. Traditional job segregation continues unabated at Wal-Mart: Women are disproportionately relegated to cashier positions, customer service, or sales positions in low-ticket departments such as apparel and jewelry, while men are disproportionately assigned to managerial positions or to lucrative departments such as appliances.

Work schedules change constantly, and if demand is slack, associates are asked and even required to leave their shifts early. Conversely, part-timers often work full-time hours without getting the corresponding benefits. Stores are often understaffed, something Wal-Mart workers blame for the stressful work environment. When the company opens a store, it hires more workers than it will eventually need, partly to help with set-up, but also to screen its new employees. After several months, Wal-Mart lets go those it does not need. Clearly, workers are bearing the brunt of the "just-in-time" system.

Not surprisingly, the company keeps a tight fist on its payroll. Starting wages are either at or close to the minimum wage. Raises are not guaranteed and top out at 30¢ a year. Even department heads start at only $8 an hour. Genuine full-time work (40 hours a week) is hard to get at Wal-Mart, because the company defines "full-time" as 28 hours a week. This odd definition allows the company to increase staffing as needed, without exceeding the limit of 40 hours a week (thereby avoiding the time-and-a-half pay mandated by federal law). Health benefits are available for full-timers, but the workers must contribute 40% from their own paychecks (a significant deduction at $5 or $6 an hour). There is no pension plan, though the employee stock ownership plan is touted as a substitute. The problem is that most workers never benefit from this system. Between high turnover and low pay, less than 2% have accumulated $50,000 or more in stock.

PROSPECTS FOR CAREER MOBILITY

Wal-Mart registered sales of $165 billion last year. The company consistently outperforms other retailers on most measures of productivity and performance. Its business model has put enormous pressure on the industry to follow suit, and will continue to prevail in the foreseeable future.

Is this really cause for concern? One common argument is that the retail sector and other low-wage service industries serve as a temporary way-station for workers—mothers wanting to get out of the house, retirees looking for something to occupy their time, and especially teenagers earning spending money. But this is a misleading or, at the very least, outdated picture. In 1996, only 16% of the workers in this industry were between the ages of 16 and 19. Fully 44% were age 35 or older. More and more, retail workers depend on their jobs for their long-term livelihood. In working-class and inner-city communities across the country, retail is in fact the main employer.

And in this dependence lies the heart of the problem, because low-wage jobs are "sticky"—once you're in, you're trapped. Moving up is tough, since many service industries have extremely flat job hierarchies. Sales and service occupations make up more than two-thirds of retail jobs, and the average ratio of managerial to front-line workers is 1:15. A typical Wal-Mart store has one store manager, four assistant managers, and 235 non-salaried workers. Moving out is equally tough, because training is almost non-existent. Retail workers get, on average, seven hours of training (last among 14 business sectors), giving them few skills with which to get better jobs.

POLICY OPTIONS

So what are the options for boosting job quality at the bottom of the service sector? The answer will probably not be found in the market. Wal-Mart has perfected a business strategy that does not build on "human capital" but that is nevertheless high-tech, efficient, and profitable. This means that the "high-road" carrot is unlikely to work here. Wal-Mart and its ilk are already taking the "high road" technologically—only with a low-wage crew. These businesses have nothing to gain by upskilling jobs. If Wal-Mart trained and paid workers to spend more quality time with customers, profits would suffer. Similarly, what would convince McDonald's to shift its Taylorized system to one based on skilled workers, given the enormous startup costs and the amount of capital it has already sunk into designing its kitchen around low-skill labor?

High-skill strategies are a hard sell at the bottom of the service sector. Ultimately, the only realistic solution to bad jobs in these industries is non-market intervention. The minimum wage and Earned Income Tax Credit are obvious candidates, though they will likely not suffice, especially since the latter ends up subsidizing low-wage employers. In the long run, what is needed is an all-out unionization assault on Wal-Mart and other firms like it. The United Food and Commercial Workers International Union (UFCW) is starting to do just that, responding to Wal-Mart's entry into the supermarket industry by mounting a national community-based organizing campaign. This spring, for example, meat cutters at a Wal-Mart store in Jacksonville, Texas, won union recognition, a first in the history of the retailer. But Wal-Mart responded by closing its meat-cutting operations in 180 stores in six states, including the one where workers had organized.

The obstacles to organizing a high-turnover service workforce are enormous. A new type of unionism will likely be needed, one that is multi-employer and occupationally based. Pursuing such a strategy will take significant reform on many fronts—not only in labor's willingness to adopt a new constituency and new organizing tactics, but more importantly, in labor law itself.

Resources: Annette Bernhardt, "Performance Without the High: Firms and Technology in Low-End Services," presented at the 2000 Annual Meetings of the Industrial Relations Research Association, Boston, Mass.; Lawrence Mishel, Jared Bernstein, and John Schmitt, *The State of Working America 1998-99*, Washington D.C.: Economic Policy Institute, 1999.

ARTICLE 4.2   *November/December 2002*

IT ALL DEPENDS ON WHO YOU ROB

BY ALEJANDRO REUSS

Considering all the stories of corporate treachery that have made headlines over the last year, you would think that accusations of massive and systematic theft at the United States' largest corporation would inspire exposés, set off investigations, perhaps even lead to arrests. So why aren't the mainstream media and the government up in arms about the "Wal-Mart scandal"?

Lawsuits filed by current and former Wal-Mart workers in 28 states have accused the company of forcing them to work "off the clock" for no pay—robbing them of wages to which they are entitled by law and by right. The recent suits—which allege that Wal-Mart supervisors make employees work, sometimes for hours, before clocking in, work through scheduled breaks, and continue working after punching out at night—are by no means small potatoes. In 2000, the company settled a class-action suit, covering nearly 70,000 Colorado workers who had been forced to work off the clock, for $50 million. A current suit, covering 200,000 Texas workers, alleges that Wal-Mart robbed them of over $150 million in wages by forcing them to work, unpaid, through their breaks.

So why haven't cops hauled Wal-Mart executives away in handcuffs? Why haven't the accusations of massive theft warranted the "scandal" treatment the press and politicians have given Enron, Halliburton, Adelphia, Tyco, WorldCom, etc.? At Enron and companies like it, the discovery of fraudulent corporate profit reports (which had inflated stock prices long enough for the executives to cash in) set off stock-price meltdowns. Stock holders were among the prominent "victims," and each new revelation made for a juicy "corrupt executives vs. deceived investors" morality play. The Wal-Mart lawsuits, which tell a story of everyday (though criminal) exploitation, just do not fit the script.

Carried away by the "irrational exuberance" of the late 1990s, the capitalist media virtually declared that a booming economy was synonymous with a booming stock market. As often as they crowed that nearly half of all U.S. households now owned stock, they apparently missed the converse—that more than half owned no stock at all. The triumphal story of the stock boom ignored this "silent majority." So do media scandals that focus on imploding stocks and investors left holding worthless paper.

As economist James K. Galbraith wrote in the *Texas Observer*, it was "not only small fry [investors], but modest millionaires in some cases, who lost their 401(k)s" in the Enron meltdown. "And there is nothing a hardworking middle manager fears more, than to end up on Social Security like ordinary folk." The power of companies over even relatively privileged employees—many of whom were barred from selling their stock holdings while company executives cashed in—is clear in the Enron scandal and others like it. By focusing on the "modest millionaires," however, the scandal coverage implicitly tells the "ordinary folk" that it's not such a big deal when they get robbed.

The "profits" at Enron may have been phony, but Wal-Mart's are very real—over $6 billion last year. The *New York Times* reports how the company has built its empire: "Many analysts say Wal-Mart's push to minimize costs is the fiercest in the industry, and holding down labor costs—including fighting off unionization at its stores—is at the heart of Wal-Mart's effort to be the nation's low-cost retailer." Low wages, meager benefits, and union busting for Wal-Mart's U.S. employees, not to mention sweatshop work and poverty pay for the Third World workers that produce the company's wares—all boost company profits and "shareholder value."

Every once in a while investors fall victim to fraud. But they are among the main beneficiaries of this daily exploitation. According to the official U.S. government National Income and Product Accounts, income from capital—including rent, dividends, interest, and realized capital gains—accounts for about one fifth of the U.S. money economy. Nearly half of that goes to the richest 1% of the U.S. population. Over seven tenths, well over $1 trillion in annual income, enrich the top 10%—just for owning property.

Fast Company founding editor Alan M. Weber writes, "Most CEOs aren't crooks—but they are incredibly competitive, financially motivated individuals … that's exactly what investors pay CEOs to be. So the real remedy is not to arrest them and send them to jail. It's to reward them for creating wealth for the company and for the shareholders." That, of course, is just what Wal-Mart executives have done. And if they have "created" that wealth by plundering workers, where's the scandal? That's just capitalism as usual.

September 1989

TO MAKE A TENDER CHICKEN

TECHNOLOGICAL CHANGE AND COSTCUTTING TAKE THEIR TOLL

BY BARBARA GOLDOFTAS

In 1983 Donna Bazemore took the best-paying job she could find in northeastern North Carolina — gutting chickens for Perdue Farms. At first she slit open carcasses; later she became a "mirror trimmer" on the night shift. As the birds moved by on the assembly line, a federal inspector next to her examined their far sides in a mirror. He pointed out unacceptable tumors, bruises, and other "physical defects," which Bazemore sliced off with huge scissors.

While the job paid better than the minimum wage she might have earned elsewhere, the conditions were grueling.

Bazemore worked in 90-degree heat as the chickens sped by, 72 to 80 a minute. Strict work rules limited bathroom breaks. The primarily black, female work force faced sexual harassment and racism from the white male supervisors. And the women endured a slew of medical problems, ranging from skin rashes to cuts to swollen, painful hands and arms.

Several months after becoming a mirror trimmer, Bazemore noticed that she had no feeling in several fingertips. The numbness progressed to pains shooting up the inside of her arm — symptoms of carpal tunnel syndrome, a potentially disabling disorder caused by overly repetitive movements.

Even after surgery, the trouble continued. "I had no strength in my hands," she says. "I couldn't do the littlest tasks around the house, like sweep a floor or stir for long periods of time. I couldn't write six or seven words without having to rest my hand."

Bazemore is one of thousands of workers hurt by their jobs in poultry processing plants—the polite term for slaughterhouses. "Work in poultry plants by every stretch of the imagination is horrible," says Artemis (her full name). She has worked for two different companies in northern Arkansas, a region thick with poultry plants. "It's stressful, demanding, noisy, dirty. You're around slimy dead bodies all the time. And it's very dangerous."

According to its trade journal, *Broiler Industry*, the industry makes "staggering" profits. Demand for poultry has grown steadily for decades, and U.S. consumers now eat more chicken and turkey than red meat. Production increased by 67% in just 10 years, from 12 billion pounds in 1977 to about 20 billion pounds in 1987.

The industry's growth and profitability have in large part come at the expense of poultry workers who, according to the Bureau of Labor Statistics, suffer twice the average private sector rates of illness and injury. As poultry processing expanded, it grew increasingly concentrated. Firms converted to large-scale assembly-line operations, ultimately speeding up and deskilling individual jobs. The resulting breakneck pace and repetitive motions tax workers' hands and arms—and can ultimately cripple them.

A CHICKEN IN EVERY POT

The poultry industry of 50 years ago hardly resembled the one that ConAgra, Tyson Foods, and Perdue now dominate. Small farmers raised most chickens and turkeys, sending them to private, local slaughterhouses. The birds were smaller and more expensive than those sold today. People ate less poultry and usually bought it whole.

In the 1940s, poultry scientists created new breeds of birds that grew faster and did not waste away in crowded conditions. The innovations made large-scale operations both feasible and efficient. In the 1940s and 1950s, giant "integrators," which already owned slaughterhouses, animal feed mills, and hatcheries, bought out the small chicken farms as well.

Since the 1960s, processing has undergone a similar transformation. Mechanizing parts of their operations enabled firms to increase the volume and size of their plants. The industry also grew more consolidated. In 1977, the top four firms slaughtered just 20% of all chickens killed in the United States. By 1987, their portion had nearly doubled to 38%. During that same period, poultry companies used the gimmick of name-brand poultry to secure a larger share of the retail market.

They began selling directly to the fast-food and retail outlets, and they introduced new, expensive products that required further processing.

A typical poultry plant now processes tens of thousands of chickens each day. One by one, live birds are hung by the feet on a moving line of hooks called shackles and mechanically stunned, decapitated, and scalded to remove the feathers. They are quickly gutted and then cut into parts, packaged whole, or sped through a deboning line.

Throughout the plant, workers perform simple, highly repetitive jobs. They draw out guts, pull livers, cut wings and gizzards, pop thigh bones. Most do a single, defined movement—cutting, slicing, lifting birds onto the shackles, or pulling breast meat from the bone with their fingers. They may repeat this motion 25, 40, 90 times a minute, hour after hour. "They treat you as if you were a machine,

POULTRY WORKERS ORGANIZE

Three-fourths of poultry processing happens in Arkansas, Georgia, Alabama, and North Carolina. The warm climate allows year-round production, and the poultry firms also prefer the southern labor climate—cheap and largely unorganized.

For many workers, poultry jobs are steadier and easier than field work. And the companies pay more than convenience stores and fastfood joints, usually between $4.50 and $6.00 an hour.

The price of the job, though, is high—a worker's safety and health—and even in anti-union areas, workers are starting to organize. At the Cargill plant in Buena Vista, Georgia, workers say the Retail, Wholesale, and Department Store Union (RWDSU), which survived a recent decertification drive there, gives them a say about their health.

"A lot of people are afraid to speak up, afraid to get fired," says Felton Toombs, who was fired three months after having carpal tunnel surgery in 1988. "You need someone to speak up for you when something goes wrong."

In northeastern North Carolina, the Center for Women's Economic Alternatives (CWEA) teaches workers that they should not have to choose between their job and their health. Organizers offer clinics about repetitive motion injuries, and they have helped hundreds of Perdue workers get medical care and workers' compensation. Workers are now asking to be sent to the doctor, says former Perdue worker Bazemore. "A couple months ago, they were losing fingers and arms and they would never complain."

plugged in, running on electricity," says Rita Eason, another former Perdue worker.

Like Bazemore, many workers do their jobs in conditions of extreme heat or cold. Processing involves both ice and scalding water, and plant temperatures reportedly vary from 26 to 95 degrees. Bazemore's department lacked ventilation, despite the heat, and in other departments, she says, "people wear three, four, five pair of socks and long underwear all year. And they're still cold."

Although the work is fast and hard, the companies allow few scheduled breaks, usually just lunch and two 10- or 15-minute rests each day. At many plants, a strict disciplinary system keeps workers in line—literally. Returning late from a break or missing part of a day, regardless of the reason, brings an "occurrence" or "write-up." After a certain number of write-ups, workers are "terminated."

> AFRAID TO ASK PERMISSION TO LEAVE THE LINE, OR FORBIDDEN TO LEAVE, WORKERS SOMETIMES URINATE, VOMIT, AND EVEN MISCARRY AS THE CHICKENS PASS BY.

"If you had to go to the bathroom more than once in two or three hours, they would threaten to write you up," says Brenda Porter, who worked at a Cargill plant in Buena Vista, Georgia, for 12 years.

Afraid to ask permission to leave the line, or forbidden to leave, workers sometimes urinate, vomit, and even miscarry as the chickens pass by. Although it has been nine years since Eason worked at Perdue, she remembers clearly seeing "a grown woman stand on the line and urinate right on herself. She was too scared to move. But then she got so cold she walked out and went home."

A constant risk of illness and injury compounds the harsh day-to-day conditions in the plants. Common ailments include warts, infections from bone splinters, and rashes from the chlorine water used to wash birds contaminated with feces. Workers often lose fingernails and toenails, and they suffer injuries from the knives, saws, and machinery.

The speed and repetition of the work cause the most serious problems. Performing the same action for hours and hours makes poultry workers highly susceptible to debilitating conditions of the nerves, muscles, and tendons. These cumulative trauma disorders, also called repetitive motion injuries, occur among a wide range of workers, from letter sorters to textile workers to typists. According to the Bureau of Labor Statistics, the disorders were the fastest-growing occupational disease of the 1980s.

Carpal tunnel syndrome, which damaged Bazemore's arms, is the most severe such disorder. When the tendons passing though a narrow channel in the wrist—the carpal tunnel—are overused, they swell and press on the nerve that controls feeling in the hand. The result can be painful—and permanently disabling.

Although Mary Smith only worked at Cargill for seven months, her brief stint at the Buena Vista plant left her with hands that hurt day and night. She started in March 1988, trimming bruises and tumors from chicken skin. The pain began in June. "At first they would swell. The nurse said it was normal; I had to get used to the job," she says. "They started hurting real bad and getting numb, especially at night. I'd wake up, shake them, lay them on the pillow. It didn't do no good."

She has not worked since last September but, says Smith, "I still have problems holding things. It hurts to wash dishes, take clothes out of the machine. My arm hurts at night, hurts all day. I get so frustrated sometimes, I feel like just cutting it off." She is hardly alone. At least 14 of her co-workers have had surgery for carpal tunnel syndrome. Union stewards at the plant estimate that more than a third of the workers there have trouble with their hands.

THEY WEAR OUT

While gutting and cutting chickens was never easy, poultry work became even harder as the industry expanded. During the 1960s and 1970s, firms increased their productivity by replacing workers with machines. A skilled worker, for example, could slaughter about 66 birds a minute, while a killing machine beheads five times as many—five a second. To meet the recent rise in demand, the plants sped up production, and workers now work at a faster pace for longer hours. Between 1975 and 1985, output per worker increased by 43%.

The U.S. Department of Agriculture (USDA), which regulates slaughterhouses, facilitated the speed-up. Federal inspectors check each bird before and after slaughter, working no faster than the rate set by the agency. Since 1979, USDA engineers have pared down the inspection time allowed for each bird. Upper limits jumped from 57 to 70 birds a minute for two inspectors, even reaching 91 for some high-speed plants.

Safe-food advocates worry about contaminated birds and rising rates of salmonella infections, but the speed-ups have also been critical to the 150,000 workers who process poultry. The changes constituted a "policy shift toward de facto deregulation," says Tom Devine of the Government Accountability Project, a whistleblower support group in Washington, D.C. that has worked with former USDA inspectors. "The idea was to keep the USDA seal of approval but get inspectors out of the way of faster line speeds."

The agency simply determines how quickly inspectors can work "comfortably," says Patrick Burke of the USDA's Food Safety and Inspection Service. "They wear out if the rate's too fast." Asked about how the speed-up might affect other workers, whose "comfort" is not monitored, Burke says that the USDA "can't legally do anything with plant employees."

The new, lucrative products of the 1980s — filleted breasts, poultry patties, chicken nuggets — have made poultry work even more physically demanding. Workers who cut or pull the meat from the bone use quick, repetitive motions that are particularly trying on their wrists and hands. Even Cargill spokesman Greg Lauser acknowledges that the "more intensive processing operations tend to have a greater incidence of repetitive motion injuries."

Many workers suffering from repetitive motion injuries have a hard time getting treatment because of hostile management, untrained nurses, and doctors who know little about their medical problems. "When you tell people you're hurting, they don't really believe you," says Perdue worker Rose Harrell, who was bounced from doctor to doctor before being diagnosed with carpal tunnel. "I told the plant manager that I didn't mind working, but my hands hurt. 'What you telling me for,' he said. 'I can't stop your hands from hurting.'"

Workers and union officials at plants throughout the South describe similar circumstances. "At Cargill [in Buena Vista] when a worker notices her hands are hurting, she'll be given Advil and told that she's just breaking them in," says Jamie Cohen, health and safety director for the Retail, Wholesale, and Department Store Union (RWDSU), which represents the plant's work force. "The previous nurse apparently even told some people, 'Go back and take the pain like the rest.'"

Workers also report being fired after they developed "hand problems." "The procedure is to keep you from going to the doctor instead of sending you to the doctor," says Zelma Ghant, a union steward at the Buena Vista plant who accompanies workers to the nurse. "Instead of facing the problems, the company tries to scare people. When a person is persistent, they find a way to terminate them, to set an example for the rest: If you don't keep quiet, this will happen to you."

Ignoring cumulative trauma disorders can aggravate them, though. Untreated, temporary damage can become permanent, and even a short delay can make a difference. Companies could help limit damage by giving employees less strenuous tasks or letting them rotate jobs. Instead, some workers report being given work that only makes their injuries worse.

Unfortunately, poultry companies have a built-in incentive to ignore injuries—it keeps workers' compensation costs down. Until recently they showed very low rates on their OSHA "200 logs," where they record work- related injuries and illnesses. The disorders are "underreported," says Roger Stephens, federal OSHA's sole ergonomist, who studies how the design of a workplace affects workers. "The reporting just doesn't go on."

Benny Bishop, plant manager of Southland Poultry in Enterprise, Alabama, says there are "few injuries" to report. "Every injury that has been reported has been recorded," he claims. RWDSU representative Linda Cromer, who worked on a recent union drive there, agrees that the past five years of Southland's OSHA logs show "virtually no repetitive motion injuries listed." But, she adds, "we hear about it on every house call."

In a written statement sent to a Congressional hearing on cumulative trauma disorders in early June, Perdue Farms claims that "grossly inaccurate media reports have created undue concern" about these disorders. Yet an internal memo from the Perdue personnel department this past February tells a different story. In response to a worker's complaint, it states that it is "normal procedure for about 60% of our work force" at the Robersonville plant to go to the nurse every morning to get pain killers and have their hands wrapped.

Perhaps in an effort to shake its reputation of ineffectualness, OSHA recently levied huge fines against meatpackers and poultry companies for failing to report repetitive motion injuries. But on both the federal and state level, OSHA has been slow to respond to the cause of repetitive motion injuries—the very nature of poultry work.

"I think there will have to be limits on the physical demands employers can make of employees," says Steve Edelstein, a North Carolina attorney who handles compensation cases for injured workers. "People shouldn't have to feel pain every day just to make a living." He says that OSHA historically overlooked the design of assembly-line work, focusing instead on safety standards and a narrow definition of illness and injury.

Companies could make some changes immediately, says Sarah Fields-Davis, director of the Center for Women's Economic Alternatives, a worker advocacy group in Ahoskie, North Carolina. "Redesigning tools and keeping scissors sharp so people don't have to use their backs to cut doesn't cost that much," she says. "Neither does rotating workers" or giving them longer breaks.

Former Perdue worker Donna Bazemore believes that companies like Perdue should retrain workers disabled by poultry work. After a woman develops carpal tunnel, they should "realize that it's going to be hard for [her] to make a living," she says.

"We're not advocating that Perdue leave," says Fields-Davis. "We just want the company to become more responsive to—and responsible for—the people who are making them rich."

> THE NEW, LUCRATIVE PRODUCTS OF THE 1980s—FILLETED BREASTS, POULTRY PATTIES, CHICKEN NUGGETS—MADE POULTRY WORK EVEN MORE PHYSICALLY DEMANDING.

November/December 2000

WHAT MIGHT WORK LOOK LIKE?

BY ROBIN HAHNEL AND CYNTHIA PETERS

It's no longer enough to point out what we don't like, we have to work out "what sort of society do we want."
—*Sheila Rowbotham*

If the mass mobilizations against the World Trade Organization, the International Monetary Fund, the World Bank, and other financial institutions are any indication, many labor, student and community activists are challenging corporate control of our lives and our workplaces. As anti-corporate-globalization activists Lori Wallach and Michelle Sforza say in their book on the WTO, "There is nothing inevitable about the model of corporate economic globalization by which our world is now being redesigned. … There are other models that would result in a more equitable, safe, ecologically sound and democratically accountable society."

But what exactly would economic justice look like? Many of us can speak passionately about what is wrong with the *status quo*, but can we articulate what we would like to replace it with? To describe a just and equitable economy, we would need to address the ideas and institutions that govern basic economic activities such as pay, organization, division of labor, the nature of work, allocation, and more. In this article, we describe how, in a better world, we might structure our jobs to be empowering and fair.

In our current economy, most jobs are relatively boring, tedious, stressful, and even hazardous. Most workers have little control over their quality of work life, let alone a say over what they produce and how it is used. A lucky few have desirable jobs that are rewarding and fulfilling and give the worker a feeling of autonomy and power in his or her daily life. But why should we accept this imbalance in people's experience of work? Why not organize work to be empowering? Why not balance work in its creative and mundane aspects?

TRUE SELF-MANAGEMENT

People should govern themselves at work as elsewhere. To exercise influence over the decisions that affect them the most, workers need more than a vote or some other formal mechanism for registering their opinion.

South End Press, a 23-year old nonprofit progressive publishing house, was founded on principles of worker democracy and self-management. But collective members realized that unless they were equally equipped with knowledge and expertise, they would not be able to participate equally in running the place. South End Press' founding members instituted a system where business jobs were shared among collective members so that everyone would learn the workings of the business, and thus be able to make informed decisions. South End Press also emphasizes extensive training, a lengthy apprenticeship for new members, and ongoing attention to creating office systems and procedures that are easily understood and accessed by all.

Anthony Arnove, a South End Press collective member since 1996, notes the way the Press responded to the development of Internet technology. Rather than hire an expert to run their web site, Press members taught themselves the basic elements of web design. Then they took the challenge of sharing knowledge about the web so that everyone could participate in substantive discussions about how to use web pages. "While not everyone knows HTML," says Arnove, "we all do have a sense that if there is some way we want to change the design or shape of the web site, or use it for a specific purpose, we know there are mechanisms for doing it."

Mondragón Bookstore and Coffee House, a nine-person enterprise in Winnipeg, Canada, has also found that when expertise is demystified and tasks, skills, and access to information, as well as empowering circumstances are shared equitably, workers can effectively manage themselves. Mondragón, like South End Press, is a small firm. Since everything must get done, of course, and there are fewer people to divide it among, it is harder than it would be in a large firm for any particular worker to choose to avoid various parts of the labor, emphasizing other components, while still doing a balanced combination of tasks. Still, even with that pressure due to limited size, Paul Burrows, one of the founders of Mondragón, says that co-workers encourage each other to take on the tasks they most shy away from. In the process, Burrows says, it has become clear that what most people lack is "skills and training, not capacity." Workers at Mondragón are trained not only as line cooks and sandwich-makers, but also as bookkeepers, event-planners, menu-planners, and bookstore staff. With self-management, says Burrows, "we gain a sense of dignity. We know from experience that we can run this business and make the hard decisions, and do it in a way that gives everyone a voice."

BALANCED JOB COMPLEXES

If all workers are to be involved in the conceptual, planning, and decision-making tasks related to their jobs (in order for them to be effective self-managers), who will be left to do the more menial work? Everyone. All jobs should feature a sensible mix of *types* of work—an idea we call "balanced job complexes."

At Mondragón, workers aim to achieve some balance in their workload over a period of weeks, says Ria Julien, a Mondragón collective member. They might spend a whole shift prepping food in the café or stocking shelves in the bookstore, but in the course of a few weeks, they will also participate in decision-making meetings, plan budgets, and consider the environmental, health, and fair-trade issues related to the way they run their restaurant. But not everyone does everything. Burrows says there are ways to account for personal preferences and still create structures that give people equal access to a range of workplace roles. For example, when it comes to representing the collective to the public, some are comfortable with public speaking and giving interviews, others prefer writing pamphlets or brochures.

As a result of balancing job complexes, there is no longer a fixed management with uniquely informative and uplifting tasks. There is no longer a set of rote jobs whose conditions are only deadening. Balancing job complexes makes for more fair and dignified work, and it lays a solid foundation for self-management. It avoids dividing the workforce into a highly empowered "coordinator class" and a subordinate, disenfranchised working class, instead giving all workers comparable empowerment in their economic lives.

WHAT ABOUT FREEDOM AND PRODUCTIVITY?

Would allowing only balanced job complexes impinge on some workers' freedom? Not as much as the *status quo* impinges on the freedom of those who get stuck with the bad jobs. If we are in favor of self-managed and fulfilling work, then we have to institute structures that make it impossible for anyone to monopolize the empowering and enriching jobs at the expense of someone else being left with menial tasks. Balanced job complexes jeopardize only the freedom of those in upper classes to continue their monopoly on empowering work.

Capitalism has norms that one must follow as well. For example, you cannot own a slave. And it isn't merely that there is a rule against it. Rather, the economy does not include that option. The roles slave and slave-owner just don't exist. Well, in a good economy and a good workplace, you cannot hire a wage slave; there is no role that is always subordinate nor others that are always dominant. There is no slot high or low in a hierarchy of influence, status, and

income, because balanced job complexes eliminate such hierarchy. Everyone has a mix of tasks balanced for empowerment and desirability of work, so the old roles of order-giving manager and order-taking worker are no longer available. Does this mean people are precluded from opting for an unbalanced job complex like folks are now precluding from opting to be a slave-owner? Yes. Each person's freedom must include respect for the freedom of others, so such options are simply ruled out by the structure of the economy.

WHAT EFFECTS WOULD BALANCED JOB COMPLEXES HAVE ON THE ECONOMY?

First, let's clarify that even if job balancing did sacrifice some output, we would not renounce dignified and empowered work as a goal. Self-management and classlessness are far more worthy aspirations than attaining maximum output. As Julien of Mondragón says, "if efficiency is how quickly a sandwich gets made or how quickly someone gets silenced if they're having a problem," then she wants nothing to do with it. "Mondragón engages your whole self. We think that's an 'efficient' thing for a workplace to do."

In other words, once economic actors have their eyes on human well-being and development, rather than their shoulders to a profit-seeking grindstone, the definition of efficiency becomes more encompassing. It begins to include not just how quickly we make something, but how the making of it affects us, how it impacts those who consume it, and how it affects the environment. It turns out, however, that productivity does not suffer with balanced job complexes.

> OUR GUIDING VALUE SHOULD NOT BE TO MAXIMIZE THE OUTPUT OF AN ECONOMY—BUT TO MEET PEOPLE'S NEEDS AND DEVELOP THEIR CAPACITIES.

Data available through the *Huenefeld Report,* an industry-wide newsletter for mid-size publishers, suggests that South End Press is at least as productive, if not more so, than other similar-sized publishers. As South End Press' Arnove suggests, "You gain an advantage by removing inefficient managers. In the rest of the business world, you have layers and layers of managers who do no work other than control employees."

Balanced job complexes offer other benefits as well. When the person with the "better" job has to do her share of more menial tasks, she'll have new interest in making all work more palatable. The more everyone is responsible for the grind, the more energy and effort will be allocated to minimizing it, and making whatever's left of it more tolerable. Consider, also, what we would gain from all those job imbalances that would get corrected in the other direction. Consider the creativity, talent, and skills that would be newly-tapped for society due to a large portion of the population now being prepared to fulfill their capabilities rather than channeled as before into rote obedience and subservience.

Our guiding value should not be to maximize the output of an economy—but to meet people's needs and develop their capacities. We can do this by furthering values such as self-management, solidarity, equity, and diversity. In societies like ours, an educated and credentialed elite monopolizes empowering and knowledge-enhancing tasks, partly due to their talents, but overwhelmingly due to their circumstantial advantages (such as their race, class, and/or gender privilege), and their willingness to trample those below. Most members of our economy are propelled into relative subservience not by lack of potential, but by socialization, schooling, and on-the-job circumstances. They could certainly partake in decision-making and creative work given the opportunity, and the gains would be enormous.

GETTING FROM HERE TO THERE

To achieve dignified work for all, we seek to balance the empowerment effect of jobs. But how might we take his long-term goal into account in our current organizing?

Redistributing Power

Clearly, South End Press and the Mondragón Bookstore and Coffee House represent the tiny fraction of workplaces that are run non-hierarchically and in a balanced fashion. For everyone else, there are social change organizations, unions, living-wage coalitions, and welfare-rights organizations, which have sought to redistribute at least some of the wealth and power that is currently disproportionately held by the top 20% of the population. Organizing, striking, and lobbying are some of the tools workers and activists have used to fight for higher wages, better benefits and job conditions, more generous welfare packages, and more dignified work for those outside the owning and coordinating class. Here are some short-term goals that activists should keep front and center in their ongoing struggle for a more just and equitable workplace.

Much work is intentionally dumbed-down precisely so that workers don't gain confidence and knowledge, which would facilitate their making demands about conditions or wages. We should demand more training for workers, and more varied job descriptions, so that they can "engage their whole selves" in their work. Members of the Harvard Union of Clerical and Technical Workers (HUCTW) recognized that, in addition to pay increases, they wanted to play a role solving problems in their departments, rather than accepting orders and mandates from above. The Union fought for and won "joint councils"—a unique decision making body, made up of equal parts management and clerical workers. In the process, HUCTW members took a step toward influencing decisions that affect their work, and are engaged not just in delivering a product to a boss, but also in defining how their work gets done. In some workplaces, unionists are critical of such arrangements, viewing them as another form of management control. But for Harvard clericals, says Adrienne Landau, president of HUCTW, joint councils have given union members a voice in a number of shop-floor decisions, such as whether there should be a dress code. "But we want to go deeper," says Landau. "Goals are still being formulated. But people in general feel that work isn't much fun. Why do I still feel intimidated to question the work reorganization plan that is put in front of me when no one asked me? Are supervisors necessary? What role do they play?"

Supporting worker ownership and worker cooperatives can be another step toward shifting conceptual and decision making labor from the "bosses" to the "bossed." Shopfloor workers want to have a say in the decisions that affect their daily work, says Adria Scharf, a *Dollars & Sense* collective member and a consultant to worker-owned firms. At a Vermont furniture manufacturer, which shares stock with its workers but is managed in a fairly traditional way, Scharf questioned several hundred workers about what changes they would most like to see in their company. A recurring theme was that they wanted their expertise and knowledge to count when it came time to making decisions about machinery purchases and other shop-floor changes. Such a change would be a straightforward way to give shop-floor workers more balance in the kinds of labor they perform.

Dignifying Our Own Work

Think about progressive media outlets, institutes, and organizations. Do they have typical corporate divisions of labor so that some folks monopolize fulfilling and empowering tasks while others have only rote and obedient ones? Will the movement "owners," "CEOs," and "managers" welcome demands from their workforces to balance movement work and employ self-management? Social change movements should develop internal work structures that benefit their members, improve their product, become congenial to working-class constituencies, and make credible their external demands. Just as people of color and women in social change movements have had to struggle with fellow activists on matters of internal race and gender relations, so too must we push within the movement for social change on matters of class divisions in our own work relations. Strategic workplace demands apply as well to our own institutions, which must serve as a model of democracy, justice, and balance in the workplace.

Resources: The Participatory Economics Project <www. parecon.org>.

CHAPTER 5

Market Structure and Monopoly

INTRODUCTION

With monopoly, we finally encounter a situation in which most economists, orthodox and otherwise, agree that unfettered markets lead to an undesirable outcome. If a firm is able to create a monopoly, it faces a downward-sloping demand curve—that is to say, if it reduces output, it can charge a higher price. The monopolist has a profit incentive to restrict output in order to charge consumers that higher price. The result is a deadweight loss—a loss to consumers that is not fully offset by the gains to the monopolist. Economists argue that competitive forces tend to undermine any monopoly, but failing this, they support antitrust policy as a backstop. The concept of monopoly not only points to an important failing of markets, but it opens the door to thinking about many possible market structures other than perfect competition—including oligopoly, in which a small group of producers dominate the market.

In this chapter, our authors are in the unaccustomed position of agreeing with much of what standard economics textbooks have to say. Still, they manage to stir up some controversy. In the first article, Chris Tilly summarizes the pluses and minuses of large and small businesses, and finds *both* wanting (Tilly, article 5.1). The next two articles focus on big business (Baker, article 5.2; Mittal and Rosset, article 5.3). The authors describe how large pharmaceutical and agribusiness concerns use monopoly power to wring extra profits from buyers, creating a variety of problems along the way. But there's a twist: the source of these monopolies is intellectual property rights—patents—which standard economic analysis sees as necessary to provide the incentive to innovate.

Edward S. Herman reviews the history of U.S. antitrust law, criticizing economists for justifying a hands-off policy toward big business mergers over the last few decades (Herman, article 5.4). Arthur MacEwan rounds out the chapter by looking *inside* large companies with market power, and asking how they set CEO salaries. He concludes that executive pay does not fit with the "one best way" analysis of business decision-making we described in the Introduction to Chapter 4. According to MacEwan, corporate directors set executive pay at high levels not because of profit-maximizing principles, but because they themselves are top executives—peers and in some cases buddies of the CEOs whose compensation they are deciding. But more fundamentally, the much higher CEO pay in the United States than elsewhere reflects the fact that work is organized differently in different countries—again, a departure from the idea of "one best way" (MacEwan, article 5.5).

The authors in this chapter agree with mainstream economics textbook authors that monopoly typically has harmful effects. They disagree about how often and how dramatically the U.S. economy differs from perfect competition. They also (at least in the case of Tilly) question whether an economy made up of small, perfectly competitive firms would be an improvement.

DISCUSSION QUESTIONS

1) (Tilly) List the pros and cons that Chris Tilly comes up with for large and small businesses. How does this compare with the problems your textbook mentions? Be sure to compare Tilly's list of small business flaws with what your textbook has to say about small business.

2) (Tilly, Baker) Dean Baker says that a company with a monopoly on a drug has "an enormous incentive to overstate the benefits and understate the risks." Tilly says that in the case of oligopoly, the incentive is for a business to pour huge amounts of money into advertising and other ways to make its brand stand out. Explain why even though both companies have an incentive to spin the truth about its product, the incentives are somewhat different in the two cases, monopoly and oligopoly.

3) (Mittal and Rosset) Anuradha Mittal and Peter Rosset claim that monopoly power in agribusiness hurts the environment by wiping out biodiversity. Explain their argument. Do you agree with it?

4) (Baker, Mittal and Rosset) Both Baker and Mittal/Rosset sharply criticize the monopoly effects of the patent system. But others argue that patents are necessary for innovation—they give companies a monopoly for a limited time so that they can recoup their research investment. How should this clash be resolved? Should patents be granted in some industries but not others? If so, how should we encourage research in areas with no patent protection?

5) (Tilly, Baker, Herman) Tilly describes how corporations fund "citizens'" groups to push policies that the corporations want. Baker says that giant drug companies fund scientists to prove that the companies' drugs work. Edward Herman states that large businesses hired economists to come up with theories that showed why huge businesses and mega-mergers can be beneficial (or at least not harmful). What are some likely results if corporations control "the marketplace of ideas"? What, if anything, should be done about it?

6) (MacEwan) Arthur MacEwan maintains that in the case of CEO pay, boards of directors pay high salaries rather than minimizing costs because they see it as the "right" thing to do. Do companies do this in areas other than executive pay? Why doesn't competition drive out such practices?

7) (General) Looking back at the readings in Chapter 4 as well as Chapter 5, the authors worry a lot about how business power can harm *both* workers and consumers. But in orthodox economics texts, almost all the attention is on how *consumers* get hurt by business power. Why do you think the emphasis is so different in the this book compared to a standard text?

8) (General) Would you rather see businesses get larger or smaller? Explain why, connecting your explanation to these readings as well as to your textbook.

KEY TO COLANDER

These readings match up with Chapters 12-15.

Tilly's description of big business fits with Chapter 12 (monopoly) and 13 (oligopoly).

The Baker and Mittal/Rosset articles relate to Chapters 12 (monopoly), as well as the discussion in Chapter 14 of the fight between monopolistic and competitive forces, and how firms protect their monopolies.

The Herman article supplements Chapter 15, "Antitrust Policy and Regulation."

MacEwan's discussion of CEO salaries adds to Chapter 14, "Real-World Competition and Regulation," which asks whether firms actually maximize profits and includes a brief look at the issue of executive pay.

July/August 1989, revised April 2002

IS SMALL BEAUTIFUL?
IS BIGGER BETTER?

SMALL AND BIG BUSINESS BOTH HAVE THEIR DRAWBACKS

BY CHRIS TILLY

Beginning in the late 1980s, the United States has experienced a small, but significant boom in small business. While big businesses have downsized, small enterprises have proliferated. Should we be glad? Absolutely, declare the advocates of small business. Competition makes small businesses entrepreneurial, innovative, and responsive to customers.

Not so fast, reply big business's boosters. Big corporations grew big because they were efficient, and tend to stay efficient because they are big—and thus able to invest in research and upgrading of technology and workforce skills.

But each side in this debate omits crucial drawbacks. Small may be beautiful for consumers, but it's often oppressive for workers. And while big businesses wield the power to advance technology, they also often wield the market power to bash competitors and soak consumers. In the end, the choices are quite limited.

BIG AND SMALL

Is the United States a nation of big businesses, or of small ones? There are two conventional ways to measure business size. One is simply to count the number of employees per firm. By this measure, small businesses (say, business establishments with less than 20 employees) make up the vast majority of businesses (Table 1). But they provide only a small fraction of the total number of jobs.

The other approach gauges market share—each firm's share of total sales in a given industry. Industries range between two extremes: what economists call "perfect competition" (many firms selling a standardized product, each too tiny to affect the market price) and monopoly (one business controls all sales in an industry). Economy-wide, as with employment, small businesses are most numerous, but control only a small slice of total sales. Sole proprietorships account for 73% of established businesses, far outnumbering corporations, which are 20% of the total (the remainder are partnerships). But corporations ring up a hefty 90% of all sales, leaving sole proprietors with only 6%. It takes a lot of mom and pop stores to equal General Motors' 1999 total of $177 billion in sales.

Industry by industry, the degree of competition varies widely. Economists consider an industry concentrated when its top four companies account for more than 40% of total sales in the industry (Table 2). At the high end of the spectrum are the cigarette, beer, and aircraft industries, where four firms account for the bulk of U.S. production.

No market comes close to meeting the textbook specifications for perfect competition, but one can still find industries in which a large number of producers compete for sales. The clothing and restaurant industries, for example, remain relatively competitive. Overall, about one-third of U.S. goods are manufactured in concentrated industries, about one fifth are made in competitive industries, and the rest fall somewhere in between.

BEATING THE COMPETITION

Those who tout the benefits of small, competitive business make a broad range of claims on its behalf. In addition to keeping prices low, they say the quality of the product is constantly improving, as companies seek a competitive edge. The same desire, they claim, drives firms toward technological innovations, leading to productivity increases.

The real story is not so simple. Competition does indeed keep prices low. Believe it or not, clothing costs us less—in real terms—than it cost our parents. Between 1960 and 1999, while the overall price level and hourly wages both increased nearly sixfold, apparel prices didn't even triple. And small businesses excel at offering variety, whether it is the ethnic restaurants that dot cities or the custom machine-tool work offered by small shops. Furthermore, however powerful small business lobbies may be in Washington, they do not influence the legislative process as blatantly as do corporate giants.

But those low prices often have an ugly underside. Our sportswear is cheap in part because the garment industry increasingly subcontracts work to sweatshops—whether they be export assembly plants in Haiti paying dollar-a-day

TABLE 1
SMALL BUSINESS NATION?

Most businesses are small, but most employees work for big businesses

Company size (number of employees)	Percent of all firms	Percent of all workers
1-4	54%	6%
5-9	20	8
10-19	13	11
20-49	8	16
50-99	3	13
100-249	2	16
250-499	0.4	10
500-999	0.2	7
1,000 or more	0.1	13

Source: County Business Patterns, 1998.

Note: "Businesses" refers to establishments, meaning business locations.

TABLE 2
WHO COMPETES, WHO DOESN'T

Industry	Percent of sales by top four firms
Light truck and utility vehicle manufacturing	99%
Breweries	90
Breakfast cereal manufacturing	83
Home center stores	75
General book stores	68
Lawn equipment manufacturing	64
Cable networks	61
Credit card issuing	54
Computer and software stores	35
Sock manufacturing	26
Hotels and motels	16
Gas stations	7
Real estate	3
Bars	1

Source: 1997 Economic Census

wages, or the "underground" Los Angeles stitcheries that employ immigrant women in virtual slavery. Struggling to maintain razor-thin profit margins, small businesses cut costs any way they can—which usually translates into low wages and onerous working conditions.

"There is a rule of survival for small business," Bill Ryan, president of Ryan Transfer Corporation, commented some years ago. "There are certain things you want to have [in paying workers] and certain things you can afford. You had better go with what you can afford." Bottom line, workers in companies employing 500 or more people enjoy average wages 30% higher than their counterparts in small businesses.

Part of this wage gap results from differences other than size—unionization, the education of the workforce, the particular jobs and industries involved. But University of Michigan economist Charles Brown and his colleagues controlled for all these differences and more, and still found a 10% premium for big business's employees. A note of caution, however: Other recent research indicates that this wage bonus is linked to long-term employment and job ladders. To the extent that corporations dissolve these long-term ties—as they seem to be rapidly doing—the pay advantage may dissolve as well.

Small business gurus make extravagant claims about small businesses' job-generation capacity. An oft-quoted 1987 report by consultant David Birch claimed that businesses with fewer than 20 employees create 88% of new jobs. The reality is more mundane: over the long run, businesses with 19 or fewer workers account for about one quarter of net new jobs. One reason why Birch's statistics are misleading is that new small businesses are created in great numbers, but they also fail at a high rate. The result is that the *net* gain in jobs is much smaller than the number created in business start-ups.

For companies in very competitive markets, the same "whip of competition" that keeps prices down undermines many of competition's other supposed benefits. The flurry of competition in the airline industry following deregulation, for example, hardly resulted in a higher quality product. Flying became temporarily cheaper, but also less comfortable, reliable, and safe.

Technological innovation from competition is also more myth than reality. Small firms in competitive industries do very little research and development. They lack both the cash needed to make long-term investments and the market power to guarantee a return on that investment. In fact, many of them can't even count on surviving to reap the rewards: only one-third to one-half of small business startups survive for five years, and only about one in five makes it to ten years. A 1988 Census Bureau survey concluded that in manufacturing, "technology use is positively correlated with plant size." Agriculture may be the exception that proves the rule. That highly competitive industry has made marked productivity gains, but its research is supported by the taxpayer, and its risks are reduced by government price supports.

Of course, the biggest myth about competition is that it

is in any way a 'natural state' for capitalism. In fact, in most markets the very process of competing for high profits or a bigger market share tends to create a concentrated, rather than a competitive, market structure. This process occurs in several ways. Big firms sometimes drive their smaller competitors out of business by selectively cutting prices to the bone. The smaller firms may lack the financial resources to last out the low prices. In the 1960s, several of IBM's smaller competitors sued it for cutting prices in a pattern that was designed to drive the smaller firms out of the market. Large corporations can also gain a lock on scarce resources: for example, large airlines like United and American operate the comprehensive, computerized information and reservation systems that travel agents tap into—and you can bet that each airline's system lists their own flights first. Or businesses may exploit an advantage in one market to dominate another, as Microsoft used its control of the computer operating system market to seize market share for its Internet browser.

Other firms eliminate competitors by buying them out—either in a hostile takeover or a friendly merger. Either way, a former competitor is neutralized. This strategy used to be severely limited by strict antitrust guidelines that prohibited most horizontal mergers—those between two firms that formerly competed in the same market. The Reagan administration's team at the Justice Department, however, loosened the merger guidelines significantly in the early 1980s. Since that time, many large mergers between former competitors have been allowed to go through, most notably in the airline industry.

THE POWER OF CONCENTRATION

Concentration, then, is as natural to market economies as competition. And bigness, like smallness, is a mixed bag for us as consumers and workers. For workers, bigness is on the whole a plus. Whereas competition forces small businesses to be stingy, big firms are on average more generous, offering employees higher wages, greater job security, and more extensive fringe benefits. In 1993, 97% of businesses with 500 or more workers provided health insurance; only 43% of businesses with 25 or fewer employees did so. Large firms also provide much more employee training. The strongest unions, as well, have historically been in industries where a few firms control large shares of their markets, and can pass along increased costs to consumers—auto, steel, and tires, for example. When profits are threatened, though, firms in concentrated markets also have more resources with which to fight labor. They are better able to weather a strike, oppose unionization, and make agreements with rivals not to take advantage of each other's labor troubles. In addition, large companies, not surprisingly, score low on workplace autonomy.

What about consumers? Corporations in industries where there are few competitors may compete, but the competitive clash is seldom channeled into prolonged price wars. The soft drink industry is a classic example. David McFarland, a University of North Carolina econo-mist, likens soft drink competition to professional wrestling. "They make a lot of sounds and groans and bounce on the mat, but they know who is going to win," he remarked.

Coke and Pepsi introduce new drinks and mount massive ad campaigns to win market share, but the net result is not lower prices. In fact, because competition between industry giants relies more on product differentiation than price, companies pass on their inflated advertising expenses to consumers. In the highly concentrated breakfast cereal market, the package frequently costs more than the contents. And of every dollar you pay for a box, nearly 20 cents goes for advertising.

It takes resources to develop and market a new idea, which gives large corporations distinct advantages in innovation. The original idea for the photocopier may have come from a patent lawyer who worked nights in his basement, but Xerox spent $16 million before it had a product it could sell. RCA invested $65 million developing the color television. RCA could take this gamble because its dominance in the television market ensured that it would not be immediately undercut by some other firm.

But market dominance can also translate into complacency. The steel industry illustrates the point. A few major producers earned steady profits through the 1950s and 1960s but were caught off-guard when new technologies vaulted foreign steel-makers to the top of the industry in the 1970s. Similarly, when IBM dominated the computer industry in the 1960s and early 1970s, innovation proceeded quite slowly, particularly compared to the frantic scramble in that industry today. With no competitors to worry about, it was more profitable for IBM to sit tight, since innovation would only have made its own machines obsolete.

And large corporations can also put their deep pockets and technical expertise to work to short-circuit public policy. In the 1980s, when Congress changed corporate liability laws to make corporate executives criminally liable for some kinds of offenses, General Electric's lobbyists and legal staff volunteered to help draft the final regulations, in order to minimize the damage.

THE BIGGEST MYTH ABOUT COMPETITION IS THAT IT IS IN ANY WAY A 'NATURAL STATE' FOR CAPITALISM. IN FACT, IN MOST MARKETS THE VERY PROCESS OF COMPETING TENDS TO CREATE A CONCENTRATED, RATHER THAN A COMPETITIVE, MARKET STRUCTURE.

Big businesses sometimes hide their lobbying behind a "citizen" smokescreen. The largest-spending lobby in Washington in 1986 was Citizens for the Control of Acid Rain. These good citizens had been organized by coal and electric utility companies to oppose tighter pollution controls. Along the same lines, the Coalition for Vehicle Choice (now, who could be against that?) was set up by Ford and General Motors in 1990 to fight higher fuel efficiency standards.

CONCENTRATION OR CONGLOMERATION

Over the last couple of decades, the mix of big and small businesses has changed, but the changes are small and—at first glance—contradictory. Over time, employment has shifted toward smaller firms, though the shift has been subtle, not revolutionary. Meanwhile, the overall level of industry-by-industry sales concentration in the economy has increased, but only slightly. As older industries become more concentrated, newer, more competitive ones crop up, leaving overall concentration relatively steady. In his book *Lean and Mean*, economist Bennett Harrison points out that there is actually no contradiction between the small business employment boomlet and big firms' continued grip on markets. Big businesses, it turns out, are orchestrating much of the flowering of small business, through a variety of outsourcing and subcontracting arrangements.

But if industry-by-industry concentration has changed little over the decades, conglomeration is a different matter. Corporate ownership of assets has become much more concentrated over time, reflecting the rise in conglomerates—corporations doing business in a variety of industries. Five decades ago, the top 200 manufacturing firms accounted for 48% of all sales in the U.S. economy. By 1993, the 200 biggest industrial businesses controlled 65% of sales.

Most mainstream economists see these groupings as irrelevant for the competitive structure of the economy. Antitrust laws place no restrictions on firms from different industries banding together under one corporate roof. But sheer size can easily affect competition in the markets of the individual firms involved. A parent company can use one especially profitable subsidiary to subsidize start-up costs for a new venture, giving it a competitive edge. And if one board of directors controls major interests in related industries, it can obviously influence any of those markets more forcefully.

A case in point is the mega-merger of Time Inc. and Warner, which will soon be joining with America Online. The resulting conglomerate will control massive sections of the home entertainment business, bringing together Time's journalists, film and television producers, and authors, Warner's entertainment machine, which includes Home Box Office, the nation's largest pay television channel, and AOL's huge share of the Internet access market. The conglomerate can influence the entertainment business from the initial point—the actors, writers, and directors—up to the point where the finished products appear on people's televisions or computers. Conglomeration also multiplies the political clout of large corporations. No wonder Disney and other entertainment giants have also hopped on the conglomeration bandwagon.

CHOOSE YOUR POISON

Competition, concentration, or conglomeration: The choice is an unsavory one indeed. Opting for lots of tiny, competing firms leaves labor squeezed and sacrifices the potential technological advantages that come with concentrated resources. Yet the big monopolies tend to dominate their markets, charge high prices, and waste countless resources on glitzy ad campaigns and trivial product differentiation. And the big conglomerate firms, while not necessarily dominant in any single market, wield a frightening amount of political and economic power, with budgets larger than those of most countries.

Of course, we don't have much to say about the choice, no matter how much "shopping for a better world" we engage in. Market competition rolls on—sometimes cutthroat, other times genteel. Industries often start out as monopolies (based on new inventions), go through a competitive phase, but end up concentrating as they mature. As long as bigness remains profitable and the government maintains a hands-off attitude, companies in both competitive and concentrated industries will tend to merge with firms in other industries. This will feed a continuing trend toward conglomeration. Since bigness and smallness both have their drawbacks, the best we can do is to use public policies to minimize the disadvantages of each.

Resources: Lean and Mean: The Changing Landscape of Corporate Power in the Age of Flexibility, Bennett Harrison, 1994; *Employers Large and Small,* Charles Brown, James Hamilton, and James Medoff, 1990.

May/June 2001

DRUG PRICES IN CRISIS

THE CASE AGAINST PROTECTIONISM

BY DEAN BAKER

In recent years, drug prices have risen to astronomical levels. In the United States, senior citizens are increasingly unable to afford prescription medication, while in developing nations, life-saving drugs are being priced out of reach for tens of millions of people with AIDS. In both cases, there is a single explanation for soaring drug prices: patent protection. If the pharmaceutical industry's patent monopolies were eliminated, most drugs would sell for only a fraction of their current cost.

Remarkably, however, the issue of drug patent monopolies rarely arises in public debate. Patent protection is a form of protectionism, but that's problematic terminology in a political climate where support for "free trade" is considered the only respectable opinion. So the pharmaceutical industry has managed to frame patent protection as a matter of "intellectual property rights" instead. Rarely has an industry been so successful in controlling the language of debate.

The industry has had a lot of help from the economics profession. Mainstream economists have developed an extensive body of research on the expected consequences of protection or monopoly pricing. If they were really as committed to efficiency and free trade as they pretend to be, they would be screaming about drug patents at the top of their lungs. The reason they don't is that they hold the drug industry in much higher esteem than manufacturing workers who might benefit from other forms of protectionism.

Of course, patent protection for prescription drugs, like all forms of protectionism, does serve a purpose—to provide industry with an incentive to research new drugs. If any firm could produce and sell every new drug that was developed, then no company would ever have a reason to spend money on research. However, the fact that drug patents *can* provide an incentive for research does not mean that they are the only or best way to support research. In fact, most biomedical research is currently supported by the federal government or private foundations, charities, and universities—not undertaken by private companies in anticipation of future sales.

We can only assess the full costs of patent protection if we recognize it as a form of protectionism, and look for all of the distortions that economists would expect protectionism to create. Once we do that, we'll see that the benefits derived from state-sanctioned monopoly protection are not justified by the quality and quantity of research that the pharmaceutical industry undertakes.

THE ECONOMICS OF PROTECTIONISM

Patent monopolies are a windfall for the pharmaceutical industry. Under the present system, a single firm gets to control the sale of a drug for the duration of its patent. Evidence from countries without effective protection for patents, or for drug prices after patents expire, indicates that most drugs would only sell for 25% of their patent protected price. In some cases, the difference is much greater. For example, the current state-of-the-art combination of anti-viral AIDS drugs sells in the United States for approximately $10,000 a year, according to the pharmaceutical industry. By contrast, a leading Indian manufacturer of generic drugs believes that it can sell the same combination profitably for $350 per year.

Why the huge gap between the monopoly patent protected price and the competitive market price? Because most drugs are relatively cheap to produce. Drugs are expensive because the government gives the industry a monopoly, not because they cost a lot to manufacture.

The costs of patent protection to consumers are enormous. The industry, which includes such giants as GlaxoSmithKline, Pfizer, and Bristol-Myers Squibb, estimates that it sold $106 billion worth of drugs in 2000. If eliminating patent protection had reduced the price of these drugs by 75%, then consumers would have saved $79 billion. This figure, to put it in perspective, is 30% more than what the federal government spends on education each year. It's more than ten times the amount that the federal government spends on Head Start. And it roughly equals the nation's annual bill for foreign oil.

What do we get for this money? Last year, the pharmaceutical industry, according to its own figures, spent $22.5 billion on domestic drug research (and another $4 billion on research elsewhere). For tax purposes, the industry claimed research expenditures of just $16 billion. Since these expenditures qualify for a 20% tax credit, the federal government directly covered $3.2 billion of the industry's research spending (20% of the $16 billion reported on tax returns). Even if we accept the $22.5 billion figure as accurate, this still means that the industry, after deducting the government contribution, spent just over $19 billion of its own money on drug research.

In other words, consumers (and the government, through Medicaid and other programs) spent an extra $79 billion on drugs because of patent protection, in order to get the industry to spend $19 billion of its own money on research. This comes out to more than four dollars in additional spending on drugs for every dollar that the industry spent on research. The rest of the money went mainly to:

> **LAST YEAR, CONSUMERS SPENT AN EXTRA $79 BILLION ON DRUGS BECAUSE OF PATENT PROTECTION, IN ORDER TO GET THE INDUSTRY TO SPEND $19 BILLION OF ITS OWN MONEY ON RESEARCH.**

• *Marketing* The industry spends tens of billions each year to convince us (or our doctors) that its new drugs are absolutely essential and completely harmless.

• *Protecting patent monopolies* Pharmaceutical companies regularly stand near the top in contributing to political campaigns. It's no accident that so many politicians are willing to push their cause.

• *Profits* The pharmaceutical industry consistently ranks at the top in return on investment. It pulled in more than $20 billion in profits for 1999.

If spending an extra four dollars on drugs in order to persuade the industry to spend one dollar on research doesn't sound like a good deal, don't worry. It gets worse.

THE INEFFICIENCIES OF PROTECTIONISM

Mainstream economists, who usually love to recite the evils of government protection, have been mostly silent on the issue of patent protection for drugs. But the evils are visible for all to see.

One major source of waste is research spending on imitation or "copycat" drugs. When a company gets a big hit with a new drug like Viagra or Claritin, its competitors will try to patent comparable drugs in order to get a slice of the market. In a world with patent protection, this can be quite beneficial to consumers, since a second drug creates some market competition. However, in the absence of patent protection, the incentive for copycat research would be unnecessary, since anyone who wanted to produce Viagra or Claritin would be free to do so, thereby pushing prices down.

How much do drug companies spend on copycat research? The industry won't say. But the Food and Drug Administration (FDA), in evaluating "new" drugs, considers only one third of them to be qualitatively new or better than existing drugs, while classifying the other two thirds as comparable to existing drugs. This doesn't mean that two thirds of research spending goes to copycat drugs; after all, the breakthrough drugs probably require more research spending, on average, than copycats. But suppose the industry wasted just 20% of its $19 billion in research spending on copycat drugs. This would bring the value of that spending down to $15 billion. That means consumers and the government are paying more than five dollars on drugs for each dollar of useful research.

The evils of protectionism don't end there. Prescription drugs present a classic case of asymmetric information: The drug companies know more about their drugs than the doctors who prescribe them, and far more than the patients who take them. The lure of monopoly profits gives the industry an enormous incentive to overstate the benefits and understate the risks of the newest wonder drugs. A June 2000 *New England Journal of Medicine* study found that the media consistently offered glowing accounts of drug breakthroughs. According to the study, the main villains in distorting the news were the public-relations departments of the drug manufacturers.

Still more serious is evidence that published research findings may be influenced by the drug industry's support. Last summer, the *New York Times* cited data showing that drugs, when tested by researchers who were supported by the drug's manufacturer, were found to be significantly more effective than existing drugs 89% of the time. By contrast, drugs tested by neutral researchers were found to be significantly more effective only 61% of the time.

Even if the industry's research could be completely trusted, there is still another problem created by the patent system—secrecy. The industry generally maintains the right to control the dissemination of findings from the research it supports. In some cases, this can mean a delay of months or even years before a researcher can disclose her findings at a conference or in a journal. In April 1996, for example, the *Wall Street Journal* reported on a British drug company's efforts to suppress a study showing that Synthroid, a drug to control thyroid problems, was no more effective than much cheaper alternatives.

In other cases, the secrecy is even more extreme. When the industry funds studies designed to prove that drugs are safe and effective enough to win FDA approval, it routinely keeps the results secret as proprietary information. This research may contain important clues about how best to use the new drug, or even about other factors affecting patients' health. Generally, however, the scientific community will not have access to it.

By creating incentives to misrepresent, falsify, or conceal research findings, patent monopolies are harmful to our pocketbooks as well as our health. At the very least, consumers may waste money on new, patent-protected drugs that are no more effective than existing drugs whose patents have expired. For example, a recent study estimated that consumers were spending $6 billion a year on a patented medication for patients with heart disease, which was no more effective than generic alternatives in preventing heart problems. As a result of industry propaganda, consumers might also spend money on drugs that could be less effective than cheaper alternatives—or on drugs that could even be hazardous to their health.

Another byproduct of monopoly drug pricing—the underground market—also has detrimental effects. When drugs can be sold profitably at prices that are much lower than their patent protected prices, consumers may seek underground sources for drugs. The most obvious way to do this is to purchase drugs in countries that either impose price controls or don't have the same patent protection as the United States. In recent years, there has been a much-publicized flow of senior citizens to Canada and Mexico in search of lower cost drugs. In the case of people traveling to Canada, the major cost to consumers is the waste of their

country; less than 20% is conducted on the campus of the Institutes themselves.) In addition, universities, private foundations, and charities fund a combined total of approximately $10 billion worth of research annually. Added together, these institutions spend 25% more on research than the pharmaceutical industry claims to spend, and nearly twice as much as the industry reports on tax returns.

Over the years, the research supported by government and non-profit institutions has led to numerous medical breakthroughs, including the discovery and development of penicillin and the polio vaccine. More recently, NIH-supported research has played a central role in developing AZT as an AIDS drug, and in developing Taxol, a leading cancer drug. The NIH's impressive list of accomplishments over the last five decades proves that the government can support effective research.

Traditionally, the NIH has focused on basic research and early phases of drug testing, while the pharmaceutical industry has engaged primarily in the later phases of drug testing—which include conducting clinical trials and carrying drugs through the FDA approval process. However, there is not a sharp division between the type of research done by the NIH and that undertaken by the pharmaceutical industry; the NIH has conducted research in all areas of drug development. There is no reason to believe that, given enough funding, the NIH could not effectively carry out all phases of drug research.

While the idea of a panel of government-supported scientists (most of whom would probably be affiliated with universities and other research institutions) deciding which drugs should be researched may seem scary, consider the current situation. Drug-company executives make their research decisions based on their assessment of a drug's profitability. In turn, that assessment depends on whether the company can get insurance companies to pay for the drug, whether it can effectively lobby legislators to have Medicaid and other government programs pay for it, and whether it can count on the courts to fully enforce its patents against competitors. It is these factors—not consideration of what will benefit the public's health—that dominate the industry's decisions about research. It is hard to believe that publicly accountable bodies that are charged with directing research for the general good would not produce better results.

The arithmetic behind a proposed switch is straightforward. If the federal government spent an additional $20 billion a year to support research at the NIH and various non-profit and educational institutions, it would more than fully replace the useful research conducted by the pharmaceutical industry. The cost to the federal govern-

THE USES OF DRUG MONEY
Drug Company Revenues, Profits, and Spending, 1999

Company	Revenues	Profits (as % of revenue)	Mrktg Costs (as % of revenue)	R&D (as % of revenue)
Merck	$32,714,000	18.0%	15.9%	6.3%
Pfizer	$16,204,000	19.6%	39.2%	17.1%
Eli Lilly	$10,003,000	27.2%	27.6%	17.8%
Schering-Plough	$9,176,000	23.0%	37.4%	13.0%
Pharmacia & Upjohn	$7,253,000	11.1%	38.6%	19.8%

Source: Families USA

time. However, when people buy drugs in countries with less stringent safety regulations, the health consequences may be severe.

THE PROVEN ALTERNATIVE

Listing the problems associated with drug patents would be an empty intellectual exercise—unless there were alternative ways to support research. Fortunately, there are. The federal government currently supports $18 billion a year in biomedical research through the National Institutes of Health (NIH) and the Centers for Disease Control (CDC). (The vast majority of NIH-funded research is carried out at universities and research centers across the ment would be less than the cost of the prescription drug plan that Al Gore advocated in last year's presidential campaign. If patent protection for drugs were eliminated, consumers would save more than $79 billion a year. These savings would increase with each passing year, since spending on drugs is currently rising at more than twice the rate of inflation.

Even assuming that the United States continues to rely on patent protection to support drug research for the immediate future, interim steps can be taken. First, it will be important to sharply restrict the worst abuses of the patent system. At the top of the list, the U.S. government should not be working with the pharmaceutical industry to impose its patents on developing countries. This is especially important in the case of AIDS drugs, since patent protection in sub-Saharan Africa may effectively be sentencing tens of million of people to death. There should also be pressure to allow the importation of drugs from nations where they are sold at lower prices, or even better, the imposition of domestic price controls.

A second priority is to create a greater opening for alternative sources of research. There should be more support for the NIH to carry some of its research through to the actual testing and approval of new drugs. The patents for these drugs should then be placed in the public domain, so that the industry can compete to supply the drugs at the lowest cost. In addition to bringing immediate benefits to consumers, this would allow for a clear test of the patent system's value as a means of supporting research, as compared with direct public support.

Back in the Middle Ages, the guild system was established to protect the secrets of masters from their apprentices. If you tried to make and sell hats but didn't belong to the hatmakers' guild, you'd be subject to arrest. Patents (and their cousin, copyrights) come out of this tradition. While most medieval restrictions have long since been discarded, patents have managed to survive and are now deeply enmeshed in our economic system. Not all forms of patent protection cause the problems associated with drug patents; in some areas, such as industrial processes, it may be reasonable to keep patent protection intact. But the case of drug patents cries out for the free market that economics say they favor, to wipe this feudal relic away.

Resources: Annals of Thoracic Surgery (September 2000): 883-888; *Wall Street Journal,* 25 April 1996, p. A1; Pharmaceutical Research and Manufacturers of America <www.phrma.org>.

ARTICLE 5.3   *March/April 2001*

GENETIC ENGINEERING AND THE PRIVATIZATION OF SEEDS

BY ANURADHA MITTAL AND PETER ROSSET

In 1998, angry farmers burned Monsanto-owned fields in Karnataka, India, starting a nationwide "Cremate Monsanto" campaign. The campaign demanded that biotech corporations like Monsanto, Novartis, and Pioneer leave the country. Farmers particularly targeted Monsanto because its field trials of the "terminator gene"—designed to prevent plants from producing seeds and so to make farmers buy new seed each year—created the danger of "genetic pollution" that would sterilize other crops in the area. That year, Indian citizens chose Quit India Day (August 9), the anniversary of Mahatma Gandhi's demand that British colonial rulers leave the country, to launch a "Monsanto Quit India" campaign. Ten thousand citizens from across the country sent the Quit India message to Monsanto's Indian headquarters, accusing the company of colonizing the food system.

In recent years, farmers across the world have echoed the Indian farmers' resistance to the biotech giants. In Brazil, the Landless Workers' Movement (MST) has set out to stop Monsanto soybeans. The MST has vowed to destroy any genetically engineered crops planted in the state of Rio Grande do Sul, where the state government has banned such crops. Meanwhile, last September more than 1,000 local farmers joined a "Long March for Biodiversity" across Thailand. "Rice, corn, and other staple crops, food crops, medicinal plants and all other life forms are significant genetic resources that shape our culture and lifestyle," the farmers declared. "We oppose any plan to transform these into genetically modified organisms."

INDUSTRIAL AGRICULTURE I: THE GREEN REVOLUTION

For thousands of years, small farmers everywhere have grown food for their local communities—planting diverse crops in healthy soil, recycling organic matter, and following nature's rainfall patterns. Good farming relied upon the farmer's accumulated knowledge of the local environment. Until the 1950s, most Third World agriculture was done this way.

The "Green Revolution" of the 1960s gradually replaced this kind of farming with monocultures (single-crop production) heavily dependent on chemical fertilizers, pesticides, and herbicides. The industrialization of agriculture made Third World countries increase exports to First World markets, in order to earn the foreign exchange they needed to pay for agrochemicals and farm machinery manufactured in the global North. Today, as much as 70% of basic grain production in the global South is the product of industrial farming.

The Green Revolution was an attempt by northern countries to export chemical- and machine-intensive U.S.-style agriculture to the Third World. After the Cuban revolution, northern policymakers worried that rampant hunger created the basis for "communist" revolution. Since the First World had no intention of redistributing the world's wealth, its answer was for First World science to "help" the Third World by giving it the means to produce more food. The Green Revolution was to substitute for the "red."

During the peak Green Revolution years, from 1970 to 1990, world food production per capita rose by 11%. Yet the number of people living in hunger (averaging less than the minimum daily caloric intake) continued to rise. In the Third World—excluding China—the hungry population increased by more than 11%, from 536 to 597 million. While hunger declined somewhat relative to total Third World population, the Green Revolution was certainly not the solution for world hunger that its proponents made it out to be.

Not only did the Green Revolution fail to remedy unequal access to food and food-producing resources, it actually contributed to inequality. The costs of improved seeds and fertilizers hit cash-poor small farmers the hardest. Unable to afford the new technology, many farmers lost their land. Over time, the industrialization of agriculture contributed to the replacement of farms with corporations, farmers with machines, mixed crops with monocultures, and local food security with global commerce.

INDUSTRIAL AGRICULTURE II: THE NEW BIOREVOLUTION

The same companies that promoted chemical-based agriculture are now bringing the world genetically engineered food and agriculture. Some of the leading pesticide companies of yesterday have become what today are euphemistically called "life sciences companies"—Aventis, Novartis, Syngenta, Monsanto, Dupont, and others. Through genetic engineering, these companies are now converting seeds into product-delivery systems. The crops produced by Monsanto's Roundup-Ready brand seeds, for example, tolerate only the company's Roundup brand herbicide.

The "life sciences" companies claim that they can solve the environmental problems of agriculture. For example, they promise to create a world free of pesticides by equipping each crop with its own "insecticidal genes." Many distinguished agriculture scientists, corporate bigwigs, and economists are jumping on the "biotechnology" bandwagon. They argue that, in a world where more than 830 million people go to bed hungry, biotechnology provides the only hope of feeding our burgeoning population, especially in the Third World.

In fact, since genetic engineering is based on the same old principles of industrial agriculture—monoculture, technology, and corporate control—it is likely to exacerbate the problems of ecological and social devastation:

• As long as chemical companies dominate the "life sciences" industry, the biotechnology they develop will only reinforce intensive chemical use. Corporations are currently developing plants whose genetic traits can be turned "on" or "off" by applying an external chemical, as well as crops that die if the correct chemical—made by the same company—is not applied.

• The biotechnology industry is releasing hundreds of thousands of genetically engineered organisms into the environment every year. These organisms can reproduce, cross-pollinate, mutate, and migrate. Each release of a genetically engineered organism is a round of ecological Russian roulette. Recently, Aventis' genetically engineered StarLink corn, a variety approved by the U.S. Department of Agriculture only for livestock consumption, entered the food supply by mixing in grain elevators and cross-pollination in the field.

• With the advent of genetic engineering, corporations are using new "intellectual property" rights to stake far-reaching claims of ownership over a vast array of biological resources. By controlling the ownership of seeds, the corporate giants force farmers to pay yearly for seeds they once saved from each harvest to the next planting. By making seed exchanges between farmers illegal, they also limit farmers' capacity to contribute to agricultural biodiversity.

THE FALSE PROMISE OF "GOLDEN RICE"

The biotech industry is taking great pains to advertise the humanitarian applications of genetic engineering. "[M]illions of people—many of them children—have lost their sight to vitamin A deficiency," says the Council for Biotechnology Information, an industry-funded public relations group. "But suppose rice consumers could obtain enough vitamin A and iron simply by eating dietary staples that are locally grown? ... Biotechnology is already producing some of these innovations." More than $10 million was spent over ten years to engineer vitamin A rice—hailed as the "Golden Rice"—at the Institute of Plant Sciences of the Swiss Federal Institute of Technology in Zurich. It will take millions more and another decade of research and development to produce vitamin A rice varieties that can actually be grown in farmers' fields.

In reality, the selling of vitamin A rice as a miracle cure for blindness depends on blindness to lower-cost and safer alternatives. Meat, liver, chicken, eggs, milk, butter, carrots, pumpkins, mangoes, spinach and other leafy green vegetables, and many other foods contain vitamin A. Women farmers in Bengal, an eastern Indian state, plant more than 100 varieties of green leafy vegetables. The promotion of monoculture and rising herbicide use, however, are destroying such sources of vitamin A. For example, bathua, a very popular leafy vegetable in northern India, has been pushed to extinction in areas of intensive herbicide use.

EACH RELEASE OF A GENETICALLY ENGINEERED ORGANISM IS A ROUND OF ECOLOGICAL RUSSIAN ROULETTE.

The long-run solutions to vitamin A deficiency—and other nutritional problems—are increased biodiversity in agriculture and increased food security for poor people. In the meantime, there are better, safer, and more economical short-run measures than genetically engineered foods. UNICEF, for example, gives high-dose vitamin A capsules to poor children twice a year. The cost? Just two cents per pill. (You can support the UNICEF Vitamin A project by calling 1-800-FOR-KIDS or visiting <www.unicefusa. org>.)

INTELLECTUAL PROPERTY RIGHTS AND GENETIC ENGINEERING

In 1998, Monsanto surprised Saskatchewan farmer Percy Schmeiser by suing him for doing what he has always done and, indeed, what farmers have done for millennia—save seeds for the next planting. Schmeiser is one of hundreds of Canadian and U.S. farmers the company has sued for re-using genetically engineered seeds. Monsanto has patented those seeds, and forbids farmers from saving them.

In recent years, Monsanto has spent over $8.5 billion acquiring seed and biotech companies, and DuPont spent over $9.4 billion to acquire Pioneer Hi-Bred, the world's largest seed company. Seed is the most important link in the food chain. Over 1.4 billion people—primarily poor farmers—depend on farm-saved seed for their livelihoods. While the "gene police" have not yet gone after farmers in the Third World, it is probably only a matter of time.

If corporations like Monsanto have their way, genetic technology—like the so-called "terminator" seeds—will soon render the "gene police" redundant. Far from being designed to increase agricultural production, "terminator" technology is meant to prevent unauthorized production—and increase seed-industry profits. Fortunately, worldwide protests, like the "Monsanto Quit India" campaign, forced the company to put this technology on hold. Unfortunately, Monsanto did not pledge to abandon "terminator" seeds permanently, and other companies continue to develop similar systems.

FUTURE POSSIBLE

From the United States to India, small-scale ecological agriculture is proving itself a viable alternative to chemical-intensive and bioengineered agriculture. In the United States, the National Research Council found that "alternative farmers often produce high per acre yields with significant reductions in costs per unit of crop harvested," despite the fact that "many federal policies discourage adoption of alternative practices." The Council concluded that "federal commodity programs must be restructured to help farmers realize the full benefits of the productivity gains possible through alternative practices."

Another study, published in the *American Journal of Alternative Agriculture,* found that ecological farms in India were just as productive and profitable as chemical ones. The author concluded that, if adopted on a national scale, ecological farming would have "no negative impact on food security," and would reduce soil erosion and the depletion of soil fertility while greatly lessening dependence on external inputs.

The country where alternative agriculture has been put to its greatest test, however, is Cuba. Before 1989, Cuba had a model Green Revolution-style agricultural economy (an approach the Soviet Union had promoted as much as the United States). Cuban agriculture featured enormous production units, using vast quantities of imported chemicals and machinery to produce export crops, while the country imported over half its food.

Although the Cuban government's commitment to equity and favorable terms of trade offered by Eastern Europe protected Cubans from undernourishment, the collapse of the East bloc in 1989 exposed the vulnerability of this approach. Cuba plunged into its worst food crisis since the revolution. Consumption of calories and protein dropped by perhaps as much as 30%. Nevertheless, today Cubans are eating almost as well as they did before 1989, with much lower imports of food and agrochemicals. What happened?

Cut off from imports of food and agrochemicals, Cuba turned inward to create a more self-reliant agriculture based on higher crop prices to farmers, smaller production units, urban agriculture, and ecological principles. As a result of the trade embargo, food shortages, and the opening of farmers' markets, farmers began to receive much better prices for their products. Given this incentive to produce, they did so, even without Green Revolution-style inputs. The farmers received a huge boost from the reorientation of government education, research, and assistance toward alternative methods, as well as the rediscovery of traditional farming techniques.

While small farmers and cooperatives increased production, large-scale state farms stagnated. In response, the Cuban government parceled out the state farms to their former employees as smaller-scale production units. Finally, the government mobilized support for a growing urban agriculture movement—small-scale organic farming on vacant lots—which, together with the other changes, transformed Cuban cities and urban diets in just a few years.

WILL BIOTECHNOLOGY FEED THE WORLD?

The biotech industry pretends concern for hungry people in the Third World, holding up greater food production through genetic engineering as the solution to world hunger. If the Green Revolution has taught us one thing, however, it is that increased food production can—and often does—go hand in hand with more hunger, not less. Hunger in the modern world is not caused by a shortage of food, and cannot be eliminated by producing more. Enough food is already available to provide at least 4.3 pounds of food per person a day worldwide. The root of the hunger problem is not inadequate production but unequal access and distribution. This is why the second Green Revolution promised by the "life sciences" companies is no more likely to end hunger than the first.

The United States is the world's largest producer of surplus food. According to the U.S. Department of Agriculture, however, some 36 million of the country's people (in-cluding 14 million children) do not have adequate access to food. That's an increase of six million hungry people since the 1996 welfare reform, with its massive cuts in food stamp programs.

Even the world's "hungry countries" have enough food for all their people right now. In fact, about three quarters of the world's malnourished children live in countries with net food surpluses, much of which are being exported. India, for example, ranks among the top Third World agricultural exporters, and yet more than a third of the world's 830 million hungry people live there. Year after year, Indian governments have managed a sizeable food surplus by depriving the poor of their basic human right to food.

THE ROOT OF THE HUNGER PROBLEM IS NOT INADEQUATE PRODUCTION BUT UNEQUAL ACCESS AND DISTRIBUTION.

The poorest of the poor in the Third World are landless peasants, many of whom became landless because of policies that favor large, wealthy farmers. The high costs of genetically engineered seeds, "technology-use payments," and other inputs that small farmers will have to use under the new biotech agriculture will tighten the squeeze on already poor farmers, deepening rural poverty. If agriculture can play any role in alleviating hunger, it will only be to the extent that we reverse the existing bias toward wealthier and larger farmers, embrace land reform and sustainable agriculture, reduce inequality, and make small farmers the center of an economically vibrant rural economy.

A BRIEF HISTORY OF MERGERS AND ANTITRUST POLICY

BY EDWARD HERMAN

Government efforts to prevent or break up monopolies are called antitrust policy. They assume that when a few companies dominate an industry, this weakens competition and hurts the public by reducing production, raising prices, and slowing technical advance. Antitrust has gone through cycles during this century. In some years, strongly pro-business presidencies (usually Republican) have allowed businesses to merge at will. These have often been followed by "reform" administrations, which tend to restrain, but not to reverse, concentrations of corporate power.

The federal government first took on a strong antitrust role with the Sherman Act of 1890, which outlawed monopoly and efforts to obtain it. In 1914 the Clayton Act also put restrictions on stock purchases and interlocking directorates that would reduce competition. This legislation responded to public anger and fears about "trusts," which brought separate firms under common control. Most notorious were Rockefeller's Standard Oil Trust and James Duke's American Tobacco Company, which employed ruthless tactics to drive their competitors out of business.

Early on the antitrust laws also treated organized labor as a "monopoly," and were used in breaking the Pullman strike in 1892. In 1908, the Supreme Court awarded damages to an employer against whom unions had organized a secondary boycott. This led to the Clayton Act exempting unions from its restrictions.

Otherwise, the federal government only minimally enforced the Sherman Act until Theodore Roosevelt was elected in 1900. Then in 1911 the Supreme Court decided that both the Standard Oil and American Tobacco trusts were "bad trusts," and ordered their dismantling. But in 1920 the Court refused to condemn the U.S. Steel consolidation, because it was a "good trust" that didn't attack its smaller rivals. This began a long period when the Antitrust Division and the courts approved mergers that produced industries with a few dominant firms, but which were "well-behaved." And in the 1920s, Republicans virtually ended antitrust enforcement.

THE GOLDEN AGE

Franklin Roosevelt revived antitrust during 1938 to 1941, and antitrust law had its golden age from 1945 to 1974, fueled by a liberal Supreme Court, anti-merger legislation passed in 1950, and mildly progressive enforcement (though less so in the Republican years). During this period Alcoa's monopoly over aluminum production was broken (1945), and the Court found the tobacco industry guilty of "group monopoly" (1946), although the companies were only assessed a modest fine.

During the 1960s, when antitrust law blocked mergers among companies in the same industry, businesses adapted by acquiring firms in unrelated industries. Many such "conglomerate" mergers took place during 1964-68, when Lyndon Johnson was president. Companies like International Telephone and Telegraph, Ling-Temco-Vought, Gulf & Western, Tenneco, and Litton Industries grew rapidly.

THE REAGAN-BUSH COLLAPSE

Antitrust policy went into recession around 1974, then plunged during the presidencies of Ronald Reagan and George Bush. They aggressively dismantled antitrust, imposing drastic cuts in budgets and manpower, installing officials hostile to the antitrust mission, and failing to enforce the laws. During 1981-89, the Antitrust Division of the Justice Dept. challenged only 16 of over 16,000 pre-merger notices filed with them.

Despite his high-profile contest with Microsoft, Bill Clinton has largely accepted the conservative view that most mergers are harmless. In recent years, federal authorities have approved or ignored many giant mergers. These include Westinghouse's buyout of CBS, the joining of "Baby Bells" Bell Atlantic and Nynex, and the combination of Chemical Bank and Manufacturers Hanover. During 1997 alone, 156 mergers of $1 billion or more, and merger transactions totalling more than *$1 trillion*, passed antitrust muster.

Clinton's failure to attack giant mergers rests nominally on the alleged efficiency of large firms and the belief that globalized markets make for competition. FTC head Robert Pitofsky said, "this is an astonishing merger wave," but not to worry because these deals "should be judged on a global market scale, not just on national and local markets."

But the efficiency of large size—as opposed to the profit-making advantages that corporations gain from market power and cross-selling (pushing products through other divisions of the same company)—is eminently debatable. And many markets are not global—hospitals, for example, operate in local markets, yet only some 20 of 3,000 hospital mergers have been subjected to antitrust challenge. Even in global markets a few firms are often dominant, and a vast array of linkages such as joint ventures and licensing agreements increasingly mute global competition.

The Clinton administration's failure to contest many giant mergers does not rest only on intellectual arguments. It also reflects political weakness and an unwillingness to oppose powerful people who fund elections and own or dominate the media. This was conspicuously true of the great media combinations—Disney and Cap-Cities/ABC, and TimeWarner and Turner—and the merger of Boeing and McDonnell-Douglas, which involved institutions of enormous power, whose mergers the stock market greeted enthusiastically.

THE ECONOMISTS SELL OUT

Since the early 1970s, powerful people and corporations have funded not only elections but conservative economists, who are frequently housed in think-tanks such as the American Enterprise, Hoover, and Cato Institutes, and serve as corporate consultants in regulatory and anti-trust cases. Most notable in hiring economic consultants have been AT&T and IBM, which together spent hundreds of millions of dollars on their antitrust defenses. AT&T hired some 30 economists from five leading economics departments during the 1970s and early 1980s.

Out of these investments came models and theories downgrading the "populist" idea that numerous sellers and decentralization were important for effective competition (and essential to a democratic society). They claimed instead that the market can do it all, and that regulation and antitrust actions are misconceived. First, theorists showed that efficiency gains from mergers might reduce prices even more than monopoly power would cause them to rise. Economists also stressed "entry," claiming that if mergers did not improve efficiency any price increases would be wiped out eventually by new companies entering the industry. Entry is also the heart of the theory of "contestable markets," developed by economic consultants to AT&T, who argued that the ease of entry in cases where resources (trucks, aircraft) can be shifted quickly at low cost, makes for effective competition.

Then there is the theory of a "market for corporate control," in which mergers allow better managers to displace the less efficient. In this view, poorly-managed firms have low stock prices, making them easy to buy. Finally, many economists justified conglomerate mergers on three grounds: that they function as "mini capital markets," with top managers allocating capital between divisions of a single firm so as to maximize efficiency; that they reduce transaction costs; and that they are a means of diversifying risk.

These theories, many coming out of the "Chicago School" (the economics department at the University of Chicago), suffer from over-simplification, a strong infusion of ideology, and lack of empirical support. Mergers often are motivated by factors other than enhancing efficiency—such as the desire for monopoly power, empire building, cutting taxes, improving stock values, and even as a cover for poor management (such as when the badly-run U.S. Steel bought control of Marathon Oil).

Several researchers have questioned the supposed benefits of mergers. In theory, a merger that improves efficiency should increase profits. But one study by Dennis Mueller, and another by F. W. Scherer and David Ravenscraft, showed that mergers more often than not have reduced returns to stockholders. A study by Michael Porter of Harvard University demonstrated that a staggering 74% of the conglomerate acquisitions of the 1960s were eventually sold off (divested)—a good indication that they were never based on improving efficiency. William Shepherd of the University of Massachusetts investigated the "contestable markets" model, finding that it is a hypothetical case with minimal applicability to the real world.

DURING 1981-89, THE ANTITRUST DIVISION OF THE JUSTICE DEPTARTMENT CHALLENGED ONLY 16 OF OVER 16,000 PRE-MERGER NOTICES FILED WITH THEM.

Despite their inadequacies, the new apologetic theories have profoundly affected policy, because they provide an intellectual rationale for the agenda of the powerful.

Resources: "Competition Policy in America: The Anti-Antitrust Paradox," James Brock, *Antitrust Bulletin*, Summer 1997; "The Promotional-Financial Dynamic of Merger Movements: A Historical Perspective," Richard DuBoff and Edward Herman, *Journal of Economic Issues*, March 1989; "Antimerger Policy in the United States: History and Lessons," Dennis C. Mueller, *Empirica*, 1996; "Dim Prospects: effective competition in telecommunications, railroads and electricity," William Shepherd, *Antitrust Bulletin*, 1997.

WHY CEO SALARIES SKYROCKET

BY ARTHUR MACEWAN

Dear Dr. Dollar,

Why do companies compensate CEOs with such high salaries and bonuses? Do the CEOs themselves decide on their pay? Isn't it always said that no one is indispensable?

— *Gwen Nottingham,*
Laurel, Montana

CEOs and other top executives of large corporations do not *formally* decide on their own salaries—that's the job of the board of directors. The board members, however, are generally high level executives of other corporations, who by supporting the big pay packages of others, win support for big pay packages for themselves.

For example, top executives of industrial companies with over $250 million in sales were compensated an averge of $870,000 in 1997, according to *Forbes*. Consider Frank Newman, who runs Bankers Trust, one of the banks that fueled the current crisis in Asia with ill-conceived loans. His 1997 salary and bonuses added up to $10.9 million. Or Harvey Golub, who oversaw the layoffs of 3,300 workers from American Express in 1997, and was compensated $33.4 million—that's about $10,000 for each layoff.

Yet the huge salaries are not only a result of executives taking good care of each other. Other countries also have "interlocking directorates" of top executives serving on other companies' boards, yet CEO salaries are not nearly so high as in the United States. Top executives in Canada, Japan, the United Kingdom, and Germany are paid only half as much as their U.S. peers (with pay including salaries, bonuses, perks, and long-term incentives). You can find individual executives in those countries who take home millions, but nowhere do top executives as a group come close to the U.S. corporate elite.

> OVER MANY DECADES, U.S. COMPANIES HAVE CREATED A HIGHLY UNEQUAL CORPORATE STRUCTURE THAT RELIES HEAVILY ON MANAGEMENT CONTROL WHILE LIMITING WORKERS' AUTHORITY.

So what's the difference? Are U.S. executives more valuable than European or Japanese executives in producing profits? The answer lies not in their productivity, but in their power.

Over many decades, U.S. companies have created a highly unequal corporate structure that relies heavily on management control while limiting workers' authority. Large numbers of bureaucrats work to maintain the U.S. system. While in the United States about 13% of nonfarm employees are managers and administrators, that figure is about 4% in Japan and Germany. So U.S. companies rely on lots of well-paid managers to keep poorly paid workers in line, and the huge salaries of the top executives are simply the tip of an iceberg.

This highly unequal corporate system is buttressed by an unequal political and social structure. Without a powerful union movement, for example, there is little pressure on Washington to adopt a tax code that limits corporate-generated inequality. Several other high-income countries have a wealth tax, but not the United States. In addition, U.S. laws governing the operation of unions and their role in corporate decision making are relatively weak (and often poorly enforced). Without powerful workers' organizations, direct challenges to high CEO pay levels are very limited (as is the power to raise workers' wages). So income distribution in the United States is among the most unequal within the industrialized world, and high executive salaries and low wages can be seen as two sides of the same coin.

CHAPTER 6

Labor Markets and the Distribution of Income

INTRODUCTION

Mainstream economics textbooks emphasize the ways that labor markets are similar to other markets. In the standard model, labor suppliers (workers) decide how much to work in the same way that producers decide how much to supply, by weighing the revenues against the costs—in this case, the opportunity costs of foregone leisure, and other potential costs of having a job, like physical injury. Labor demand is derived demand: consumer demands for goods and services drive firms' production decisions, which in turn dictate the amount of labor to use. Workers are paid based on their marginal products—the amount that they contribute, per hour, to output.

The same principles explain income differences in the orthodox model. Workers earn different wages because they contribute different marginal products to output. People who supply other inputs—investors or lenders supplying capital, land-owners supplying land—are rewarded according to the marginal products of those inputs. Of course, economists of every stripe acknowledge that in reality many non-market factors, such as government assistance programs, unionization, and discrimination, affect incomes. But in most economics textbooks these produce limited deviations from the basic laws of supply and demand.

The authors in this chapter focus on these "deviations." They contend that non-market factors are not exceptions to a universal rule, but part of a complex *set* of rules that produce poverty and inequality. Marc Breslow describes the reasons for a widening wage and employment gap between black and white men, including racial discrimination (Breslow, article 6.2). David Bacon describes the post-9/11 crackdown on immigrant workers (Bacon, article 6.4). Amy Gluckman points out the persistent wage gap between men and women, and outlines "comparable worth" policies that compensate female-dominated jobs equally with male-dominated ones (Gluckman, article 6.1). As her article suggests, the analyses in this chapter demand ambitious public policy—not simply ensuring the smooth operation of markets for labor and other inputs, but creating a better set of rules.

Randy Albelda and Chris Tilly examine situations in which the earnings from labor fail to lift a family out of poverty. Albelda describes how welfare-to-work programs place women who are not "work-ready" into jobs that are not "mother-ready"—that lack flexibility and family supports such as child care—moving them from the ranks of the welfare poor to the working poor (Albelda, article 6.3). Tilly analyzes the impact of living wage laws, which set a minimum wage above the federal minimum for selected groups of workers (Tilly, article 6.5).

The last three articles spotlight inequality. Phineas Baxandall tries to make Bill Gates's unimaginable wealth imaginable (Baxandall, article 6.8). Thad Williamson places inequality in a global context (Williamson, article 6.6). And Alejandro Reuss explores the effects of inequality on death rates (Reuss, article 6.7).

DISCUSSION QUESTIONS

1) (Gluckman) "Equal pay for equal work" has not proven sufficient to equalize women's and men's pay. Why not? Contrast the explanations of mainstream economic commentators with those of comparable worth advocates. Where do you come down in this debate?

2) (Gluckman, Breslow) Race and gender discrimination mean that women and African American workers (among others) are "underpriced" relative to their true marginal products. If this is so, why don't rational, cost-minimizing businesses snap up these low-cost workers, bidding their wages back up to their marginal product?

3) (Gluckman) At the close of her article, Amy Gluckman contrasts comparable worth with a "far more radical" revaluation of different types of work. Explain the difference between the two. How does each of these programs of reform relate to the idea that wages are set to equal marginal product?

4) (Bacon) Based on the standard economic model, what would you expect to be the likely effects of tougher immigration laws on labor supply and wages? David Bacon maintains that the crackdown has had different effects from these expected ones. Explain.

5) (Albelda) Welfare-to-work programs compel welfare recipients to take paid jobs. What effects will this have on the total supply of labor, and on the elastic-

ity of labor supply? What effects would you expect on the wages of less-skilled workers?

6) (Albelda) Should we use public policy to make jobs more "mother-ready"? First, what does this mean, and how could it be done? Second, is it a good idea?

7) (Tilly) Chris Tilly claims that for modest increases in the living wage (or, for that matter, the minimum wage), the Law of Demand does not apply—the quantity of labor demanded will not decrease. How can this be? However, he adds that as increases grow larger, the Law of Demand will eventually kick in. Does this mean that cities should not set a high living wage?

8) (Williamson) Thad Williamson says it would be "easy" to make "serious, rapid progress toward the complete eradication of global poverty." But clearly this has not happened. Why not? Consider various possible explanations.

9) (Reuss) Death rates are higher where inequality is higher. These mortality differences apply at all income levels, even after taking into account differences in poverty. How can this be explained?

10) (General) A number of *Real World Micro* authors, including Bacon, Breslow, Gluckman, and Tilly in this chapter, claim that labor unions are much-needed equalizers that help low-wage workers. Orthodox economists tend to be much more negative about unions, arguing that they interfere with the smooth functioning of labor markets and pit the interests of a small group of workers against the broader interests of all workers and consumers. Explain how these differing assessments of unions are connected to differing views of *how the labor market works*. Where do you come down in this debate?

11) (General) The authors in this chapter view inequality as a bad thing. In contrast, many economic conservatives see inequality as a natural and unavoidable outcome of an economy based on incentives (with the added implication that attempts to reduce inequality risk undermining these important incentives). State and justify your own opinion about this.

12) (General) Neoclassical textbooks use the ideas of supply and demand and marginal product to explain pay levels. Can these ideas explain why dangerous, physically difficult, and boring jobs like asbestos abatement are also some of the worst paid? If so, how? If not, what might explain these jobs' low pay?

September/October 2002

COMPARABLE WORTH

BY AMY GLUCKMAN

There must be something to an idea that the business press has recently labelled "crackpot," "more government humor," an attempt "to Sovietize U.S. wage scales," and one of ten "dumbest ideas of the century." The idea is comparable worth (or "pay equity"), a broad term for a range of policies aimed at reducing the pay gap between occupations traditionally filled by women and those traditionally filled by men.

Comparable worth proposals first appeared in the 1970s, when women's rights campaigners began to recognize that much of the pay gap between men and women occurred not because women were paid less for doing the exact same work, but because women workers were concentrated in occupations that paid less than male-dominated occupations.

Consider a nurse who earns less than a maintenance worker working for the same employer. (This is typical of the pay gaps researchers uncovered in studies of municipal pay scales in several U.S. cities in the 1970s.) The nurse is responsible for the well-being and even the lives of her patients, and the job typically requires at least two years of postsecondary education. The maintenance worker may have far less serious responsibilities and probably did not even need a high-school diploma to get the job. Why might he earn more? His job may be physically demanding and may entail unpleasant or risky working conditions (although so may hers!). But in many cases, any reasonable evaluation of the two jobs supports the nurse's claim that she should earn the higher salary.

Comparable worth advocates argue that this kind of pay gap is the result of gender bias. Historically, they claim, employers set wages in various occupations based on mistaken stereotypes about women—that women had little to contribute, that they were just working for "pin money." These wage differences have stuck over time, leaving the 60% of women who work in female-dominated occupations (as well as the small number of men who do) at a disadvantage. Studies show that even after other factors affecting wages are accounted for, the percentage of women in an occupation has a net downward effect on that occupation's average wage.

Mainstream economists take issue with this view. How do they explain the persisting wage gap between male-dominated and female-dominated occupations? The market, of course. Wages are not set by evaluating the requirements of each job, they claim, but rather by shifts in the supply of and demand for labor. In this view, the nurse-janitor pay gap represents the outcome of past employment discrimination against women. Discrimination in hiring kept women out of many occupations, resulting in an oversupply of women entering the traditionally-female jobs such as nursing. This oversupply kept wages in those fields low. Not to worry: as gender bias against women wanes and women are able to enter the full range of occupations, some economists argue, this situation will resolve itself and the pay gap between female- and male-dominated occupations will disappear.

As it turns out, the majority of women workers continue to labor within the confines of the "pink-collar" ghetto. Women have indeed entered certain professions in significant numbers over the past thirty years. Physicians were 10% female in 1972, but 27.9% female in 2000. Lawyers and judges were 3.8% female in 1972, but 29.7% female in 2000. But the extent of sex segregation in a wide range of occupations has barely budged during this time. Teachers (K-12) were 70% female in 1972; 75.4% female in 2000. Secretaries were 99.1% female in 1972; 98.9% female in 2000. Hairdressers were an identical 91.2% female in 1972 and in 2000! Retail sales clerks were 68.9% female in 1972; 63.5% female in 2000. On the other side, automobile mechanics were 0.5% female in 1972; 1.2% female in 2000. Plumbers were 0.3% female in 1972; 1.9% female in 2000. (Women moved into a few blue-collar jobs in greater—but still relatively low—numbers. For example, telephone installers were 0.5% female in 1972, but 13.1% female in 2000.) So either employers are still discriminating directly against women to a significant degree, or else the mainstream economists' predictions about the effects of waning job discrimination are wrong—or both.

Another analysis points to the lower wages women earn as the price they pay for choosing jobs that give them the flexibility to fulfill parenting responsibilities. For example, many women (and a few men) choose to become teachers so that they can be home with their children in the late afternoon and during school vacations. But leaving gender aside, do employees typically trade off lower wages for greater flexibility? Higher-paid jobs tend to have more flexibility, not less. If this argument has some relevance for women in female-dominated professions such as teaching, it ignores entirely the vast number of women in low-wage, female-dominated occupations: retail clerk, direct care worker, waitress, beautician. These jobs certainly don't offer their occupants flexibility in return for their low wages.

Conservative commentators also stress that the overall wage gap between men and women—women employed full time, year round earn about 74% as much as men—is reasonable because women on average have fewer years of work experience and less seniority. That's true, but accounts for only about 40% of the gap. That leaves about 15 to 16 cents on every dollar unaccounted for. (Ironically, it is deindustrialization and the resulting decline in men's wages—not growth in women's wages—that has been primarily responsible for the shrinking of the gender wage gap, down from 59% in 1970.)

> EVEN AFTER OTHER FACTORS ARE ACCOUNTED FOR, THE PERCENTAGE OF WOMEN IN AN OCCUPATION HAS A NET DOWNWARD EFFECT ON THAT OCCUPATION'S AVERAGE WAGE.

So the work force continues to be segregated by sex, and women's wages continue to lag behind men's, if not as much as in the past. What can be done? Comparable worth advocates have used a variety of strategies: legislation, lawsuits, collective bargaining agreements. Typically, advocates call for employers to use job evaluation instruments that rate different jobs according to several criteria such as skill, responsibility, and working conditions. Job evaluation instruments like these are not new; many large corporations already use them in their ordinary personnel procedures.

Of course, a job rating scale does not automatically indicate how to weight different factors in determining compensation, and so does not in itself determine how much a job should pay. Usually, this piece of the puzzle comes from information about what employers actually do pay. In other words, these instruments don't exclude the market from consideration. Instead, they usually take market wages for various occupations as baseline data to determine how much value to assign to different job characteristics. Then, however, employees and employers can recognize jobs that fall off the curve—jobs that pay much more or much less than the broad average of jobs with the same rating. On this basis, workers can then push employers to raise the wages of "underpaid" jobs.

The comparable worth movement made a lot of headway in the 1970s and early 1980s, primarily in unionized, public-sector workplaces. However, comparable worth barely made a dent in the private sector. Even in the public sector, the movement's momentum slowed by the late 1980s. Today, Congress is again considering legislation authorizing workers to sue their employers in order to correct pay inequities between male- and female-dominated job titles and also between race-segregated job titles.

Comparable worth legislation, if enacted, could potentially give an enormous boost to low-wage women workers. One study estimates that "among those currently earning less than the federal poverty threshold for a family of three, nearly 50 percent of women of color and 40 percent of white women would be lifted out of poverty" by a national comparable worth policy that addressed both race-segregated and sex-segregated occupations.

However, comparable worth is not a cure-all. Since comparable worth typically addresses wage gaps within a single workplace, it does not help workers whose employers pay everyone the minimum wage. Without strong unions, comparable worth won't get very far even if new legislation were enacted; for one thing, it is unions that are most likely to be able to fund the expensive litigation necessary to force companies to revise their pay scales. At a deeper level, existing comparable worth policies largely accept how the U.S. economic system has typically rewarded different job factors. It is one thing to even out pay inequities between jobs that rate the same on existing job-evaluation instruments. It would be far more radical to rebuild our notions of fair compensation in a way that values the skills of caring, communication, and responsibility for people's emotional well-being that are critical to many female-dominated occupations.

Resources: Deborah M. Figart and Heidi I. Hartmann, "Broadening the Concept of Pay Equity: Lessons for a Changing Economy" in Ron Baiman, Heather Boushey, Dawn Saunders, eds., *Political Economy and Contemporary Capitalism: Radical Perspectives on Economic Theory and Policy* (M. E. Sharpe, 2000); "In Pursuit of Pay Equity" in Dollars & Sense, *Women at Work: Gender and Inequality in the '80s*; Paula England, "The case for comparable worth," *Quarterly Review of Economics and Finance* 39:3, Fall 1999; *Forbes*, 27 December 1999; *Statistical Abstract of the United States*.

January/February 1997

LAST IN, FIRST OUT: BLACK MEN TAKE THE HEAT

BY MARC BRESLOW

The widely-syndicated economics columnist Robert Samuelson recently wrote, "Most men, whatever their race, shouldn't regularly be without work. If they are, the main reason is that they lack the skills, discipline or desire to find and keep jobs." Samuelson went on to argue that since most blacks have jobs, for those who don't the problem must be within themselves rather than resulting from racism or the structure of the U.S. economy.

Contrary to Samuelson's moralizing, the truth is that African Americans are victims of an economy that has been failing most workers for more than two decades, of employment trends that increasingly confer benefits only on those with advanced degrees, and of continued racism. Equally destructive, the current political climate blames them for their own suffering.

Since the early 1970s real wages for American workers have been falling, while unemployment rates have risen. For African Americans, and particularly young male workers, the trend has been worse. Average wages have fallen more than 15%, while unemployment, even during the current economic "boom," remains above 11% for all black men, and around 25% for those under the age of 25.

Racists, such as Charles Murray and his *Bell Curve* supporters, claim that this trend can be explained by genetics, or by the moral failure of black families. Conservatives blame the government for interfering with free markets, arguing that the minimum wage, welfare and other federal policies have reduced the available jobs and destroyed work incentives. Yet another explanation, favored by moderate economists, says that whites have more "human capital"—education and experience—than blacks, so they are worth more on the job market.

The racist arguments are so offensive that I would rather ignore them. But, briefly, consider—is it reasonable to suppose that either the genetic endowments, or the cultural backgrounds, of African Americans deteriorated so quickly as to explain a rise in unemployment from 8% during 1970 to 15% during the recession of the mid-1980s?

The answer is no—blacks have always been the last hired and the first fired in the United States. When the U.S. economy provided close to full employment, white employers hired African Americans even when they might have preferred not to. But when there are many applicants for every available job, it is far easier for employers to discriminate—and to indulge the racist preferences of their white employees and customers.

Job opportunities for all Americans have been on a long downward trend, and they are far lower today than the official five point something percent unemployment rate indicates. Because federal statistics ignore all potential workers who are too discouraged to have looked for work in the past month, and all those who want full-time jobs but can only find part-time ones, the real "underemployment" rate is actually about 12% at present.

And while the classified ads may show many jobs available for skilled workers in the largely-white suburbs, there are few openings for people in poor inner-city neighborhoods—who often cannot get to suburban jobs due to lack of public transportation. For example, 14 people applied for every job opening at fast food restaurants in the predominantly black central Harlem neighborhood of New York City during one five-month period in 1993, according to a study by Katherine Newman for the Russell Sage Foundation. Among those people who applied for such jobs but were rejected, 73% still lacked jobs a year later.

Blaming the existence of welfare or other low-income government policies for blacks' worsening plight also makes little sense, since the real value of such programs has been steadily decreasing. How can the minimum wage, for example, be a main cause of job losses when it had (until the rise in October 1996 from $4.25 to $4.70) lost 30% of its value since 1970? Similarly, how can welfare benefits cause joblessness when the value of welfare grants fell by 45% since 1970, even before the new legislation radically downsized the welfare system?

The real causes of the severe drop in black men's earnings versus white men's lies in the restructuring of the U.S. labor market. Economists John Bound of the University of Michigan and Richard Freeman of Harvard University attribute this drop first to the rapid disappearance of factory jobs in the United States, where black men had been highly concentrated. In 1973 42% of black men in the Midwest held manufacturing jobs, compared to 33% of white men. But by 1989 there was a dramatic turnaround—only 12% of blacks held such relatively well-paying jobs, compared to 21% of whites.

This incredible shift occurred because workers who had the most seniority got to keep the much-reduced number of union jobs. African American men, who had less seniority because discriminatory barriers had only recently come down and because they were on average younger, were the first to be laid off.

Second, the one-third fall in the inflation-adjusted value of the minimum wage harmed blacks more than whites since more black Americans held jobs paying the minimum. And third, the decline of unions in America has particularly hurt African Americans, 32% of whom held unionized jobs in 1983, compared to 22% of whites.

For black women, average wages have fallen only slightly, in contrast to the severe 15% drop for men. But their situation relative to white women has gotten worse, since white women's wages have risen significantly over the past two decades.

The declining minimum wage has hurt African-American women, as has reduced funding for education and government. Racial and gender discrimination has been less severe in the public than the private sector, so that many black women found jobs there during the 1960s and 1970s. But as government spending has dropped, these jobs have dried up. In 1973, for example, 70% of young college-educated black women, and 57% of white women, found jobs in education. But by 1989 only 20% of young female college graduates, both black and white, were employed in education.

Although genetics, culture, and welfare policies do not explain the worsened circumstances of African Americans, the "human capital" argument does have some truth. Even though African American educational levels have been catching up to whites (68% of blacks had high school degrees in 1992 versus 31% in 1970), whites still have twice as high a proportion of college graduates as blacks (thanks in part to falling funding for public education). Whereas in years past a high school degree was enough to provide access to reasonably-paying jobs, it no longer does so. In today's restructured labor market only people with college and graduate degrees (and not all of them) have seen their wages rise over time.

Moreover, Bound and Freeman's data show that even among college graduates the gap between white and black earnings has widened in recent years. One reason for this is the continued prevalence of racist attitudes among employers. In 1991 the Urban Institute conducted a study in which they sent out pairs of "testers," one black and one white, to apply for the same jobs. The pairs were carefully matched to have equal qualifications for the jobs, including not only paper qualifications, but also personal qualities such as openness and articulateness. One striking finding of the study was that in 15% of cases only the white tester received a job offer, while only the black tester received an offer in a mere 5% of cases.

Such evidence tends to undermine the validity of the "human capital" argument, since the paired testers had the same education and experience. And the implied discrimination is enough to explain much of the difference between black and white unemployment rates.

The U.S. economy is badly serving the needs both of those who have jobs and those who want them, and people of color are particularly hard hit. There are no easy answers to our long-term economic decline. But it is high time to stop blaming the victims.

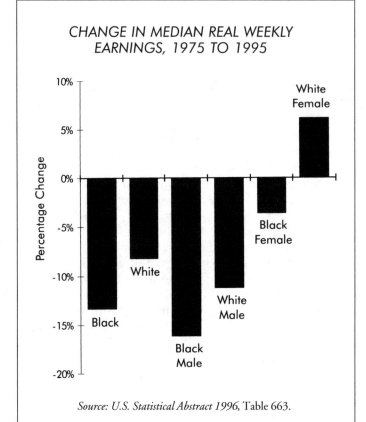

CHANGE IN MEDIAN REAL WEEKLY EARNINGS, 1975 TO 1995

Source: U.S. Statistical Abstract 1996, Table 663.

Resources: This article draws heavily on "The Racial Divide Widens," *Dollars & Sense,* Jan/Feb 1995, and "To Be Young, Black, and Female," *Dollars & Sense,* May/June 1995. Also see "What Went Wrong? The Erosion of Relative Earnings and Employment Among Young Black Men in the 1980s," John Bound and Richard B. Freeman, *Quarterly Journal of Economics,* 1992; "Finding Work in the Inner City: How Hard is it Now? How Hard will it be for AFDC Recipients?," Katherine Newman and Chauncy Lennon, NY: Russell Sage Foundation Working Paper #76, October 1995.

September/October 2000

WHAT'S WRONG WITH WELFARE-TO-WORK

BY RANDY ALBELDA

"Ending welfare as we know it" has rapidly become ending welfare. Time limits virtually assure that the majority of families who receive welfare will be cut off at least from federal funding. The current trend is to replace welfare with earnings and is best summed up by the ever-present term "welfare-to-work."

The welfare-to-work "solution" can be thought of as a match made in hell. It puts poor mothers who need the most support and flexibility into jobs in the low-wage labor market which often are the most inflexible, have the least family-necessary benefits (vacation time, health care, sick days), and provide levels of pay that often are insufficient to support a single person, let alone a family. This mismatch is not going to be resolved by providing short-term job training, work vans, poor-quality child care, or even refundable earned income tax credits. It is a political, social, and economic problem that must be addressed in our policies but also in our national psyche. It starts with valuing the work that families do. Raising children—in any and all family configurations—is absolutely vital work to our individual and collective well-being. And it is deserving. Recognizing this will not only transform how we think about welfare, it can and must change how we think about the structure of paid work. We must have access to paid work that allows us to take care of our families and have a family life without relegating all women to the home.

BEEN THERE, DONE THAT

Ending welfare poses some historically familiar alternatives for women. Getting married and staying married—thus being dependent on a man—was of course the fond hope and major inspiration for conservatives who sponsored the 1996 Personal Responsibility and Work Opportunity Reconciliation Act (PRWORA). The Act leads with these two "findings": 1) Marriage is the foundation of a successful society; and 2) Marriage is an essential institution of a successful society which promotes the interests of children.

The path most proponents of welfare reform promote publicly, however, is "welfare-to-work." There is a wide range of methods for promoting paid work instead of welfare, from the punitive "work-first" strategies pursued by over half the states to the more liberal strategies (which include a generous package of training and education options, day care, transportation, and health care) put forth by Mary Jo Bane and David Ellwood when they were welfare reform policymakers in the Clinton administration. Despite its current popularity, the notion of putting welfare mothers to "work" is hardly new. Work requirements have long been part of AFDC, and were seen as an important way to get women, particularly black women, off the welfare rolls. It was only in the early 1990s, however, that paid work became the main alternative in light of benefit time limits.

Most states, as well as the ancillary not-for-profit agencies and for-profit companies that get lucrative welfare-related contracts, are putting significant energies into getting adult welfare recipients to "work." Work in this case means paid employment or unpaid community or public-service placements (workfare). But there are problems with welfare-to-work, some of which states readily recognize and are working to cope with (however inadequately), and others which states do not even recognize.

INADEQUATE SUPPORTS FOR WELFARE-TO-WORK MOMS

One aspect of states' welfare-to-work policy has always been their concern with the "job readiness" of welfare mothers. From vast amounts of published research we know many welfare mothers have low educational attainment and many lack recent job experience (although the vast majority have been employed at some point). Both of these characteristics impede entry into the labor market and, once there, all but assure low wages. This is too bad since welfare-to-work ideology rests on short-term training, which is reinforced by precluding most education from qualifying as "work-related activities" in the work quotas established in PRWORA. This of course means that many state programs will be ineffectual in improving women's skills.

More and more research is uncovering another set of barriers to work, including learning disabilities, severe bouts of depression, and experiences with domestic violence. The prediction is that the easy-to-place recipients will soon be thrown out of the welfare system and those who remain will require much more training and support to get paid employment. Ironically, or perhaps cynically, welfare will become exactly how it was portrayed for years—a system that serves very low-functioning women with children who need long-term assistance. Recent studies show that over 41% of current recipients have less than a high school diploma, and between 10% and 31% of welfare recipients are currently victims of domestic violence. Helping women overcome barriers to employment will take time, quality counseling, and long-term training, something welfare reform is discouraging or prohibiting.

What distinguishes welfare recipients from other poor people is that two thirds of them are children being raised, most often, by a mother on her own. Welfare has always been a program for families with young children. Therefore, welfare-to-work requires a substantial set of ancillary supports that *mothers* with small children *need* to get to work, such as health insurance, transportation, and child care. Since many jobs available to welfare-to-work mothers do not provide health insurance, states allow women to stay on Medicaid, but typically only for one year after leaving welfare. Then they're on their own. Some states have recognized the transportation challenge mothers face—efficiently getting children to and from day care and school, and getting themselves to and from work in a timely fashion—and some are trying to solve this problem with loaner cars, work vans, and public transportation vouchers. In rural and suburban areas, however, the problems are much more difficult since adequate transportation is just not there. Regarding child care, policy makers recognize the need for it, but their solutions should make us shiver. Very few states pay any attention to the quality of care. Any care seems to do for poor mothers. In Massachusetts, for example, the state encourages mothers to find low-cost caretakers with reimbursements of $15 a day. Assuming you get what you pay for, such child care is a disaster for mothers and children. Moreover, it impoverishes and exploits the caregivers.

AND WHAT ABOUT THE PROBLEMS WITH NO NAME?

Will welfare-to-work actually ensure economic "independence"? Many are avoiding this question because the economic expansion, which has both accompanied and accommodated welfare-to-work, has at least fulfilled one premise of welfare reform—moving women from the rolls to a job. However, come the downturn, many who did get jobs will lose them and caseloads will creep back up. Further, the expansion has allowed states to be slack, if not entirely unimaginative, in their training and education efforts, relying on the economic expansion to reduce rolls and thereby claim victory in the welfare reform battle.

Will finding a job mean earning a living wage? Not likely. What is almost always ignored or conveniently forgotten in the blind faith that all too often accompanies the welfare-to-work mentality is that the U.S. labor market has always failed women who have little formal education and sporadic job experiences. Women have a very hard time supporting themselves, let alone families, on wages from waitressing, sales clerking, cleaning hotel rooms, or even assisting administrators. Yet these are exactly the kinds of jobs welfare-to-work mothers are likely to get.

In addition to the problems of a fickle labor market and chronically low wages, women in the welfare-to-work pipeline must cope with the fact that most jobs are not "mother ready." That is, they do not accommodate mothers' needs, even when training, work, and child care arrangements are in place. These are not unknown or new needs. They include the remarkably mundane events such as children getting sick, school and medical appointments, school vacations, and early-release school days. Employers, especially those who employ low-wage workers, do not want workers who come in late because a school bus didn't show up, miss days because there was no child care, or worry about their children at 3:00 p.m.—instead of doing their tedious low-wage-earning tasks. Unfortunately, low-wage employers of current and former welfare recipients are least likely to grant sick leave and vacation time. According to a report in last year's *American Journal of Public Health,* 46% of women who had never been on welfare got sick leave and vacation pay at their jobs, as compared to 24% of women who had been on welfare less than two years, and 19% of women who had been on welfare more than two years.

Most state administrators, politicians, journalists, and researchers see the work of taking care of children as a cost of welfare-to-work, but not as an important and valuable family activity. Devaluing women's unpaid work in the home is clearly evident in studies of welfare reform. Typically, researchers compare welfare families' and employed families' material well-being without imputing any value to women's time. In short, the value of women's unpaid labor in the home when she is receiving welfare is zero. As a policy, welfare-to-work fails to grapple with the fact that adults responsible for children cannot (and probably should not) put their jobs—especially low-wage ones—before the needs of their children.

FAMILY VALUES/VALUING FAMILIES

The ideologues who concern themselves with poor mothers exhibit split personalities when it comes to getting women to work. The conservative architects of welfare reform who want to force poor mothers to do lousy jobs are now busy enacting tax cuts to encourage middle-class moms to stay at home and trying hard to eliminate the "marriage penalty" in the tax code. Liberals, on the other hand, seem preoccupied with providing inadequate supports for full-time employment for poor mothers. What's going on?

One way to make sense of the obsession with employment for poor mothers is to see the emphasis on paid work in welfare reform as a major change in thinking about women and public assistance. Indeed, it is a major value shift. The Social Security Act of 1935 made all poor single mothers entitled to receive Aid to Families with Dependent Children (AFDC), although the levels received were far lower than the other two major programs (Social Security and Unemployment Insurance) in that historic legislation. At that time, the notion of having to "work" for one's benefits was not an expectation of most single mothers. Women who were not attached to male breadwinners received income, but not much.

Another old value set guiding single mothers' receipt of cash assistance pivoted on how women became single mothers. Widows were seen as deserving, while divorced, separated, and never-married mothers were not. Benefit levels reinforced these "values."

What makes a single mother "deserving" today has changed. The salient factor is no longer how she happened to become a single parent, but rather if she is engaged in paid labor. This sentiment is only possible in an age when most women are in the paid labor market and when the moral repugnance of women without men has dissipated. Ironically, both of these accomplishments can be attributed in part to the successes of the women's movement, coupled with modern industrialization. As more and more women are drawn into the labor force, they tend to have fewer children and are not as likely to get or stay married. Interestingly, both conservatives and liberals have lent weight to the idea that working single mothers are more deserving.

The positive value of employment was accompanied by the negative value placed on receiving welfare. Led by Ronald Reagan and conservative thinker Charles Murray in the 1980s, welfare opponents referred to AFDC recipients as "welfare queens." They were presumed to have loads of children, leech resources from the state, and then pass their dysfunctional behavior on to their children. In the mid-1980s through the 1990s, many "liberal" poverty researchers carried this banner as well. "Underclass" authors, notably William Julius Wilson and Christopher Jencks, as well as their left detractors, such as William Darity and Samuel Myers, discussed welfare receipt as a pathology—one of the many "bad" behaviors that helps reproduce poverty. Jencks even referred to women receiving welfare as the "reproductive underclass." Further, when adult recipients have earnings, even if they receive hefty supplements, they are not perceived as receiving "hand-outs" and hence are deserving. It would seem, then, putting welfare mothers to work solves the problem of growing welfare rolls and plays into American values that will help restore safety nets for the poor. On both the Right and the Left, putting poor mothers to work is the prescribed cure to their "dysfunctional" tendencies.

A PROGRESSIVE AGENDA

I do not want to argue here that paid work is bad. Indeed, earnings can and do buy economic security and some independence from men, especially from abusive relationships. In a society that values paid work, doing it can build your self-esteem as well. However, welfare-to-work is a set-up. The types of jobs poor mothers get and can keep provide neither much dignity nor sufficient wages. Working enough hours at low wages to support a family is often untenable. Women fail too often. This is not only demoralizing, but economically debilitating. If we don't think both about valuing women's work at home as well as when they do paid work, welfare-to-work is a cruel hoax that makes legislators feel better about themselves, but leaves poor families in the lurch.

WELFARE-TO-WORK FAILS TO GRAPPLE WITH THE FACT THAT ADULTS RESPONSIBLE FOR CHILDREN CANNOT (AND PROBABLY SHOULD NOT) PUT THEIR JOBS BEFORE THE NEEDS OF THEIR CHILDREN.

Instead of trying to reform poor mothers to become working poor mothers, we need to take a closer look at job structures and what it will take to make work possible for mothers who support families. This might include a shorter work week or at least income supplements to those who take a part-time job so that families can still pay for basic needs like housing, health insurance, child care, food, and clothing. Paid family and medical leave and expanded unemployment insurance to cover less continuous and low-paying part time work must also be in place. A mother shouldn't lose her job or her weekly pay because her child gets chicken pox. Herein lies the true opportunity of welfare-to-work welfare reform. (For more policy initiatives, see "An Immodest Proposal, Rewarding Women's Work to End Poverty," p. 36).

A national discussion about the value of women's work in the home is much needed for all women, not just those who turn to public assistance. It would raise several important sets of policy issues, including:

• seriously considering the provision of publicly funded family care such as child care centers, extended day programs, and child allowances;
• working to make sure that welfare is not punitive, and is at least comparable to social security and unemployment insurance; and
• focusing not just on making mothers "job ready," but promoting policies that make paid work "mother-

ready"—in other words, conducive to mothers' needs, paying a living wage, and offering opportunities for advancement.

If we as a nation recognized the value of women's work, we wouldn't have welfare reform that merely replaces public assistance with forcing mothers into working jobs at low wages and a shallow set of supports that vanishes quickly. Seeing the work of raising children as a benefit to society, not merely a cost of going to work, would mean developing a welfare-to-work regime that truly supports part-time waged work. Further, it might make us more cognizant that for some families at some points in their lives, having the sole adult in the labor force is not possible or desirable. Public income supports for poor single mothers will always need to exist precisely because we value the work of mothers taking care of their children.

Resources: Gwendolyn Mink, *Welfare's End*, Cornell University Press, 1998. P. Loprest and S. R. Zedlewski, November 1999, "Current and Former Welfare Recipients: How Do They Differ?" *Discussion Paper 17* (Washington: The Urban Institute). Sandra Danziger, et al., *Barriers to the Employment of Welfare Recipients*, revised ed. 9/99, University of Michigan Press. S. Jody Heymann and Alison Earle, "The Impact of Welfare Reform on Parents' Ability to Care for their Children's Health," *American Journal of Public Health*, April 1999.

ARTICLE 6.4

January/February 2003

IMMIGRANT WORKERS IN THE CROSSHAIRS

BY DAVID BACON

Erlinda Valencia came from the Philippines almost two decades ago. Like many Filipina immigrants living in the San Francisco Bay area, she found a job at the airport, screening passengers' baggage.

For 14 years she worked for Argenbright Security, the baggage-screening contractor used by airlines across the country. For most of that time, it was a minimum-wage job, and she could barely support her family working 40 hours a week. Then, two years ago, organizers from the Service Employees International Union (SEIU) began talking to the screeners. Erlinda Valencia decided to get involved, and eventually became a leader in the campaign that brought in the union. "We were very happy," she remembers. "It seemed to us all that for the first time, we had a real future." The new contract the union negotiated raised wages to over $10 an hour, and workers say harassment by managers began to decrease.

Erlinda Valencia's experience reflected a major national shift in immigrant workers' organizing. In recent years, immigrant workers made hard-fought gains in their rights at work, and in using these rights to organize unions and fight for better wages and conditions. De-spite the hostile reaction embodied in measures like California's Propositions 187 and 227, which sought to penalize undocumented immigrants and ban bilingual education, the political and economic clout of immigrants has increased, in large part because of successful labor organizing efforts. Some, like the janitors' strike in Los Angeles, have become well-known.

As a result, the AFL-CIO changed its position on immigration, and began calling for the repeal of employer sanctions, the federal law making it illegal for an undocumented worker to hold a job. The national movement for amnesty for undocumented workers began to grow, and the U.S. and Mexican governments started to negotiate over variants of the proposal. Under pressure from unions and immigrant rights organizations, the Immigration and Naturalization Service (INS) reduced the number of raids it carried out from 17,000 in 1997 to 953 in 2000.

Then the airplanes hit the twin towers in New York and the Pentagon in Washington. The mainstream media universally portrayed the September 11 attacks as the actions of immigrants. Political figures across the board proposed restrictions on immigration (by students, for instance) and crackdowns against undocumented workers, despite the fact that none of this would have prevented the attacks. The movement towards amnesty, and away from immigration raids and heavy-handed enforcement tactics, halted abruptly. Many public agencies, from local police departments to the Social Security Administration, which previously faced pressure to stop aiding the INS, took up immigration enforcement as a new responsibility. The Bush administration took advantage of the anti-immigrant fever to undermine the rights of workers, especially the foreign-born. The nativist scapegoating also provided a rationale for attacks on civil liberties, including the open use of racial profiling, indefinite detention, and other repressive measures.

EVERYTHING CHANGES—FOR TRANSPORTATION WORKERS

Screeners like Erlinda Valencia were among the first, and hardest, hit. Media and politicians blamed the screeners for allowing terrorists to board airplanes in Boston and New York with box cutters and plastic knives, despite the fact that these items were permitted at the time. But the whispered undercurrent beneath the criticism, that the screeners were undependable, and possibly even disloyal, was part of the rising anti-immigrant fever which swept the country.

Screeners in California airports, like those in many states where immigrants are a big part of the population, are mostly from other countries. In fact, the low pay for screeners was one of the factors that led to the concentration of immigrants and people of color in those jobs. In the search for scapegoats, they were easy targets.

In short order, Congress passed legislation setting up a new Transportation Security Authority (TSA) to oversee baggage and passenger screening at airports, and requiring that screeners be federal government employees. That could have been a good thing for Valencia and her coworkers, since federal employees have decent salaries, and often, because of civil service, lots of job security. Federal regulations protect their right to belong to unions, as well—at least they used to.

The TSA, however, was made part of the recently established Homeland Security Department. Legislation passed after the November elections—and after some Democrats did an about face and voted for it—allows Homeland Security czar Tom Ridge to suspend civil-service regulations in any part of the new department. By doing so, he can eliminate workers' union rights, allow discrimination and favoritism, and even abolish protection for whistleblowers.

In the anti-immigrant fever of the times, moreover, Congress required that screeners be citizens. Valencia had never become one, because of a catch-22 in U.S. immigration law. She is petitioning for visas for family members in the Philippines. As a citizen, however, she would actually have to wait longer to petition for them than she has to as a legal resident.

At the San Francisco airport, over 800 screeners were non-citizens. The INS, however, refused to establish any fast-track to citizenship, to help them qualify for the new federalized jobs. So just as she and her coworkers finally made the job bearable and capable of supporting a family, she lost it in November, when the citizenship requirement went into effect nationwide. "It's so unfair," she said. "I've done this job for 14 years, and we're all really good at it. Instead of wanting us to continue, they're going to hire people with no experience at all, and we'll probably have to train them too. You can fly the airplane, even if you're not a citizen, and you can carry a rifle in the airport as a member of the National Guard doing security, without being a citizen either. But you can't check the bags of the passengers."

In recent years, screeners working for private contractors like Argenbright have organized unions at airports in a number of cities, including San Francisco and Los Angeles. By federalizing the workforce, the government was also, in effect, busting those unions and tearing up their newly won contracts. The act creating the Homeland Security Department—which, with 170,000 employees, will be the largest in the federal government—may be invoked to prevent the new screener workforce from forming new unions and bargaining with the TSA. The American Federation of Government Employees, which represents federal workers, has protested against the exemption of the TSA from federal regulations recognizing employees' collective bargaining rights, and announced its intention of organizing the new workforce. But it does not challenge the citizenship requirement for screeners.

TAKING THE "WAR" TO THE WORKPLACE

Valencia was caught up in a wave of anti-immigrant legislation and repression that has profoundly affected immigrants and workers across the country in the wake of the September 11 terrorist attacks. The INS has launched a series of large-scale raids—Operation Tarmac. In airports around the country, the agency has told employers to provide the I-9 form for their employees. Using this information, agents have organized raids to pick up workers, and demanded that employers terminate those it says lack legal status. Close to 1,000 workers have been affected.

Initially, the INS stated publicly that it would only concentrate on workers who had access to the planes themselves, using aviation security as a pretext (hence the name Operation Tarmac). But once the raids got going, the crackdown expanded to workers in food preparation, and even in food service within passenger areas of the airports. A late-August raid at the Seattle-Tacoma International Airport led to the arrest of workers at the Sky Chef facility, which prepares on-board meals for airlines. The Hotel Employees and Restaurant Employees International Union (HERE), which is negotiating a contract with the company, claims that workers were called to an employee meeting, where they were met by INS agents in company uniforms. Some arrested workers had worked as long as 10 years at the facility, which ironically is owned by a foreign airline, Lufthansa.

Another 81 airport workers were arrested in raids on the Los Angeles, Orange County, Ontario (Calif.), Palm

Springs, and Long Beach airports on August 22. The detained immigrants were working in janitorial, food service, maintenance, and baggage-handling jobs. They were picked up because they apparently were using Social Security numbers which didn't match the INS database. While federal authorities admit that none of them—in fact none of the people arrested in any Operation Tarmac raid—are accused of terrorist activity, U.S. Attorney Debra Yang claimed that "we now realize that we must strengthen security at our local airports in order to ensure the safety of the traveling public." Eliseo Medina, executive vice-president of the SEIU, which has mounted organizing drives among many of the workers in Southern California airports, called the arrests unwarranted. "These people aren't terrorists," he fumed. "They only want to work." Unions like the Communications Workers of America (CWA) have protested Operation Tarmac raids in Washington, D.C., and elsewhere.

THERE IS NO LOGIC THAT CONNECTS A WORKER'S IMMIGRATION STATUS WITH NATIONAL SECURITY. AND PROPONENTS OF ANTI-IMMIGRANT CRACKDOWNS DON'T EVEN BOTHER TRYING TO PRODUCE AN EXPLANATION THAT DOES.

While the anti-immigrant campaign may have started at U.S. airports, it has now expanded far beyond their gates. The agency taking the new anti-immigrant attitude most to heart has been the Social Security Administration (SSA). Following the September 11 attacks, the SSA has flooded U.S. workplaces with "no-match letters," which the agency sends to employers informing them of employees whose Social Security numbers don't correspond to the SSA database.

In the last few years, employers have used no-match letters to fire immigrant workers during union organizing drives, or to intimidate those attempting to enforce worker protection laws. Until September 11, unions were making some headway in preventing these abuses. Two years ago, San Francisco's hotel union, HERE Local 2, won an important arbitrator's decision, which held that finding the name of a worker in a no-match letter was not, by itself, sufficient reason for terminating her. In addition, pressure on the SSA resulted in the inclusion, in the text of the letter, of a similar caveat, saying that inclusion in a no-match list was not to be taken as evidence of lack of immigration status.

In the wake of September 11, however, SSA has consciously embraced the no-match letter as an immigration-enforcement device. In 2001, the agency sent out 110,000 letters, and only when there were more than ten no-matches at a company or if the no-matches represented at least 10% of a company's total workforce. This year it plans to increase the number of letters to 750,000, and all it takes is one no-match to generate a letter. The pretext is September 11: "Concerns about national security, along with the growing problem of identity theft, have caused us to accelerate our efforts," according to SSA Commissioner Jo Anne Barnhart. The Internal Revenue Service has also sharply increased the number of letters sent to employers questioning incorrect numbers, and has threatened to begin fining employers who provide them. As in the case of Valencia and the screeners, however, there is no logic that connects a worker's immigration status with national security. And proponents of these changes don't even bother trying to produce an explanation that does.

The new attitude at Social Security marks an important change. In Nebraska in 1998, Operation Vanguard, a large-scale INS program to enforce employer sanctions, relied on the SSA's database to sift out the names of possible undocumented immigrants from the rolls of all the state's meatpacking employees. Over 3,000 people lost their jobs as a result. The INS had plans to extend the operation to other states, but was unable to do so when the SSA expressed misgivings about the INS's use of its database, and denied further access. The SSA had faced pressure from immigrants' rights groups and labor unions, who questioned why information intended to ensure that workers receive retirement and disability benefits was suddenly being used to take their jobs. After September 11, 2001, such objections were brushed aside.

The net effect of the new enforcement efforts has been to turn the Social Security card into a *de facto* national ID card, especially for employment, without any act of Congress creating one. Immigrant rights and civil liberties advocates have fought for years against the creation of a national ID, saying that it would inevitably lead to abuse by government and employers, and that it would eventually become a kind of internal passport. And Congress has been unwilling to establish such a national identification system, at least until September 11.

AN INJURY TO ALL

The wave of repression against immigrant workers hasn't just affected immigrants themselves. Limitations on workers' rights affect all workers. But because immigrants have been in the forefront of organizing unions and fighting sweatshop conditions, the threat against them has increased the danger that such conditions will spread, and affect workers throughout the labor force.

INS enforcement has increased the pressure on undocumented workers to avoid anything that could antagonize their employers, whether organizing a union, asking for a raise, or filing a complaint about unpaid overtime. There are almost 8 million undocumented people in the United States—4% of the urban workforce, and over half of all farm workers—according to a recent study by the Pew Hispanic Trust. When it becomes more risky and difficult for these workers to organize and join unions, or even to hold a job at all, they settle for lower wages. And when the price of immigrant labor goes down as a result, so do wages for other workers.

Attacks on immigrant workers have an especially big effect on unions trying to organize industries where immigrants are a large part of the workforce. The Operation Tarmac raids, for instance, hurt hotel unions' efforts to organize food service workers. The unions organizing immigrants are some of the most progressive in the labor movement. Unions like the Hotel Employees and Restaurant Employees have been disproportionately hit by the anti-immigrant offensive. Other unions, like the Teamsters and Laborers, have also led immigrant rights activity in many local areas, and suffered the impact of no-match letters and raids. Although the Bush administration has courted these unions' national leaders, the relationship doesn't seem to have provided any political leverage for stopping anti-immigrant abuses.

ORGANIZING A FIGHTBACK

Today, employers illegally fire workers for union activity in 31% of all union organizing campaigns, affecting immigrant and native-born workers alike. Companies treat the cost of legal battles, reinstatement, and back pay as a cost of doing business, and many consider it cheaper than signing a union contract. Labor rights for all workers need to be strengthened, not weakened. But, as former National Labor Relations Board chair William Gould IV points out, "There's a basic conflict between U.S. labor law and U.S. immigration law." In its recent *Hoffman* decision, the Supreme Court has held that the enforcement of employer sanctions, which makes it illegal for an undocumented immigrant to hold a job, is more important than the right of that worker to join a union and resist exploitation on the job.

Despite the decision, however, and the growing anti-immigrant climate, immigrants workers are still organizing. In May, four hundred workers won a hard-fought union election at the ConAgra beef plant in Omaha, a city where INS raids destroyed immigrant-based union committees only a few years ago. New Jersey recycling workers at KTI also finally won a union vote, on their fourth attempt to join the Laborers Union, which is also organizing successful campaigns among asbestos workers on Long Island. HERE won a 22-year battle for a contract at San Francisco's flagship Marriott Hotel, the hotel chain's first corporate-managed property to sign a union agreement.

The union-based efforts for amnesty and the repeal of employer sanctions were dealt a serious blow by the post-September 11 climate, but there are signs of renewed forward movement. SEIU Local 790, in cooperation with Filipinos for Affirmative Action and the Phillip Veracruz Justice Project, led efforts to fight for screeners' jobs at the San Francisco airport. The SEIU also initiated a national postcard campaign, called A Million Voices for Justice, to restart the national campaign for amnesty. In August, the SEIU and the ACLU sued the Department of Transportation over the citizenship requirement, and in mid-November Federal District Court Judge Robert Takasugi ruled the requirement illegal. The decision, however, only applies to the nine workers in whose names the suit was filed. Lawyers for the plaintiffs hope to broaden it to a class-action, while federal authorities predictably announced they would appeal.

Last summer, HERE announced plans for a Freedom Ride on Washington, D.C., for immigrant rights. The union deliberately chose the name and used the language of the civil-rights movement in an effort to establish a greater level of unity between African Americans, Latinos, and Asian Americans. HERE officials also said they intended to challenge the color line—employers have kept African Americans out of hotel employment, while hiring immigrants at lower wages—in hotels across the country. Massive layoffs and the economic downturn in tourism made plans to challenge hiring discrimination a moot point, but in the spring, HERE announced that it would again begin organizing its Freedom Ride, and set it for fall 2003.

And while Erlinda Valencia was one of the nine named plaintiffs in the suit against the citizenship requirement, the favorable court decision only means, at best, that she can take a test to qualify for her old job. If she takes it and passes, she will be put on a list of eligible potential employees. Her old job at the airport and those of her coworkers have already been filled. Preliminary studies indicate that many new hires are ex-members of the military and law enforcement agencies, and that the new workforce does not include nearly as many immigrants or people of color as the old one.

Valencia, like may other former screeners, has found herself looking for another job. The labor councils, unions, and immigrant rights activists who supported the screeners mounted food drives, tried to help former screeners get retraining, and tried to help them find stable new employment. But the larger challenge, they believe, is building a political movement to roll back the anti-immigrant atmosphere in which Valencia, and many like her, have become ensnared.

September/October 2001

NEXT STEPS FOR THE LIVING-WAGE MOVEMENT

BY CHRIS TILLY

This past May, Harvard University students made national headlines by occupying a university building for three weeks to demand that Harvard and its contractors pay employees a living wage. While Harvard refused to grant the $10.25 wage that the students demanded, they did agree to form a study committee with ample student and union representation. In the days that followed, Harvard also ended a contract negotiation deadlock with food service workers by offering an unprecedented wage increase of over $1 per hour—a surprise move that many attributed to the feisty labor-student alliance built through the living-wage push.

Harvard's living-wage activists represent the tip of a much larger national iceberg, most of which has taken the form of attempts to pass local living-wage ordinances. Over 60 local governments have passed living-wage laws—almost all since a ground-breaking Baltimore ordinance passed in 1994—with more coming on board each month. Such ordinances typically require the local government, along with any businesses that supply it, to pay a wage well above the current federal minimum of $5.15. Living-wage coalitions originally set wage floors at the amount needed by a full-time, year-round worker to keep a family of four above the poverty line (currently about $8.40 per hour), but like the Harvard students, they are increasingly campaigning for higher figures based on area living costs. The community organization ACORN (Alliance of Community Organizations for Reform Now) has spearheaded many of the coalitions, and an up-to-date living-wage scorecard can be found on its web site <www.livingwage campaign.org>. At the heart of the campaigns are low-wage workers like Celia Talavera, who joined Santa Monica's successful living-wage campaign last May. Referring to her job as a hotel housekeeper, she said, "I am fighting for a living wage because I want to work there for a long time."

The spread of living-wage laws reflects deep public concern about the unfairness of today's economy to those at the bottom of the paid workforce. A recent *USA Today* poll rated "lack of livable wage jobs" as Americans' top worry, even ahead of such perennial favorites as "decline of moral values." This sentiment makes living-wage laws eminently winnable. But it is worth pausing to ask: What, exactly, has the living-wage movement won? And how can we adapt this strategy to win more?

LIMITED VICTORIES

Opponents of living-wage laws argue that they will increase costs to local taxpayers, and drive business away from the locality. Living-wage boosters have two responses. First, fairness is worth the cost. And second, studies have shown that such ordinances have *not* escalated costs, nor repelled businesses. But why not? After all, economic theory suggests that companies compelled to pay higher costs will either seek to pass them on, or move on to greener pastures.

One reason is that living-wage ordinances typically affect very few workers. At passage, an average of only about 1,000 per locality actually have their wages boosted (in part because many of those covered already earn the mandated wage or more). This number is stunningly small, given that living-wage adopters include Los Angeles, New York, Chicago, and numerous other large cities and counties.

But smallness cannot be the entire explanation. Johns Hopkins University economist Erica Schoenberger and others followed specific contracts to the City of Baltimore, looking at changes from before that city's living-wage law went into effect to two years after. They found that contract costs increased only about 1%, far less than inflation. One possibility, of course, is that the wage floor spurred contractors to find new ways to increase true efficiency—getting the same amount of work done with less labor and less effort. For instance, this can happen if higher wages allow employers to hold on to the same employees longer, shrinking employer expenditures on recruitment, hiring, and training. Or perhaps the businesses have simply accepted lower profit margins.

But there are three less pleasant possibilities as well. Contractors may have sped up their workers, extracting more work in return for the higher pay. They may have reduced the quality of goods or services they delivered. Or, they may simply have failed to comply with the law. The poor track record of many laws that declare labor rights without adequate enforcement mechanisms suggests that this last possibility may be quite real. Even the federal minimum wage is ignored by growing numbers of employers, says economist Howard Wial of the AFL-CIO's Working for America Institute.

EXTEND THE LAWS?

How should the living-wage movement respond to this evidence of limited impact? One possibility is to widen and sharpen living-wage laws' bite. Recent living-wage ordinances have set minimums as high as $12 per hour (in Santa Cruz, California). In Santa Monica, California, campaigners extended coverage to tourist-district businesses that had received city subsidies for redevelopment, and elsewhere coalitions aim to expand the law to include any business that receives substantial subsidies or tax abatements from the local government. Activists are also setting their sights on living-wage agreements with large private businesses—starting with those most vulnerable to political and public relations pressure, especially nonprofits such as Harvard. Even more ambitious are the advocates proposing state and federal living-wage laws; legislative proposals are pending in Hawaii, Vermont, and at the federal level. (See "Vermont's Livable Income Law," p. 83)

Others are pursuing area-wide minimum wages set at levels closer to a living wage. Washington, D.C., has long had a minimum wage $1 above the federal minimum. Similar referenda were defeated in Houston and Denver, but New Orleans citizens will vote on a local minimum wage this coming February.

These initiatives are important, because there is certainly room for significant wage increases before we can expect negative effects on employment. When adjusted for inflation, hourly wages for the lowest-paid tenth of the workforce jumped by 9% between 1995 and 1999, in large part due to living-wage laws and federal minimum-wage increases. Yet the unemployment rate at the end of the 1990s fell to its lowest level in 30 years. More fine-grained studies of state and federal minimum-wage increases yield the same result: Such increases have caused little or no worker displacement over the last ten years. One reason is that wages for the bottom tenth were beaten so far down over the 1980s and early 1990s—even after the recent wage surge, inflation-adjusted 1999 wages remained 10% below their 1979 level.

But if the movement succeeds in extending and increasing living wages, at some point economic theory is bound to be proven right: costs to taxpayers will climb, employment will decrease, or both. Even in the most positive scenario—that businesses find ways to increase productivity—remember that rising productivity typically means doing the same work with fewer workers. This was the experience of the Congress of Industrial Organizations (now part of the AFL-CIO), which unionized core manufacturing industries in the 1930s and 1940s. The CIO succeeded in hiking pay, and in the decades that followed, U.S. manufacturers avidly hunted for ways to boost productivity. The good news is that U.S. manufacturing became the most productive in

LIVING WAGES OVERSEAS

A movement-building perspective helps us think about living wages in an international context. If people in rich countries try to decide the appropriate wage floor for people in poor countries, they run a serious risk of destructive paternalism. Consider the case of Haiti. A few years back, the National Labor Committee (the folks who blew the whistle on the sweatshops behind Kathie Lee Gifford's designer label) and others—me included—made much of the fact that Haiti's export assembly factories paid as little as 11 cents an hour. True enough, but it's also true that in the context of economic collapse, many in the Haitian countryside view this as a sufficiently handsome wage to crowd into shacks in Port-au-Prince for a chance to get one of these jobs. A U.S. trade law that barred goods produced by workers earning less than, say, $1 an hour would effectively shut Haitian goods out of this country, causing job loss in Haiti.

The alternative is to find ways to beef up Haitians' ability to place greater demands on employers, allowing Haitians to decide for themselves what is a living wage. That meant backing President Jean-Bertrand Aristide's adoption of a $2.50 per day minimum wage in 1991. It means supporting Batay Ouvriye (Workers' Struggle) when they help export-sector workers form unions. In general, it means taking a lead from workers, peasants, and pro-people governments in the global South, and conditioning trade privileges on respect for workers' right to organize rather than on any particular wage level. Consistently applying this principle means that goods produced by companies in the United States that flout labor laws—not just such companies in Haiti, Mexico, or China—should likewise be penalized.

the world for several decades. The bad news is that heightened efficiency shrank labor requirements dramatically. In fact, this is the main reason for declining U.S. manufacturing jobs, far overshadowing shifts in the global division of labor. Manufacturing is a slightly larger share of U.S. domestic output today than it was in 1960, but factory employment has dropped from 31% to 14% of the workforce.

If extending the living wage's impact will eventually either raise costs to taxpayers or diminish employment, it may be tempting to adopt the other major argument advocates use: fairness is worth the cost. And this answer makes a great deal of sense. Think for a moment about the federal *minimum* wage's effect. The average person who eats at McDonald's earns more than the average person who works at McDonald's, so if bumping up the minimum wage raises the cost of burgers, cash is shifting in more or less the right direction. By the same token, over the 1980s and 1990s, local and state privatization and tax cuts redistributed income from low-income workers to taxpayers who have higher incomes on average—so if living wages help to reverse this flow, that's a plus for equality.

> HARVARD'S LIVING-WAGE ACTIVISTS REPRESENT THE TIP OF A MUCH LARGER NATIONAL ICEBERG, MOST OF WHICH HAS TAKEN THE FORM OF ATTEMPTS TO PASS LOCAL LIVING-WAGE ORDINANCES.

What about job losses? Few would object to shutting down companies that rely on slavery or child labor. The same logic extends to exploitatively low wages. As with child labor laws, laws that bar low wages will put some workers out of a job. So it is important to view living-wage laws as part of a broader program that includes job creation, training, and income support for those unable to work. To achieve this broader program, we need a powerful movement. And the red-hot living-wage movement offers one of the strongest potential building blocks for such a broader movement.

BUILD THE MOVEMENT?

That brings us to another response to the limited impact of living-wage laws to date: using the living wage as a movement-building tool. The living-wage issue encourages labor, community, and religious organizations to coalesce around genuine shared interests, creating an opportunity to open an even broader dialogue on wage fairness and inequality.

The goal should be to build movements that can address some of the weaknesses of current living-wage laws, including non-compliance and the potential for speed-up or job loss. Of course the U.S. institution that has been most effective in monitoring compliance with labor laws, curbing speed-up, and lobbying for job creation is the labor movement—and living-wage laws provide a golden opportunity for strengthening unions. Baltimore activists who won that city's 1994 living-wage ordinance, considered the spark of the current living-wage prairie fire, sought above all to slow down union-busting privatization. Living-wage laws close off low wages as a competitive strategy, dulling the edge of employer resistance to unions. Some coalitions have also won clauses requiring covered businesses to be neutral in union organizing campaigns or even to immediately recognize any union that signs up a majority of workers, foreclosing employers' usual anti-union tactics. A lower profile way to disarm anti-union employers is to ban retaliation against workers organizing for a living wage—which basically puts a local law against union-busting on the books to supplement weak federal laws.

In addition, living-wage advocates need to pay attention to winning laws that nurture the living-wage movement itself. For instance, some laws give living-wage coalition constituents the first crack at applying for jobs covered by the living wage, in some cases through coalition-controlled hiring halls. Patronage usually gets a bad name, but this kind of community control over hiring can help cement a living-wage movement's strength by giving it the ability to reward its members and supporters. Moreover, although advocates dream of short-cutting the process of passing hundreds of local laws by winning federal legislation, in reality the local mobilizations are the key to success with compliance. Any federal law is likely to remain a dead letter unless we have built those hundreds of robust place-based coalitions ready to monitor the law's implementation and use it as an organizing tool.

The biggest challenge in movement building is reaching beyond wages and jobs to the less obvious issues. For instance, how do we defend the quality of public services? Many nonprofits and community-based organizations have been drawn into the game of privatizing social services. Sometimes these agencies enter unholy alliances with private businesses and city officials to oppose a living-wage law, because they fear it will threaten their job programs for disadvantaged workers. Organizations representing workers, communities, service providers, and clients must search for common ground based on high wages and adequate services. In Massachusetts, for example, unions and service providers have campaigned jointly for a state-funded living wage for human-service workers employed by hundreds of state contractors.

Another tough nut to crack is how to win adequate income for those who are unable to work for pay, or who end up working on a very part-time or part-year basis. Unfortunately, some of the same public attitudes that make it easy to build coalitions around living wages—equating work with virtue, for example—make it hard to defend welfare for people not working for wages. The principals from the living-wage movement—unions, churches, and ACORN itself—have also joined efforts to demand more adequate and less restrictive welfare benefits, but so far with much less success.

MORE THAN JUST A LIVING

The sixty local living-wage laws to date represent a tremendous victory for working people, but one that is, so far, narrow in scope. The challenge now is to extend the reach of the laws, while building and broadening the living-wage movement at the same time. Extending the laws' reach means bringing more cities on board, but even more importantly, boosting the numbers and types of workers covered within each city. To the extent that advocates succeed in passing stronger laws, they will engender fiercer resistance—both direct challenges to the legislation and more covert attempts to flout the laws or shift the costs. To successfully counter this resistance, movement-building efforts must go beyond the boundaries of the current living-wage movement. The end result will look less like a living-wage movement, more like a broad insurgent movement to redistribute income and other resources.

Resources: Robert Pollin and Stephanie Luce, *The Living Wage: Building a Fair Economy* (W.W. Norton, 1998); Lawrence Mishel, Jared Bernstein, and John Schmitt, *The State of Working America 200-2001* (Cornell University Press 2001); David Card and Alan B. Krueger, *Myth and Measurement: The New Economics of the Minimum Wage* (Princeton University Press 1995).

VERMONT'S LIVABLE INCOME LAW

While Vermont politics are famously progressive, its low wages (9% below the national average) and high living expenses (15% above national average) are anything but worker-friendly. Armed with these and other findings detailed in its *Vermont Job Gap Study*, the Burlington-based Peace and Justice Center set out to change those statistics with its Livable Wage Campaign.

The Vermont Livable Wage Campaign has achieved two significant legislative victories. Act 21, passed in 1999, raised the minimum wage by 50 cents, to $5.75 an hour (60 cents above the national minimum, though still a dollar less than in neighboring Massachusetts). The measure also provided funding for the state legislature to form a Study Committee on a Livable Income.

In 2000, the state's General Assembly agreed to some of the Study Committee's recommendations and passed Act 119, which took three more steps on the livable-wage issue:

- an increased minimum wage, now at $6.25 per hour
- a budget of $3.5 million (up 7%) for Vermont's Earned Income Tax Credit
- the publication of four annual reports by the state Joint Fiscal Office of Basic Needs Budgets / Livable Wage Figures.

Another bill, which would raise the minimum wage to $6.75, passed Vermont's Senate this year. This bill will be taken up in 2002 by the state House of Representatives, where its passage is uncertain. After the 2000 elections, conservatives gained a majority, in a backlash against recent legislation permitting same-sex "civil unions."

The Livable Wage Campaign, however, continues on several fronts, including a multi-year strategy to increase wages for some of Vermont's worst-paid workers—child care staff and public-school support staff at K-12 schools and state colleges.

— *Beth Burgess*

Resources: Vermont's Livable Wage Campaign <www.vtlivablewage.org>; Ellen Kahler, Vermont Peace and Justice Center.

THE STORY YOUR NEWSPAPER IGNORES:
GLOBAL INEQUALITY

BY THAD WILLIAMSON

What's the most important piece of economic news we need to understand the effects of our political and economic systems on human life? The daily stock market numbers? Monthly unemployment figures? Quarterly figures on GDP growth?

All of those indicators have their use, but perhaps the most important source of information isn't to be found on the business page—or, quite often, anywhere at all in the newspaper. That source is the annually-released United Nations Human Development Report, a comprehensive overview of global trends in poverty, development, and human well-being. The Annual Report is both an indispensable guide to the human condition at the turn of the century and an important attempt to raise consciousness about the grossly absurd way the world's resources are now distributed. For instance, the 1999 report noted that....

• The world's richest 20% now pocket 86% of the world's gross domestic product; the middle 60% has just 13%; and the poorest 20% have but 1%. The income gap between the top fifth and the bottom fifth is now 74 to 1, compared to just 30 to 1 in 1960.

• 1.3 billion people—over one-fifth of the world's population—lack access to clean water; 1.3 billion people live on less than one dollar a day; 840 million people are malnourished. According to the United Nations Hunger Project, roughly 24,000 people a day die from hunger-related causes.

• The assets of the world's 200 richest people more than doubled between 1994 and 1998, to over $1 trillion. The world's three richest people have assets, the report notes, greater than the combined economic output of the 48 poorest countries.

• Fifty-five nations have seen real per capita incomes decrease over the last decade.

THE WORLD'S THREE RICHEST PEOPLE HAVE ASSETS GREATER THAN THE COMBINED ECONOMIC OUTPUT OF THE 48 POOREST COUNTRIES.

Simply reporting these basic facts helps check our tendency to accept as normal the highly abnormal world in which we live, especially for those who do not experience economic hardship firsthand. Yet even more stunning than the simple facts of human poverty and growing inequality is how easy it would in fact be to make serious, rapid progress toward complete eradication of global poverty.

In 1997, for instance, the *Human Development Report* noted that for just $40 billion a year, basic health and nutrition, basic education, reproductive health and family planning services, and water sanitation services could be extended to the entire world's population. That figure, equivalent to roughly 15% of the annual Pentagon budget, totals less than one-fifth of one percent of the world's income. As the 1999 *Report* observes, "a yearly contribution of 1% of the wealth of the 200 richest people could provide universal access to primary education for all ($7-8 billion)." A 5% contribution would suffice to provide a full complement of social services universally.

And, it might be added, in a world where $1.5 trillion a day crosses borders via international financial transactions, a simple tax of 0.1% on such transactions for one month would raise about $45 billion—more than enough to carry out the core of the UN's anti-poverty agenda.

Forty billion dollars amounts to about 0.5% of the annual gross domestic product of the United States; a relatively minor adjustment in priorities could yield an incredible human achievement—the universal provision of basic social services. In fact, the U.N. has estimated that a well-spent $80 billion would suffice to provide not only basic social services but also income transfers sufficient to lift all of the world's poorest people out of conditions of extreme poverty.

May/June 2001

CAUSE OF DEATH: INEQUALITY

BY ALEJANDRO REUSS

INEQUALITY KILLS.

You won't see inequality on a medical chart or a coroner's report under "cause of death." You won't see it listed among the top killers in the United States each year. All too often, however, it is social inequality that lurks behind a more immediate cause of death, be it heart disease or diabetes, accidental injury or homicide. Few of the top causes of death are "equal opportunity killers." Instead, they tend to strike poor people more than rich people, the less educated more than the highly educated, people lower on the occupational ladder more than those higher up, or people of color more than white people.

Statistics on mortality and life expectancy do not provide a perfect map of social inequality. For example, the life expectancy for women in the United States is about six years longer than the life expectancy for men, despite the many ways in which women are subordinated to men. Take most indicators of socioeconomic status, however, and most causes of death, and it's a strong bet that you'll find illness and injury (or "morbidity") and mortality increasing as status decreases.

Men with less than 12 years of education are more than twice as likely to die of chronic diseases (e.g., heart disease), more than three times as likely to die as a result of injury, and nearly twice as likely to die of communicable diseases, compared to those with 13 or more years of education. Women with family incomes below $10,000 are more than three times as likely to die of heart disease and nearly three times as likely to die of diabetes, compared to those with family incomes above $25,000. African Americans are more likely than whites to die of heart disease; stroke; lung, colon, prostate, and breast cancer, as well as all cancers combined; liver disease; diabetes; AIDS; accidental injury; and homicide. In all, the lower you are in a social hierarchy, the worse your health and the shorter your life are likely to be.

THE WORSE OFF IN THE UNITED STATES ARE NOT WELL OFF BY WORLD STANDARDS.

You often hear it said that even poor people in rich countries like the United States are rich compared to ordinary people in poor countries. While that may be true when it comes to consumer goods like televisions or telephones, which are widely available even to poor people in the United States, it's completely wrong when it comes to health.

In a 1996 study published in the *New England Journal of Medicine*, University of Michigan researchers found that African-American females living to age 15 in Harlem had a 65% chance of surviving to age 65, about the same as women in India. Meanwhile, Harlem's African-American males had only a 37% chance of surviving to age 65, about the same as men in Angola or the Democratic Republic of Congo. Among both African-American men and women, infectious diseases and diseases of the circulatory system were the prime causes of high mortality.

It takes more income to achieve a given life expectancy in a rich country like the United States than it does to achieve the same life expectancy in a less affluent country. So the higher money income of a low-income person in the United States, compared to a middle-income person in a poor country, does not necessarily translate into a longer life span. The average income per person in African-American families, for example, is more than five times the per capita income of El Salvador. The life expectancy for African-American men in the United States, however, is only about 67 years, the same as the average life expectancy for men in El Salvador.

HEALTH INEQUALITIES IN THE UNITED STATES ARE NOT JUST ABOUT ACCESS TO HEALTH CARE.

Nearly one-sixth of the U.S. population lacks health insurance, including about 44% of poor people. A poor adult with a health problem is only half as likely to see a doctor as a high-income adult. Adults living in low-income areas are more than twice as likely to be hospitalized for a health problem that could have been effectively treated with timely outpatient care, compared with adults living in high-income areas. Obviously, lack of access to health care is a major health problem.

But so are environmental and occupational hazards; communicable diseases; homicide and firearm-related injuries; and smoking, alcohol consumption, lack of exercise, and other risk factors. These dangers all tend to affect lower-income people more than higher-income, less-educated people more than more-educated, and people of color more than whites. African-American children are more than twice as likely as white children to be hospitalized for asthma, which is linked to air pollution. Poor men are nearly six times as likely as high-income men to have elevated blood-lead levels, which reflect both residential and workplace environmental hazards. African-American men are more than seven times as likely to fall victim to homicide as white men; African-

MORTALITY AMONG BRITISH CIVIL SERVANTS
Based on a ten-year study beginning in 1967

Death rate over 10-year period (%)

16
14
12
10
8
6
4
2
0

Top   Second   Third   Bottom

Job Grade

Source: Michael Marmot, "Social Differentials in Mortality: The Whitehall Studies," *Adult Mortality in Developed Countries: From Description to Explanation,* 1995.

American women, more than four times as likely as white women. The less education someone has, the more likely they are to smoke or to drink heavily. The lower someone's income, the less likely they are to get regular exercise.

Michael Marmot, a pioneer in the study of social inequality and health, notes that so-called diseases of affluence—disorders, like heart disease, associated with high-calorie and high-fat diets, lack of physical activity, etc.—are most prevalent among the *least affluent* people in rich societies. While recognizing the role of such "behavioral" risk factors as smoking in producing poor health, he argues, "It is not sufficient … to ask what contribution smoking makes to generating the social gradient in ill health, but we must ask, why is there a social gradient in smoking?" What appear to be individual "lifestyle" decisions often reflect a broader *social* epidemiology.

GREATER INCOME INEQUALITY GOES HAND IN HAND WITH POORER HEALTH.

Numerous studies suggest that the more unequal the income distribution in a country, state, or city, the lower the life expectancies for people at all income levels. One study published in the *American Journal of Public Health,* for example, shows that U.S. metropolitan areas with low per capita incomes and low levels of income inequality have lower mortality rates than areas with high median incomes and high levels of income inequality. Meanwhile, for a given per capita income range, mortality rates always decline as inequality declines.

R.G. Wilkinson, perhaps the researcher most responsible for relating health outcomes to overall levels of inequality (rather than individual income levels), argues

that greater income inequality causes worse health outcomes independent of its effects on poverty. Wilkinson and his associates suggest several explanations for this relationship. First, the bigger the income gap between rich and poor, the less inclined the well off are to pay taxes for public services they either do not use or use in low proportion to the taxes they pay. Lower spending on public hospitals, schools, and other basic services does not affect wealthy people's life expectancies very much, but it affects poor people's life expectancies a great deal. Second, the bigger the income gap, the lower the overall level of social cohesion. High levels of social cohesion are associated with good health outcomes for several reasons. For example, people in highly cohesive societies are more likely to be active in their communities, reducing social isolation, a known health risk factor.

Numerous researchers have criticized Wilkinson's conclusions, arguing that the real reason income inequality tends to be associated with worse health outcomes is that it is associated with higher rates of poverty. But even if they are right and income inequality causes worse health *simply by bringing about greater poverty*, that hardly makes for a defense of inequality. Poverty and inequality are like partners in crime. "[W]hether public policy focuses primarily on the elimination of poverty or on reduction in income disparity," argue Wilkinson critics Kevin Fiscella and Peter Franks, "neither goal is likely to be achieved in the absence of the other."

DIFFERENCES IN STATUS MAY BE JUST AS IMPORTANT AS INCOME LEVELS.

Even after accounting for differences in income, education, and other factors, the life expectancy for African Americans is less than that for whites. U.S. researchers are beginning to explore the relationship between high blood pressure among African Americans and the racism of the surrounding society. African Americans tend to suffer from high blood pressure, a risk factor for circulatory disease, more often than whites. Moreover, studies have found that, when confronted with racism, African Americans suffer larger and longer-lasting increases in blood pressure than when faced with other stressful situations. Broader surveys relating blood pressure in African Americans to perceived instances of racial discrimination have yielded complex results, depending on social class, gender, and other factors.

Stresses cascade down social hierarchies and accumulate among the least empowered. Even researchers focusing on social inequality and health, however, have been surprised by the large effects on mortality. Over 30 years ago, Michael Marmot and his associates undertook a landmark study, known as Whitehall I, of health among British civil servants. Since the civil servants shared many characteristics regardless of job classification—an office work environment, a high degree of job security, etc.— the researchers expected to find only modest health differences among them. To their surprise, the study revealed a sharp increase in mortality with each step down the job hierarchy—even from the highest grade to the second highest. Over ten years, employees in the lowest grade were three times as likely to die as those in the highest grade. One factor was that people in lower grades showed a higher incidence of many "lifestyle" risk factors, like smoking, poor diet, and lack of exercise. Even when the researchers controlled for such factors, however, more than half the mortality gap remained.

Marmot noted that people in the lower job grades were less likely to describe themselves as having "control over their working lives" or being "satisfied with their work situation," compared to those higher up. While people in higher job grades were more likely to report "having to work at a fast pace," lower-level civil servants were more likely to report feelings of hostility, the main stress-related risk factor for heart disease. Marmot concluded that "psycho-social" factors—the psychological costs of being lower in the hierarchy—played an important role in the unexplained mortality gap. Many of us have probably said to ourselves, after a trying day on the job, "They're killing me." Turns out it's not just a figure of speech. Inequality kills—and it starts at the bottom.

Resources: Lisa Berkman, "Social Inequalities and Health: Five Key Points for Policy-Makers to Know," February 5, 2001, Kennedy School of Government, Harvard University; *Health, United States, 1998, with Socioeconomic Status and Health Chartbook*, National Center for Health Statistics <www.cdc.gov/nchs>; Ichiro Kawachi, Bruce P. Kennedy, and Richard G. Wilkinson, eds., *The Society and Population Health Reader, Volume I: Income Inequality and Health*, 1999; Michael Marmot, "Social Differences in Mortality: The Whitehall Studies," *Adult Mortality in Developed Countries: From Description to Explanation*, Alan D. Lopez, Graziella Caselli, and Tapani Valkonen, eds., 1995; Michael Marmot, "The Social Pattern of Health and Disease," *Health and Social Organization: Towards a Health Policy for the Twenty-First Century*, David Blane, Eric Brunner, and Richard Wilkinson, eds., 1996; Arline T. Geronimus, et al., "Excess Mortality Among Blacks and Whites in the United States," *The New England Journal of Medicine* 335 (21), November 21, 1996; Nancy Krieger, Ph.D., and Stephen Sidney, M.D., "Racial Discrimination and Blood Pressure: The CARDIA Study of Young Black and White Adults," *American Journal of Public Health* 86 (10), October 1996; *Human Development Report 2000*, UN Development Programme; *World Development Indicators 2000*, World Bank.

ARTICLE 6.8   *January/February 2000*

HOW RICH IS BILL?

BY PHINEAS BAXANDALL

Even with Microsoft's legal worries, Bill Gates is sitting pretty on $72 billion worth of Microsoft stock. While it might be hard to imagine how much that really is, a bunch of committed souls have tried and posted their efforts on various web sites.

For instance, one person calculated that if you earned the minimum wage (now $5.15 an hour) and worked continuously, 24 hours a day, 7 days a week, and saved every bit of your earnings (and didn't pay taxes), you would need to work for about 1.6 million years to earn Bill's money. If you took the wimpy approach, and only worked 40 hours a week, then it would take 6.7 billion years. (Note that humankind's oldest known hominid ancestor, Australopithecus, lived between 3.5 and 4 million years ago.)

If you began traveling along a line of one dollar bills laid end to end and started picking up each note on the day Microsoft first issued stock in its company—March 13, 1986—you would need to travel that line of bills at 58.15 mph in order to accumulate wealth at the same rate as Bill has since that time.

Gates's wealth is almost double what the gold in Fort Knox is worth. Gates himself is worth (if he weighs about 180 lbs.) over $27 million an ounce. Michael Jordan—who made $35 million his last year with the NBA's Chicago Bulls—would have had to play basketball at that salary for over 2,302 years to make as much as Gates. Gates's fortune is worth more than the economic output of Pakistan, Egypt, or Ireland. If you laid his money out in $1 bills end to end, the trail would reach to the moon and back 14.6 times. Bill could give each of the 760,000 homeless people in America $94,822.52.

Finally, consider that Gates has made this money in the 24 years or so since Microsoft was founded in 1975. If you presume that he has worked 14 hours a day on every business day of the year since then, that means he's been making a staggering $1 million per hour, around $300 per second. Which means that if he should see or drop a $1,000 bill on the ground, it just would not be worth his time to bend over and pick it up.

Resources: www.quuxuum.org/~evan/bgnw.html. As of November 5, 1999 4:41pm ET Microsoft was selling for $91.5625 a share. Bill's 787,059,300 shares represent $72,065,117,156.25 worth of Microsoft stock. We have assumed above that stopping to pick up a bill from the ground takes perhaps four seconds.

CHAPTER 7

Market Failure, Government Policy, and Corporate Governance

INTRODUCTION

Markets sometimes fail. Mainstream economists typically focus on failures in which existing markets fall short of facilitating exchanges that would make both parties better off. When a factory pollutes the air, people downwind suffer a cost, and might be willing to pay the polluter to curb emissions—but there is no market for clean air. In cases like this, the logical solution is for the government to step in with regulations that ban industries from imposing pollution costs on others. The same goes when private markets do not provide sufficient amounts of public goods—things like vaccines, which everyone benefits from whether they contribute to paying for them or not. Again, government must step in. But what percentage of pollution should industries be required to eliminate? How much should be spent on public health? To decide how *much* government should step in, economists propose cost-benefit analysis, suggesting that the government weigh benefits against costs like a firm deciding how many cars to produce.

Orthodox economists typically see market failures as fairly limited in scope. In fact, they do not consider many negative consequences of markets to be failures at all. When workers are paid wages too low to meet their basic needs, economists do not usually call their poverty and overwork "market failures," but "incentives" to get a higher-paying job. As we saw in the last chapter, mainstream economists are less concerned about how equally the pie is distributed than the overall size of the pie, although most would agree that governments should help those most in need. Still, when economists do recognize market failures, most argue that they are best solved by markets themselves—so pollution should be reduced by allowing firms to trade for the right to pollute, and failing schools should be improved by introducing competition with vouchers and charter schools. Finally, orthodox economists worry about *government* failure—the possibility that government responses to market failures may cause more problems than they solve. They conclude that the "invisible hand" of the market works pretty well, and that alternatives to it may be far worse.

The authors in this chapter see market failures as far more widespread and systemic. They place a high value on outcomes beyond "the size of the pie": environmental sustainability, equality, economic democracy. And some of

them step beyond the "market vs. government" dichotomy to propose other systems of economic governance. Chris Tilly launches the debate by explaining why the invisible hand does not work as well as mainstream theory suggests (Tilly, article 7.1). Heidi Vogt follows up, describing how "marketizing" the supply of water has brought dire consequences in South Africa (Vogt, article 7.2). Lisa Heinzerling and Frank Ackerman point out key flaws in the use of cost-benefit analysis to guide government action (Heinzerling and Ackerman, article 7.4). And Eban Goodstein argues that, contrary to some economic predictions, environmental regulation has *not* cost jobs (Goodstein, article 7.3).

The final three articles address a topic to which most economics textbooks devote little ink: how should we get businesses to do the right thing? Jonathan Rowe considers a wide range of options for improving corporate behavior (Rowe, article 7.5). Elaine Bernard zeroes in on one particular tool: labor law that will facilitate a larger role for unions rather than obstructing them (Bernard, article 7.6). Thad Williamson suggests community ownership of business (Williamson, article 7.7). This broad spectrum of proposals contrasts with the relatively narrow discussion of government regulation found in most standard texts.

DISCUSSION QUESTIONS

1) (Tilly) Chris Tilly highlights several important exceptions to the principle that "markets work for the greater good of all." These are exceptions that standard textbooks acknowledge as well. The disagreement comes over how serious these shortcomings are. Given the flaws in the principle of the invisible hand, do you think it is still a useful principle in guiding economic policy? If your answer is no, why do you think it is so widely used?

2) (Vogt) Read over Heidi Vogt's article about water privatization in South Africa, keeping in mind the standard textbook's list of possible shortcomings of markets: externalities, public goods, information problems, and income distribution. Which of these apply in this case? Explain as concretely as possible.

3) (Heinzerling and Ackerman) Make a list of types of goods that are harder to put a price on than others. Why is it so hard to price these types of goods?

4) (Heinzerling and Ackerman) Lisa Heinzerling and Frank Ackerman point out a number of flaws in cost-benefit analysis. These weaknesses suggest that the cost-benefit approach will work better in some situations, worse in others. Describe when you would expect it to work better and worse, and explain.

5) (Goodstein) Eban Goodstein says that even though environmental regulation has costs for business, it has not resulted in fewer jobs. This goes against the logic of deadweight loss. How can it be true? (Hint: The answer lies in macro, not micro.)

6) (Rowe, Williamson) Standard theory offers support for "market-based" environmental reforms, such as systems that allow companies to buy and sell the right to pollute. Jonathan Rowe (and for that matter, Marc Breslow in Chapter 2, article 2.2) also sees advantages to this kind of reform. However, such reforms run counter to Thad Williamson's vision of an economy governed by grassroots democracy. Outline the strengths and weaknesses of such market-based environmentalism, referring to the articles and your main textbook as appropriate.

7) (Williamson) Williamson's core proposal is community ownership of business. How does he say this will address the failures of both market and government control of the economy? Do you agree with his solution?

8) (Bernard, Rowe, Williamson) These articles offer a wide range of alternative forms of business governance. Identify the main alternatives they suggest. Which proposals (if any) do you find particularly promising, and why?

KEY TO COLANDER

These articles accompany Chapters 18 and 20.

The Tilly and Vogt articles (along with questions 1-2) connect most closely to discussions of market failure in Chapter 18, and to the short mention of distributional issues in Chapter 20.

Goodstein's article (along with questions 5-6) relates to the Chapter 18 discussion of "Alternative Methods of Dealing with Externalities."

Heinzerling and Ackerman discuss cost-benefit analysis, which Colander addresses in Chapter 20.

The Bernard, Rowe, and Williamson articles about how to govern business relate in a general way to Chapters 18 and 20, and also touch on some themes that come up in Chapter 15's section on "Regulation, Government Ownership, and Industrial Policy." Bernard's article also speaks to the impact of unions (Chapter 16).

SHAKING THE INVISIBLE HAND

THE UNCERTAIN FOUNDATIONS OF FREE-MARKET ECONOMICS

BY CHRIS TILLY

"It is not from the benevolence of the butcher, the brewer or the baker that we expect our dinner, but from their regard to their own interest... [No individual] intends to promote the public interest... [rather, he is] led by an invisible hand to promote an end which was no part of his intention."

Adam Smith, The Wealth of Nations, *1776*

Seen the Invisible Hand lately? It's all around us these days, propping up conservative arguments in favor of free trade, deregulation, and tax-cutting.

Today's advocates for "free," competitive markets echo Adam Smith's claim that unfettered markets translate the selfish pursuit of individual gain into the greatest benefit for all. They trumpet the superiority of capitalist free enterprise over socialist efforts to supplant the market with a planned economy, and even decry liberal attempts to moderate the market. Anything short of competitive markets, they proclaim, yields economic inefficiency, making society worse off.

But the economic principle underlying this fanfare is shaky indeed. Since the late 19th century, mainstream economists have struggled to prove that Smith was right—that the chaos of free markets leads to a blissful economic order. In the 1950s, U.S. economists Kenneth Arrow and Gerard Debreu finally came up with a theoretical proof, which many orthodox economists view as the centerpiece of modern economic theory.

Although this proof is the product of the best minds of mainstream economics, it ends up saying surprisingly little in defense of free markets. The modern theory of the Invisible Hand shows that given certain assumptions, free markets reduce the wasteful use of economic resources—but perpetuate unequal income distribution.

To prove free markets cut waste, economists must make a number of far-fetched assumptions: there are no concentrations of economic power; buyers and sellers know every detail about the present and future economy; and all costs of production are borne by producers while all benefits from consumption are paid for by consumers (see box for a complete list). Take away any one of these assumptions and markets can lead to stagnation, recession, and other forms of waste—as in fact they do.

In short, the economic theory invoked by conservatives to justify free markets instead starkly reveals their limitations.

THE FRUITS OF FREE MARKETS

The basic idea behind the Invisible Hand can be illustrated with a story. Suppose that I grow apples and you grow oranges. We both grow tired of eating the same fruit all the time and decide to trade. Perhaps we start by trading one apple for one orange. This exchange satisfies both of us, because in fact I would gladly give up more than one apple to get an orange, and you would readily pay more than one orange for an apple. And as long as swapping one more apple for one more orange makes us both better off, we will continue to trade.

Eventually, the trading will come to a stop. I begin to notice that the novelty of oranges wears old as I accumulate a larger pile of them and the apples I once had a surplus of become more precious to me as they grow scarcer. At some point, I draw the line: in order to obtain one more apple from me, you must give me more than one orange. But your remaining oranges have also become more valuable to you. Up to now, each successive trade has made both of us better off. Now there is no further exchange that benefits us both, so we agree to stop trading until the next crop comes in.

Note several features of this parable. Both you and I end up happier by trading freely. If the government stepped in and limited fruit trading, neither of us would be as well off. In fact, the government cannot do anything in the apple/orange market that will make both of us better off than does the free market.

Adding more economic actors, products, money, and costly production processes complicates the picture, but we reach the same conclusions. Most of us sell our labor time in the market rather than fruit; we sell it for money that we then use to buy apples, oranges, and whatever else we need. The theory of the Invisible Hand tells us a trip to the fruit stand improves the lot of both consumer and seller; likewise, the sale of labor time benefits both employer and employee. What's more, according to the theory, competition between apple farmers insures that consumers will get apples produced at the lowest possible cost. Government intervention still can only make things worse.

This fable provides a ready-made policy guide. Substitute "Japanese autos" and "U.S. agricultural products" for apples and oranges, and the fable tells you that import quotas or tariffs only make the people of both countries worse off. Change the industries to airlines or telephone services, and the fable calls for deregulation. Or re-tell the tale in the labor market: minimum wages and unions (which prevent workers from individually bargaining over their wages) hurt employers and workers.

FRUIT SALAD

Unfortunately for free-market boosters, two major shortcomings make a fruit salad out of this story. First, even if free markets perform as advertised, they deliver only one benefit—the prevention of certain economically wasteful practices—while preserving inequality. According to the theory, competitive markets wipe out two kinds of waste: unrealized trades and inefficient production. Given the right assumptions, markets ensure that when two parties both stand to gain from a trade, they make that trade, as in the apples-and-oranges story. Competition compels producers to search for the most efficient, lowest-cost production methods—again, given the right preconditions.

Though eliminating waste is a worthy goal, it leaves economic inequality untouched. Returning once more to the orchard, if I start out with all of the apples and oranges and you start out with none, that situation is free of waste: no swap can make us both better off since you have nothing to trade! Orthodox economists acknowledge that even in the ideal competitive market, those who start out rich stay rich, while the poor remain poor. Many of them argue that attempts at redistributing income will most certainly create economic inefficiencies, justifying the preservation of current inequities.

But in real-life economics, competition does lead to waste. Companies wastefully duplicate each other's research and build excess productive capacity. Cost-cutting often leads to shoddy products, worker speedup, and unsafe working conditions. People and factories stand idle while houses go unbuilt and people go unfed. That's because of the second major problem: real economies don't match the assumptions of the Invisible Hand theory.

Of course, all economic theories build their arguments on a set of simplifying assumptions about the world. These assumptions often sacrifice some less important aspects of reality in order to focus on the economic mechanisms of interest. But in the case of the Invisible Hand, the theoretical preconditions contradict several central features of the economy.

For one thing, markets are only guaranteed to prevent waste if the economy runs on "perfect competition": individual sellers compete by cutting prices, individual buyers compete by raising price offers, and nobody holds concentrated economic power. But today's giant corporations hardly match this description. Coke and Pepsi compete with advertising rather than price cuts. The oil companies keep prices high enough to register massive profits every year. Employers coordinate the pay and benefits they offer to avoid bidding up compensation. Workers, in turn, marshal their own forces via unionization—another departure from perfect competition.

Indeed, the jargon of "perfect competition" overlooks the fact that property ownership itself confers disproportionate economic power. "In the competitive model," orthodox economist Paul Samuelson commented, "it makes no difference whether capital hires labor or the other way around." He argued that given perfect competition among workers and among capitalists, wages and profits would remain the same regardless of who does the hiring. But unemployment—a persistent feature of market-driven economies—makes job loss very costly to workers. The sting my boss feels when I "fire" him by quitting my job hardly equals the setback I experience when he fires me.

PERFECT INFORMATION?

In addition, the grip of the Invisible Hand is only sure if all buyers and sellers have "perfect information" about the present and future state of markets. In the present, this implies consumers know exactly what they are buying—an assumption hard to swallow in these days of leaky breast implants and chicken à la Salmonella. Employers must know exactly what skills workers have and how hard they will work—suppositions any real-life manager would laugh at.

Perfect information also means sellers can always sniff out unsatisfied demands, and buyers can detect any excess supplies of goods. Orthodox economists rely on the metaphor of an omnipresent "auctioneer" who is always calling out prices so all buyers and sellers can find mutually agreeable prices and consummate every possible sale. But in the actual economy, the auctioneer is nowhere to be found, and markets are plagued by surpluses and shortages.

Perfect information about the future is even harder to come by. For example, a company decides whether or not to build a new plant based on whether it expects sales to rise. But predicting future demand is a tricky matter. One reason is that people may save money today in order to buy (demand) goods and services in the future. The problem comes in predicting when. As economist John Maynard Keynes observed in 1934, "An act of individual saving means—so to speak—a decision not to have dinner today. But it does not necessitate a decision to have dinner or to buy a pair of boots a week hence...or to consume any specified thing at any specified date. Thus it depresses the business of preparing today's dinner without stimulating the business of making ready for some future act of consumption." Keynes concluded that far from curtailing waste, free markets gave rise to the colossal waste of human and economic resources that was the Great Depression—in part because of this type of uncertainty about the future.

FREE LUNCH

The dexterity of the Invisible Hand also depends on the principle that "You only get what you pay for." This "no

ASSUMPTIONS AND REALITY

The claim that free markets lead to efficiency and reduced waste rests on seven main assumptions. However, these assumptions differ sharply from economic reality. (Assumptions 1, 3, 4, and 5 are discussed in more detail in the article.)

ASSUMPTION ONE: No market power. No individual buyer or seller, nor any group of buyers or sellers, has the power to affect the market-wide level of prices, wages, or profits.

REALITY ONE: Our economy is dotted with centers of market power, from large corporations to unions. Furthermore, employers have an edge in bargaining with workers because of the threat of unemployment.

ASSUMPTION TWO: No economies of scale. Small plants can produce as cheaply as large ones.

REALITY TWO: In fields such as mass-production industry, transportation, communications, and agriculture, large producers enjoy a cost advantage, limiting competition.

ASSUMPTION THREE: Perfect information about the present. Buyers and sellers know everything there is to know about the goods being exchanged. Also, each is aware of the wishes of every other potential buyer and seller in the market.

REALITY THREE: The world is full of lemons—goods about which the buyer is inadequately informed. Also, people are not mind-readers, so sellers get stuck with surpluses and willing buyers are unable to find the products they want.

ASSUMPTION FOUR: Perfect information about the future. Contracts between buyers and sellers cover every possible future eventuality.

REALITY FOUR: Uncertainty clouds the future of any economy. Futures markets are limited.

ASSUMPTION FIVE: You only get what you pay for. Nobody can impose a cost on somebody else, nor obtain a benefit from them, without paying.

REALITY FIVE: In a free market, polluters can impose costs on the rest of us without paying. And when a public good like a park is built or roads are maintained, everyone benefits whether or not they helped to pay for it.

ASSUMPTION SIX: Self-interest. In economic matters, each person cares only about his or her own level of well-being.

REALITY SIX: Solidarity, jealousy, and even love for one's family violate this assumption.

ASSUMPTION SEVEN: No joint production. Each production process has only one product.

REALITY SEVEN: Even in an age of specialization, there are plenty of exceptions to this rule. For example, large service firms such as hospitals or universities produce a variety of different services using the same resources.

free lunch" principle seems at first glance a reasonable description of the economy. But major exceptions arise. One is what economists call "externalities"—economic transactions that take place outside the market. Consider a hospital that dumps syringes at sea. In effect, the hospital gets a free lunch by passing the costs of waste disposal on to the rest of us. Because no market exists where the right to dump is bought and sold, free markets do nothing to compel the hospital to bear the costs of dumping—which is why the government must step in.

Public goods such as sewer systems also violate the "no free lunch" rule. Once the sewer system is in place, everyone shares in the benefits of the waste disposal, regardless of whether or not they helped pay for it. Suppose sewer systems were sold in a free market, in which each person had the opportunity to buy an individual share. Then any sensible, self-interested consumer would hold back from buying his or her fair share—and wait for others to provide the service. This irrational situation would persist unless consumers could somehow collectively agree on how extensive a sewer system to produce—once more bringing government into the picture.

Most orthodox economists claim that the list of externalities and public goods in the economy is short and easily addressed. Liberals and radicals, on the other hand, offer a long list: for example, public goods include education, health care, and decent public transportation—all in short supply in our society.

Because real markets deviate from the ideal markets envisioned in the theory of the Invisible Hand, they give us both inequality and waste. But if the theory is so far off the mark, why do mainstream economists and policymakers place so much stock in it? They fundamentally believe the profit motive is the best guide for the economy. If you believe that "What's good for General Motors is good for the USA," the Invisible Hand theory can seem quite reasonable. Business interests, government, and the media constantly reinforce this belief, and reward those who can dress it up in theoretical terms. As long as capital remains the dominant force in society, the Invisible Hand will maintain its grip on the hearts and minds of us all.

ENVIRONMENTAL JUSTICE IN SOUTH AFRICA

WATER SANITATION, PRIVATIZATION, AND THE LEGACY OF APARTHEID

BY HEIDI VOGT

There's a new hero fighting on the edge of illegality to get clean drinking water to Johannesburg's poor. The "struggle plumber" knows how to uninstall the blocks that prevent free water from flowing from central pipes into peoples' homes. Yes, that's against the law. But poor communities depend on the struggle plumbers to help them survive as water prices rise in South Africa.

The residents of the country's poor neighborhoods are fighting for access in the face of multinational corporations' increasing control of the water supply. The government's answer has been to send armed security guards to shut off the water. "Out of desperation people are reconnecting their water. The council can call them thieves but obviously people have become so desperate that they can't do without water," said Orlean Naidoo, who lives in the poor neighborhood of Bayview in Chatsworth.

The people who are struggling for water access find justification in the South African constitution, one of the most progressive in the world on basic economic rights. The constitution promises clean water to all its citizens as a right, not a privilege. "Everyone has the right to have access to sufficient food and water," reads the six-year-old document. Still, change is slow, infrastructure is spotty, and millions of South Africans are still waiting for this promise to translate into drinkable water.

PERILS OF PRIVATIZATION

The ongoing privatization of utilities in South Africa stands in the way. In 2000, the French company Suez Lyonnaise des Eaux signed one of the largest water con-tracts in the world, taking over a large section of South Africa's water utilities. Others have followed: multinationals Biwater, Vivendi, and Saur all now own a chunk of South Africa's water supply.

When private companies take over utility contracts, prices go up, water quality goes down, and the poor lose out. South Africans have seen the price increases firsthand. In 1995, Biwater signed a contract to supply the city of Nelspruit with water. Over the next five years, rates in-creased more than 400%.

But these costs have not deterred the advocates of "free market" water. In December 2002, the U.S. Agency for In-ternational Development (USAID) sponsored a report suggesting that the privatiza-tion of water utilities in South Africa could help bring the price of water under control. The report, written for USAID by the Washington, D.C., consulting firm Padco, admits that "there have been fail-ures" of water privatization, but claims that critics "ignore … unforeseen changes" responsible for price increases. A copy of the report, originally commissioned for the South African government, found its way into the hands of pri-vate water companies interested in investing in South Af-rica. So the funding that was supposed to help bring clean water to South Africans has created a tool for multination-als to justify privatization—with the approval of the United States government.

The World Bank, unsurprisingly, is also on the water-privatization bandwagon. The Bank-approved "cost recov-ery" program in South Africa proceeds from the principle that water should be made available to people only if the company providing it can recover its costs plus a profit. Taxes are not to subsidize utility prices and those who can't pay are not to get services. Since the South African govern-ment introduced cost recovery as part of the Growth, Em-ployment and Redistribution (GEAR) program in 1996, more than 10 million people have had their water cut off. GEAR didn't meet mass opposition in South Africa when it was first introduced. But as the program began to take effect, jobs and services started disappearing, and protests started to become the norm for every new move towards privatization.

The poor (mostly black) majority has paid the price for South Africa's new economic model. By 2000, piped water had become too expensive for many residents of KwaZulu

Natal—where unemployment hovers around 40%. When water was cut off, citizens resorted to drinking untreated water from rivers, ponds, and puddles. By the end of 2001, more than 100,000 residents had been infected with cholera, a disease virtually unseen in South Africa for decades. After the cholera outbreaks, the government decided to give 6,000 free liters of water a month to people who couldn't afford water. However, the people wouldn't get the free water until they had paid outstanding debts for water—which they didn't have the money for. "When water's a private commodity at a market rate, it's not rich white people in the suburbs that are going to suffer," says Sara Grusky of the California-based activist group Public Citizen, which is currently working with a number of community groups in South Africa on water issues.

Since the end of apartheid in 1994, pipes that used to supply the poorer neighborhoods of Johannesburg with free, clean water have been slowly replaced with pre-paid pumps. The pumps, which private multinationals are putting in place, are among the government's most controversial moves. In this system, each water pump has a counter that deducts units from a pre-paid card. This system eliminates the difficulty of issuing and collecting bills. It also means days without clean water for cash-strapped families.

Since 1998, pre-paid water meters have been outlawed in Britain as a threat to public health. But pre-paid meters have not disappeared in South Africa. Suez Lyonnaise des Eaux is currently beginning a pre-paid meter trial in Orange Free State.

So the struggle plumbers have gone to work. They've dismantled pre-pay meters and hacked into company pipes in the name of the right to water. A copper disk placed inside the pipes prevents water from flowing to those who haven't paid. The struggle plumbers open up the pipes and remove that disk.

The people of South Africa are also fighting back politically. Since 1999, the Congress of South African Trade Unions (COSATU) has held two-day general strikes to protest the privatization of utilities. In October 2002, COSATU led a demonstration of 70,000 in Johannesburg to protest job cuts and the commercialization of services. "COSATU remains opposed to the government selling off state companies which provide essential services to the community," spokesperson Patrick Craven told Afrol News. "We will continue to demand that the government … maintain these organizations in the public sector and make them deliver affordable and accessible services, especially to the poor."

ARTICLE 7.3

May/June 1997

DOES PRESERVING THE EARTH THREATEN JOBS?

BY EBAN GOODSTEIN

Back in 1990, the U.S. Business Roundtable published a study predicting that the Clean Air Act amendments, which were passed later that year, would lead to massive job loss: There is "little doubt," they claimed, "that a minimum of two hundred thousand (plus) jobs will quickly be lost, with plants closing in dozens of states. This number could easily exceed one million jobs—and even two million jobs—at the more extreme assumption about residual risk." Because of these concerns, the amendments bud-

geted retraining funds of $50 million per year for displaced workers.

Six years later, a front page *New York Times* article seemed to confirm this prediction. Titled "Eastern Coal Towns Wither in the Name of Cleaner Air," it detailed the five-year impact of the amendments on Appalachian communities, as electric companies switched to low sulfur western coal to meet tougher air pollution standards. Curiously, though, the article never gave a number for job losses—perhaps because a number would have undercut the headline. By reading carefully, and doing some math, one could calculate that at most 1,000 job losses per year, over a multistate region, could be attributed to regulation. From another source, we know that by 1995 fewer than 3,000 workers nationwide had applied for Clean Air Act retraining funds.

I do not mean to downplay the devastating impact that layoffs have in communities—especially small communities that depend on natural resource industries. But the facts suggest that perceptions and reality are way out of line concerning jobs and the environment. The job losses in the coal industry have been as bad as they get from environmental regulation, but nevertheless were of little significance in a nation with more than 100 million people working. The same week that the *Times* ran the coal story on the front page, buried in the business section was the news that "trade and technology" had eliminated a whopping 100,000 textile jobs in the previous year *alone*.

BLAME THE FEDERAL RESERVE, NOT THE EPA

When a sentence begins with "all economists agree," it is a good idea to head for the door. But stay seated for these three facts: (virtually) all economists agree that, for the economy as a whole, there is no trade-off between jobs and the environment. Moreover, as the coal case suggests, actual layoffs from regulation have been, relatively speaking, quite small. Finally, regulation has not damaged the international competitiveness of U.S. manufacturing.

The first fact—no economy-wide trade-off—is an easy one to check, simply by looking at U.S. economic growth in recent years. In 1995, in spite of spending $160 billion per year on environmental protection, the U.S. economy was growing too fast from the Federal Reserve Bank's point of view. Too many people were employed in the United States, according to the Bank, raising the specter of inflation. As a result, the Federal Reserve hiked interest rates several times, in an effort to cool the economy down and *raise* unemployment rates towards the 6% level. Put another way, in 1995 the brake on job growth was clearly not excessive environmental regulation, but rather the (excessively) firm hand of the Fed.

Regulation is indeed expensive. Spending on a cleaner environment raises the costs of other goods and services, and reduces their consumption. This is the cost that we, as consumers, pay for regulation. In exchange, of course, we get the truly valuable benefit of a cleaner environment.

But it is a mistake to confuse costs of environmental protection with job losses from environmental protection. At a nationwide level, unemployment rates ultimately depend on the health of the macroeconomy, which has not been impaired by environmental regulation.

Indeed, environmental costs translate into environmental spending, which also provides jobs. As I document in a recent report, most studies find that jobs created in environmental and related sectors outweigh jobs lost due to higher regulatory costs, leading to small overall "net" employment *gains*.

Net increases in employment can happen in several ways. First, environmental spending pumps demand into the economy during recessions, dampening business cycles. Second, some environmental production (recycling, for example) is more labor intensive than the alternative (incineration), leading to more jobs per dollar of Gross Domestic Product.

Third, environmentally preferable means of meeting our energy needs (a sector that currently causes much of the nation's air pollution) would yield more jobs than our current reliance on burning fossil fuels and uranium. This is because energy conservation, wind energy and solar energy substitute for capital-intensive electricity generation plants and for imports of oil and natural gas. Such spending contributes little to employment in the United States.

But what about the quality of jobs? More labor intensive jobs are generally lower paid, whether in the service or manufacturing sector. On the other hand, much environmental spending, like defense spending, is heavily concentrated in the manufacturing sector. Spending on pollution control equipment, sewage treatment facilities or plastic liners for landfills promotes both direct and indirect job growth in traditional blue collar industries.

In fact, one study found that environmental protection provides employment heavily weighted to the transportation, communication and utility sectors, and away from services, both private and governmental. While only 22% of all non-farm jobs were in the manufacturing, transportation, communication and utility sectors in 1991, 57% of jobs generated by environmental spending fell in one of these categories. By contrast, only 22% of environmentally-related jobs were in wholesale and retail trade, finance, insurance, real estate or services, compared to 55% for the economy as a whole. And in spite of criticisms that environmental regulation only creates jobs for pencil-pushing regulators, only 11% of environmental employment was governmental, compared to an overall 17% share for government employment.

BLAME DOWNSIZING, NOT THE EPA

If there is no job trade-off nationally, what about at the local level? Again, in contrast to the conventional wisdom, the number of workers laid off due primarily to environmental regulations has been quite small. A series of studies found that manufacturing layoffs due to environmental regulation were on the order of 1,000 to 3,000 jobs per year nationwide in the late 1970s and 1980s.

More recently a U.S. Department of Labor survey, covering 57% of the manufacturing workforce, identified an average of four plant closings and 648 workers laid off due to environmental and safety regulation each year during the late 1980s. This was *less than one-tenth of one percent* of all major layoffs in manufacturing. The major source of job loss has been "corporate restructuring"—the 4,400 layoffs that Aetna Insurance Company announced last October, for example, were double the total number of jobs lost nationwide due to environmental regulation over the four-year period of the Labor Department survey.

A paper released by the Economic Policy Institute (EPI) this spring looks carefully at manufacturing job losses in heavily regulated southern California. Boston University economist Eli Berman finds no reduction in businesses' demand for workers—indeed, perhaps because of large investments in pollution abatement equipment in the oil industry, employment actually rose slightly after the introduction of stricter air quality regulations.

Local trade-offs between jobs and the environment are most severe in the timber and mining industries—but even in the eastern coal-fields and the logging communities of the Pacific Northwest, total job losses from regulation have been in the low thousands—well below the total from a single corporate downsizing. These cases take on a high media profile because the jobs pay well, because reemployment opportunities are limited for many (but not all) laid-off rural workers, and because the industries in question are facing larger scale layoffs due to automation, import competition and/or declining natural resources. In the coal case, for example, even the *Times* attributed less than half of the job loss in the first half of the 90s to the Clean Air Act.

Again, this is not to minimize the impact that any plant closing has on a community. Clearly, in a world of increasing job instability, we need good legislation to protect workers who are faced with plant closings, expanded educational opportunities for laid-off workers, and affordable health care coverage that stays with workers when they lose their jobs. But the reasons for this have very little to do with environmental regulation, and much, much more to do with international trade, technology, and corporate downsizing.

REGULATION AND COMPETITIVENESS

OK, so maybe there is no national job trade-off, and layoffs due to regulation have been small. But aren't we losing manufacturing jobs to countries overseas that have lax environmental standards? Again, the answer is no. The overall competitiveness of U.S. firms has not been damaged by regulation. Moreover, few firms are relocating to take advantage of lightly regulated "pollution havens" in poor countries. For decades economists have been looking quite hard for exactly these effects. But in their recent survey article on this topic, Harvard economist Adam Jaffe and his co-authors report, "studies attempting to measure the effect of environmental regulation on net exports, overall trade-flows, and plant location decisions have produced estimates that are either small, statistically insignificant, or not robust to tests of model specification." In other words—no observable impact.

Why? One answer is that most trade flows and foreign investment in manufacturing occur between developed countries, all of whom have comparable environmental regulations. A second answer is that, for most industries, environmental costs remain low—on the order of 1% of total business costs.

A third, intriguing answer comes from Harvard Business School professor Michael Porter. Porter argues that regulation, while imposing short run costs on firms, actually enhances their competitiveness in the long run. This can happen if regulation favors companies that are for-

ward-looking, meaning, for example, those that anticipate trends, invest in modern production processes, and stress research and development.

There is some evidence for the Porter view. In a forthcoming EPI report I show that heavily regulated industries actually faced less growth in import competition during the 1980s than the average for all industries.

PERCEPTION AND REALITY

In a poll taken in the early 90s, one-third of working adults in America felt that *their own job* was somewhat or very threatened by environmental regulation. It is not, unfortunately, hard to see how beliefs like this get shaped and reinforced. In 1990 the Business Roundtable offered up their take on environmental regulation: Job losses from the Clean Air Act alone are on the order of two million. The media widely reported their prediction. The reality, six years later, has been closer to 3,000 total layoffs, yet you wouldn't know it from reading the *New York Times*.

These skewed perceptions take a heavy political toll. On the table this year are proposals by the EPA to tighten air quality regulations and expand the chemical emission reporting requirements for manufacturing industries. Congress is also considering weakening the Superfund legislation, which provides for the clean-up of hazardous waste sites. In all cases, the anti-environment argument boils down to one word: jobs.

In spite of the conventional wisdom, however, the underlying economic realities are clear:

• national employment levels are determined largely by federal fiscal and monetary policies, not environmental regulation;

• regulation causes small local job losses in manufacturing;

• regulation has no negative impact on the international competitiveness of U.S. industry; and

• there is little capital flight to pollution havens.

These points run so counter to the popular perception—manufactured by corporate lobbyists and repeated daily in the press—that I suspect that having read this article, many readers probably still don't believe them.

Resources: "Environmental Regulation and Labor Demand: Evidence From the South Coast Air Basin," Eli Berman and Linda T. Bui, forthcoming from Economic Policy Institute, Washington, DC; "Why No Pollution Havens? Environmental Regulation and U.S. Net Export Performance," *EPI Working Paper,* Eban Goodstein, 1996, Economic Policy Institute; "Jobs and the Environment: An Overview," *Environmental Management,* Eban Goodstein, 1996; "Environmental Regulation and the Competitiveness of U.S. Manufacturing: What Does the Evidence Tell Us?", Adam B. Jaffe, Steven R. Peterson, Paul R. Portney and Robert N. Stavins, *Journal of Economic Literature* 33-1, 1995.

March/April 2003

PRICING THE PRICELESS

INSIDE THE STRANGE WORLD OF COST-BENEFIT ANALYSIS

BY LISA HEINZERLING AND FRANK ACKERMAN

How strictly should we regulate arsenic in drinking water? Or carbon dioxide in the atmosphere? Or pesticides in our food? Or oil drilling in scenic places? The list of environmental harms and potential regulatory remedies often appears to be endless. In evaluating a proposed new initiative, how do we know if it is worth doing or not? Is there an objective way to decide how to proceed? Cost-benefit analysis promises to provide the solution—to add up the benefits of a public policy and compare them to the costs.

The costs of protecting health and the environment through pollution control devices and other approaches are, by their very nature, measured in dollars. The other side of the balance, calculating the benefits of life, health, and nature in dollars and cents, is far more problematic. Since there are no natural prices for a healthy environment, cost-benefit analysis creates artificial ones. Researchers, for example, may ask a cross-section of the affected population how much they would pay to preserve or protect something that can't be bought in a store. The average American household is supposedly willing to pay $257 to prevent the extinction of bald eagles, $208 to protect humpback whales, and $80 to protect gray wolves.

Costs and benefits of a policy, however, frequently fall at different times. When the analysis spans a number of years, future costs and benefits are *discounted,* or treated as equivalent to smaller amounts of money in today's dollars. The case for discounting begins with the observation that money received today is worth a little more than money received in the future. (For example, if the interest rate is 3%, you only need to deposit about $97 today to get $100 next year. Economists would say that, at a *3% discount rate,* $100 next year has a *present value* of $97.) For longer periods of time, or higher discount rates, the effect is magnified. The important issue for environmental policy is whether this logic also applies to outcomes far in the future, and to opportunities—like long life and good

health—that are not naturally stated in dollar terms.

WHY COST-BENEFIT ANALYSIS DOESN'T WORK

The case for cost-benefit analysis of environmental protection is, at best, wildly optimistic and, at worst, demonstrably wrong. The method simply does not offer the policy-making panacea its adherents promise. In practice, cost-benefit analysis frequently produces false and misleading results. Moreover, there is no quick fix, because these failures are intrinsic to the methodology, appearing whenever it is applied to any complex environmental problem.

It puts dollar figures on values that are not commodities, and have no price.

Artificial prices have been estimated for many benefits of environmental regulation. Preventing retardation due to childhood lead poisoning comes in at about $9,000 per lost IQ point. Saving a life is ostensibly worth $6.3 million. But what can it mean to say that one life is worth $6.3 million? You cannot buy the right to kill someone for $6.3 million, nor for any other price. If analysts calculated the value of life itself by asking people what it is worth to them (the most common method of valuation of other environmental benefits), the answer would be infinite. The standard response is that a value like $6.3 million is not actually a price on an individual's life or death. Rather, it is a way of expressing the value of small risks of death. If people are willing to pay $6.30 to avoid a one in a million increase in the risk of death, then the "value of a statistical life" is $6.3 million.

It ignores the collective choice presented to society by most public health and environmental problems.

Under the cost-benefit approach, valuation of environmental benefits is based on individuals' private decisions as consumers or workers, not on their public values as citizens. However, policies that protect the environment are often public goods, and are not available for purchase in individual portions. In a classic example of this distinction, the philosopher Mark Sagoff found that his students, in their role as citizens, opposed commercial ski development in a nearby wilderness area, but, in their role as consumers, would plan to go skiing there if the development was built. There is no contradiction between these two views: as individual consumers, the students would have no way to

SHOULD WE LAUGH—OR CRY?

When it comes to cost-benefit analysis, nothing is out of bounds: everything has a price, and no inference is too heartless for the "hard science" of economics. The following stories are not the work of a lunatic fringe, but on the contrary, reflect how some of the most influential and well-known cost-benefit practitioners view the world.

Several years ago, states were suing tobacco companies for medical expenditures resulting from cigarette smoking. At that time, W. Kip Viscusi, a professor of law and economics at Harvard, concluded that states, in fact, *saved* money as the result of smoking by their citizens. Why? Because they died early, saving the states expenses on nursing home care and other services associated with an aging population! Viscusi even suggested that "cigarette smoking should be subsidized rather than taxed."

Take the problem of lead poisoning in children. One of the most serious and disturbing effects of lead is the neurological damage it can cause in young children, including permanently lowered mental ability. Randall Lutter, a researcher at the AEI-Brookings Joint Center for Regulatory Studies, put a dollar figure on the damage by looking at how much parents spent on a treatment designed to cause excretion of lead from the body. Parental spending on this treatment, according to Lutter, supports an estimate of $1,500 per IQ point lost due to lead poisoning. Previous economic analyses by EPA, based on the decrease in the children's expected future earnings, have estimated the value to be much higher—up to $9,000 per IQ point. Based on his lower figure, Lutter suggest that "agencies should consider relaxing their lead standards."

For sheer analytical audacity, Lutter's study faces some stiff competition from another study concerning children. Here, researchers examined mothers' car-seat fastening practices. They calculated the difference between the time required to fasten the seats correctly and the time mothers actually spent fastening their children into their seats. Then they assigned a monetary value to this interval of time based on the mothers' hourly wage rate (or, in the case of non-working moms, based on a guess at the wages they might have earned). When mothers saved time—and, by hypothesis, money—by fastening their children's car seats incorrectly, they were, according to the researchers, implicitly placing a finite monetary value on the life-threatening risks to their children posed by car accidents. Building on this calculation, the researchers were able to answer the vexing question of how much a statistical child's life is worth to her mother: $500,000.

express their collective preference for wilderness preservation. Their individual willingness to pay for skiing would send a misleading signal about their views as citizens.

It is often impossible to arrive at a meaningful social valuation by adding up the willingness to pay expressed by individuals. What could it mean to ask how much you personally are willing to pay to clean up a major oil spill? If no one else contributes, the clean-up won't happen regardless of your decision. As the Nobel Prize-winning economist Amartya Sen has pointed out, if your willingness to pay for a large-scale public initiative is independent of what others are paying, then you probably have not understood the nature of the problem.

It systematically downgrades the importance of the future.

One of the great triumphs of environmental law is that it seeks to avert harms to people and to natural resources in the future, and not only within this generation, but in future generations as well. Indeed, one of the primary objectives of the National Environmental Policy Act, which has been called our basic charter of environmental protection, is to nudge the nation into "fulfill[ing] the responsibilities of each generation as trustee of the environment for succeeding generations."

The time periods involved in protecting the environment are often enormous—even many centuries, in such cases as climate change, radioactive waste, etc. With time spans this long, any discounting will make even global catastrophes seem trivial. At a discount rate of 5%, for example, the deaths of a billion people 500 years from now become less serious than the death of one person today. Seen in this way, discounting looks like a fancy justification for foisting our problems off onto the people who come after us.

It ignores considerations of distribution and fairness.

Cost-benefit analysis adds up all the costs of a policy, adds up all the benefits, and compares the totals. Implicit in this innocuous-sounding procedure is the assumption that it doesn't matter who gets the benefits and who pays the costs. Yet isn't there is an important difference between spending state tax revenues, say, to improve the parks in rich communities, and spending the same revenues to clean up pollution in poor communities?

The problem of equity runs even deeper. Benefits are typically measured by willingness to pay for environmental improvement, and the rich are able and willing to pay for more than the poor. Imagine a cost-benefit analysis of locating an undesirable facility, such as a landfill or incinerator. Wealthy communities are willing to pay more for the benefit of not having the facility in their backyards; thus, under the logic of cost-benefit analysis, the net benefits to society will be maximized by putting the facility in a low-income area. In reality, pollution is typically dumped on the poor without waiting for formal analysis. Still, cost-benefit analysis rationalizes and reinforces the problem, allowing environmental burdens to flow downhill along the income slopes of an unequal society.

CONCLUSION

There is nothing objective about the basic premises of cost-benefit analysis. Treating individuals solely as consumers, rather than as citizens with a sense of moral responsibility, represents a distinct and highly questionable worldview. Likewise, discounting reflects judgments about the nature of environmental risks and citizens' responsibilities toward future generations.

These assumptions beg fundamental questions about ethics and equity, and one cannot decide whether to embrace them without thinking through the whole range of moral issues they raise. Yet once one has thought through these issues, there is no need then to collapse the complex moral inquiry into a series of numbers. Pricing the priceless just translates our inquiry into a different language, one with a painfully impoverished vocabulary.

This article is a condensed version of the report *Pricing the Priceless*, published by the Georgetown Environmental Law and Policy Institute at Georgetown University Law Center.

The full report *Pricing the Priceless* is available on-line at <www.ase.tufts.edu/gdae/publications/C-B%20pamphlet%20final.pdf>. Ackerman and Heinzerling's book on these and related issues, *Priceless: Human Health, the Environment, and the Limits of the Market*, will be published by The New Press in January 2004.

THE USE AND MISUSE OF COST-BENEFIT ANALYSIS: ARSENIC IN DRINKING WATER

One thing is certain: arsenic is bad for you. It causes cancers of the bladder, lungs, skin, kidneys, nasal passages, liver, and prostate, as well as other cardiovascular, pulmonary, neurological, immunological, and endocrine problems. It is found naturally in rock formations and dissolves into drinking water supplies, the principal source of exposure.

Starting in 1942, federal law set the standard limiting arsenic in drinking water to 50 parts per billion (ppb). In 1962, the U.S. Public Health Service recommended that drinking water should not contain more than 10 ppb. In January 2001, EPA finally adopted this standard (recommended by the World Health Organization and adopted by many European countries). Less than two months later, the Bush administration withdrew the new rule—only to accept it again after eight months of further review and debate.

In developing the new standard, EPA considered four possible standards: 3, 5, 10, and 20 ppb. On the cost side, detailed engineering descriptions are available for an array of possible technologies for water treatment and disposal of resulting residues. EPA's estimates express only a narrow range of uncertainty about costs. If the chosen pollution control technologies become cheaper once the arsenic rule is implemented—as often happens when environmental rules are enforced—the cost estimates will prove too high.

On the benefit side, reduction in arsenic in drinking water has many health advantages. However, EPA's analysts were only able to produce quantitative estimates of the health effects for bladder and lung cancer; all numerical analysis of benefits refers to preventing these two cancers alone. EPA set the value of an avoided death at $6.1 million in 1999 dollars, based on "wage-risk" studies measuring the wage premium required to attract workers to dangerous jobs. For other health effects, EPA found that there was no "willingness-to-pay" value available for nonfatal cancers—so it used the value of reducing chronic bronchitis instead! EPA did not provide a dollar equivalent at all for health effects other than bladder and lung cancers.

The range between the upper and lower estimates of health benefits reflects solely the uncertainty about the number of avoided cancers. Costs and monetized benefits are roughly comparable for 20 ppb and 10 ppb. At 5 ppb and 3 ppb, the monetized benefits are below the costs.

AEI-BROOKINGS ANALYSIS

The AEI-Brookings Joint Center for Regulatory Studies has been a vocal proponent of cost-benefit analysis of environmental rules. Nevertheless, when EPA first issued its new arsenic rule, AEI-Brookings produced a highly critical study authored by Robert Hahn and Jason Burnett. EPA had erred in two ways, the AEI-Brookings study concluded, which led to overestimates of the benefits of arsenic reduction.

First, the study criticized EPA for failing to discount the lives saved by the arsenic rule. Because exposure to arsenic leads to cancer only after a latency period, Hahn and Burnett thought EPA should have discounted the benefits of the rule. Without citing any arsenic-related scientific evidence, Hahn and Burnett picked a latency period of 30 years as their "best estimate." This guess, combined with a 7 percent discount rate, had the effect of reducing the present value of a life saved from $6.1 million to $1.1 million.

Second, the AEI-Brookings study criticized EPA for assuming that the number of cancer cases due to arsenic is proportional to total exposure. Making up a different relationship between exposure and cancer, Hahn and Burnett, neither of whom is a scientist, guessed that there were only one-fifth as many cases of cancer due to arsenic as EPA had projected. With these and other adjustments, Hahn and Burnett found the costs of arsenic reduction to be roughly ten times the benefits, costing a shocking $65 million per life saved. They speculated that even 50 ppb might be too strict a standard, in light of the low benefits.

When the National Academy of Sciences (NAS) reviewed the arsenic standard yet again, in 2001, it found exactly the opposite of Hahn and Burnett's "best estimate." That is, NAS concluded that arsenic would cause more cancer cases than EPA had projected. This finding, no doubt combined with the public outcry over the issue, helped persuade the Bush administration to relent and accept the 10 ppb standard.

PUBLIC DEBATE

Once the rival EPA and Hahn-Burnett numbers made their way into the public forum, the assumptions, qualifications, and uncertainties surrounding them were forgotten.

The *Washington Post,* for example, ran a series of opinion pieces criticizing EPA's 10 ppb standard when originally issued in early 2001. Because the rule was predicted to cost $210 billion and the benefits were valued at $170 billion, these essays concluded that the rule was not worth it. They completely ignored the many unquantified benefits EPA had felt certain would flow from the rule.

The articles also referred to the Hahn-Burnett analysis without even mentioning the discounting and the dubious estimates that so influenced its results. Journalist Michael Kinsley noted the $65 million price tag per life saved according to Hahn and Burnett's analysis, and opined, without dwelling on the details, that its assumptions seemed "reasonable."

The public dialogue in the aftermath of the Bush administration's initial withdrawal of the new arsenic rule was not about discounting future life-saving, or cancer risk assessment, or the value of a life. Yet the numerical estimates of the benefits turn almost entirely on these issues, and the theories on which they rest. Cost-benefit analysis has not enriched the public dialogue; it has impoverished it, covering the topic with poorly understood numbers rather than clarifying the underlying clash of values.

July/August 1998

BAD COMPANY

HOW TO CIVILIZE THE CORPORATION

BY JONATHAN ROWE

If a council of wise elders were to recommend a design for the basic business organization of this age, the current form of corporation would not likely be their choice.

Today's version of the corporation evolved about 150 years ago, at a time when space seemed vast and earth's resources even vaster. The economic task was simple: cover the continent, exploit its resources, build a muscular industrial machine equal to those of Europe. It was simply to grow. Today the task is more complex. The habitat can no longer absorb all the effluents of our striving—nor, for that matter, can we. The noxious side effects of production often loom larger than the supposed benefits; the factory that employs hundreds may befoul the water that is used by millions.

The corporation is not responsible for all this harm, of course. But it is the central engine of the economy for better or worse. It wields the most resources, cuts the widest swath. If the economy is to meet not just its age-old obligations to workers but its newer challenge of treading more lightly upon the earth, a remade corporation will have to play a central role.

As it stands, the corporation is not designed to deal with the negative dimensions of its activities, the way a person can. Like the 19th-century economic assumptions it embodies, it has little capacity to think beyond the boundaries of its own balance sheet. The large "publicly traded" corporation—one with shares of ownership traded on the stock exchanges—is especially captive to its form. A CEO fails to maximize monetary return and Wall Street analysts breathe fire. Shareholders can even sue if the company doesn't fulfill its legally enshrined duty to gain for them the greatest possible return.

Markets and corporations are whatever we choose to make them. The corporation does not exist in nature; unlike real persons it has no existence independent of the government that creates it. And it is past time for the corporation to grow up. It is a little like seeing the appetite of a 13-year-old in a body pushing forty—19th-century assumptions bumping up against a crowded world on the threshold of the 21st. The corporation needs a broader concept of the bottom line, and more ability to think about things besides itself.

The strange part is that's pretty much where the corporation started—a broader bottom line. The early corporations of Europe were not businesses but literally embodiments of social stability and cohesion—monasteries and universities, boroughs and guilds. They reconciled individual behavior with larger social ends. Even the early business corporations were defined largely by a public purpose (by the lights of the era). Only in the last century did this connection unravel.

To piece it together again, we need to understand that the original business corporations in the United States grew out of a bargain. Individual responsibility is a bedrock principle of common law. Owners were once personally responsible for the activities of the business, including the employees who toiled on their behalf. Your employee fouled a neighbor's well, the neighbor could sue you. That principle endured for centuries, but it broke down as business ventures grew in scale. When the British Crown sought to explore the New World, for example, few would put up capital if they could be personally on the line if something went wrong—a shipwreck, say. In today's terms, it would be like getting sued for the Valdez oil spill because you owned a hundred shares of Exxon stock.

To resolve this impasse, the Crown established the principle of limited liability for investor-owners. This new privilege could not be dispensed willy-nilly. It went only to companies chartered specifically to carry out a mission of state, such as the trading companies which returned large revenues to the Crown. This was the concept of the corporation which took root in the New Land.

The trading companies had come to embody all that American colonists detested about British rule, and their suspicions regarding legal agglomerations of all kinds. So the colonists kept the corporation on a very tight leash. The colonial (and later state) legislatures granted corporate charters one by one, to enterprises that served a clearly public purpose, such as operating a toll road or a ferry service. They loaded the charters with provisions to ensure that the public interest was served. There were restrictions on how large the corporation could become and even how long it could exist.

During the nineteenth century this bargain unraveled. The burgeoning enterprise of the era, the rise of factories and railroads, and the national market the latter made possible, were simply too much for the old restraints. First the states enacted "free incorporation laws" which enabled anyone to form a corporation to do just about anything they wanted. Historians have hailed this as part of "Jacksonian Democracy," a blow for the common folk against special privilege. There was that element; the bestowal of charters had become a bastion of cronyism and political deals. But the free incorporation laws led directly to the huge industrial monopolies of the end of the century, and scrapped the premise of the corporate arrangement. The corporation kept its exemption from common law principles of responsibility, but shed the inconvenient obligation to serve the public in return.

Even so, there were lingering echoes of the old bargain. For example, many states still imposed size limits; as late as 1890, New York State permitted corporations to be no larger than $5 million in capital. (It was to evade such restrictions that John D. Rockefeller put together the web of secret agreements that became known as the Standard Oil Trust.)

But then a governor of New Jersey had a supply-side inspiration: Lure enough corporations with weak, permissive laws and you could collect enough revenue in incorporation fees to cut taxes substantially for individuals. That set off a race to the bottom, in which the states competed to enact the most permissive laws and thus attract the most corporations. The eventual champ was Delaware, where many of the nation's largest corporations exist today as files in a lawyer's office in the state capital of Wilmington. The relationship between the corporation and the states had turned upside down. Once the creature of the states, the corporation was now the demanding taskmaster which played them off against one another.

EVENTUALLY, THE CORPORATION COULD DO WHATEVER IT WANTED, GROW AS BIG AS IT WANTED.

The Supreme Court contributed to this shift when in 1886 it declared, with no explanation, that the Fourteenth Amendment applied to corporations. These legal "persons" now had all the Constitutional protections that real people had; an amendment intended to guarantee the rights of the most vulnerable in the land was turned into a bill of rights for the most powerful. This decision would shape permanently the legal context for regulation and the nature of politics itself. One of the Constitutional rights now extended to corporations was freedom of speech. As things now stand, business lobbies can buy all the time and space they want to tell the public that global warming is not a problem. Real people who lack that kind of money don't get any time or space at all.

Eventually, the corporation could do whatever it wanted, grow as big as it wanted; it could even live forever. In the case of railroads, the first mega-corporations, they could take the vast portions of the public (originally native American) domain—bestowed on them by legislatures to help support rail service—and use these gifts for their own gain instead. At the same time the corporation shed most of the corresponding obligations that were built into its organic structure. Instead of a creature of society, it became the dominant institution in it besides the government (and some would say including the government).

The result today is that the corporation is an anomaly. It developed in a way that the seminal thinkers about democracy and the economy could not have foreseen. When Adam Smith wrote *The Wealth of Nations* (1776), for example, the modern corporation did not exist. The corporation of his experience was a government franchise along the lines of the East India Company, a form of business he did not consider promising. In one of his less prescient passages, Smith wrote that the corporation would never amount to much in the international marketplace; it was too cumbersome and bureaucratic, too lacking in the "dexterity and judgement" of individual entrepreneurs who assuredly would run circles around it.

Thus it was possible for Smith to envision an economy of individual shopkeepers and entrepreneurs whose atomistic strivings would keep one another in check—and whose social affinities as members of a community would tend to keep their enterprises on a tether of community norms. Similarly with the Founding Fathers: The homegrown corporations within their ken were local franchises that ran bridges and the like. They were a state and local issue. Matters seemed well in hand and it did not occur to most of the authors of the Constitution to include the corporation within the scheme of checks and balances by which they sought to restrain agglomerations of power in the body politic.

This helps explain why the corporation has come to so dominate the nation's politics and market. With the original bargain broken, there is nothing in our institutional genetic coding to reconcile the corporation with the larger whole. The odd part is that pollution occupies a similar place in our economics. At the end of the 18th century, when Adam Smith wrote, the earth still seemed immense. It took six weeks to get a wagon from Smith's Edinburgh to London and back. That there might be limits to the ability of the habitat to absorb the effluents of human activity could seem remote. Remote too was the possibility that commercial transactions might one day have a greater effect upon the millions who aren't party to them than upon those who are, thus upsetting the central calculus of market economics.

Today economists try to deal with these environmental ripple effects under the rubric of "externalities," a revealing term. The toxic emissions from a smelter are not "external" to the lives of the neighbors who must suffer them; they are so only to the preconceptions of economists who regard the smelter and its customers as the core reality, and everything besides that as "external." The large literature on "externalities" suggests that a central fact of modern economic life—degradation of the habitat—fits awkwardly with a central assumption of the discipline: that the center of the economic universe is still an isolated transaction between a buyer and a seller.

There's a need for a new economics that integrates the toxic impacts of economic activity into the core reality, and which seeks to promote human well-being instead of just money-making transactions. At the same time, there's a need to integrate the most important part of the economy—the corporation—into economic and political reality. In environmental terms, the corporation is going to have to take more responsibility for its impacts upon others, just as we expect real people to do.

The most prominent corner in the environmental debate today is called "market based" environmentalism. The basic idea is to establish financial carrots and sticks instead of ordinary regulation. Instead of mandating a smokestack scrubber, say, charge the company heavily for what it emits and let it find the most efficient way to clean up its discharges. There's a tendentious quality to a lot of market-based environmentalism, especially when its advocates dismiss ordinary regulation as "command and control," with the Stalinist overtones of that phrase. The fact is, there will always be a need for plain old regulation; you can't let some people poison others just because they pay a market price to do so.

Still, the market-basers have a point. If you can build environmental and other concerns into a company's ordinary financial metabolism—make them the warp and woof of the market calculus—then the need for external regulation will be less. Very likely you will achieve your goals in a more elegant and efficient way. The discussion usually starts with taxes, which is where public policy affects prices most directly. Tax petroleum and other fuels more heavily, and you set up a dynamic in which companies strive to conserve in order to save money. Less pollution should be the result. The revenues could be used to cut the payroll tax on work. It is insane to tax work heavily but the use of natural resources hardly at all.

But the tax system is just one way to use the infrastructure of the market to prod corporations towards a broader bottom line. The information system is another. Even in orthodox market theory, buyers are supposed to have complete information about the implications of their buying so they can make choices that express their values. Today such information is in short supply. We have little idea where the stuff we buy comes from, the conditions under which it is made, or the effluents and other impacts created in the process.

THE CHARTER CHALLENGE

Some environmentalists are starting to confront corporations by challenging the privileges granted to them by state charters. "Battles with regulatory agencies are very limited," says Richard Grossman, whose Cambridge, Mass.-based Program on Corporations, Law, and Democracy has led the intellectual charge to rethink corporate charters. "It is challenging corporate behavior one item at a time"—and tacitly upholds corporate political rights Grossman believes are illegitimate.

After regulators failed to rein in Waste Management, the huge garbage conglomerate, Pennsylvania environmentalists asked their attorney general to revoke its charter and thus its ability to operate in the state. When the attorney general refused, the Community Environment Legal Defense Fund took him to court in 1996. The Fund lost its case, but Tom Linzey of the Legal Defense Fund explains the principle at stake: A charter is "a contract between the people of the state, who charter corporations to create wealth... and the corporation agrees to abide by the state's laws. Somebody has to police these contracts."

If state officials do not bow to grassroots pressure, the activists plan to lobby for local ordinances to hold corporations accountable. The idea, according to Grossman, is to "provoke a crisis of jurisdiction" by creating more stringent laws than that of the states or feds, igniting a debate on state officials who shirk their duty to challenge corporate misdeeds.

— *Loren McArthur*

Sixty years ago, in the midst of the Depression, Congress established the Securities and Exchange Commission to require rigorous financial reporting by corporations. The idea was that informed investors would help avert another financial crash. Today we need more environmental-impact reporting so that informed buyers can help avert an environmental crash. The so-called Toxics Release Inventory, enacted in the 1980s, requires plants to disclose to their neighbors the toxic substances they use and emit. It has been an environmental success story and a model for the way disclosure can affect corporate behavior.

More broadly, there's a need for more and better indicators of environmental well-being that establish a context of concern about these matters. Today, readers of the daily papers find out about the stock and bond markets and baseball standings in great detail. About environmental conditions they learn very little. If people seem indifferent to such matters as the emissions from their sport utility vehicles, it is partly because there is little in our daily cognitive environments to impress such a concern upon us, and much advertising to make us want to buy the SUVs. The nation's current index of economic progress, the Gross Domestic Product or GDP, is perverse in this regard. It merely adds up all economic activity—constructive or destructive. The more gas we guzzle, the worse the air gets and the more medical problems that result, the more the GDP goes up. Walk or ride a bike and the GDP goes down because you are spending less money.

This is idiotic. The nation needs an index of economic well-being, not just of money spent. Starting close to home, over 200 states and localities around the country are developing their own indicators of well-being.

Such steps could affect the context in which the corporation operates. Eventually the corporation must change internally, through new forms of ownership which embody environmental concerns so they don't have to be injected from without. One example is local ownership along the lines of the Green Bay Packers football team, owned entirely by residents of Green Bay, Wisconsin. Local owners are likely to think a little longer about fouling their own nest (and about such things as moving their own or their neighbors' jobs abroad). There is no guarantee, but at least the decision takes on a personal dimension that is lacking now in the abstracted Wall Street calculus.

Employee ownership can work in similar fashion, especially regarding workplace environmental issues. There also should be new corporate structures offering tax breaks and other advantages in exchange for high levels of environmental performance. The law offers special privileges for people who want to assemble a real estate investment empire. Why not for people who want to do environmental good?

There's also a need to revive the corporate charter as a genuine agreement between the institution and society. Today it is little more than a permissive carte blanche for management, and that won't change as long as states must grovel to attract corporate charter business. Early in the century, President Taft proposed federal chartering for very large corporations. This is a good Republican idea whose time has come. Global corporations should operate under ground rules in proportion to their impact and scale, and that means more than a file drawer in a law office in per-

missive Delaware. The growing movement to reopen the corporate charter debate at the state level could lead eventually in this direction (see box); at the very least there needs to be a floor that limits the ability of corporations to play states off against one another.

At the same time, the political impact of the corporation needs to be brought back into scale with the rest of society. If, as Congressional Republicans argue, labor unions should have to get the consent of their members to make political contributions, shouldn't corporations have to get the consent of their customers who are the source of the corporation's political funds? At the very least, shouldn't they have to inform their customers about which politicians get a cut of the money shoppers spend at the store?

Ultimately the nation is going to have to revisit the question of corporate personhood, which the Supreme Court declared but never really justified. As long as corporations have the same speech rights as individuals, they will have more such rights, because they have so much more by way of money and resources to make use of them. The next strict-constructionist Supreme Court nominee should be asked to explain where precisely the Constitution says that artificial persons should have the same rights and protections that real people do.

Techno-futurists say the new information-based economy will make most environmental concerns moot. But paper use has burgeoned along with computers. Pressures on forests, offshore oil, and mineral deposits have not abated. If some forms of physical pollution have diminished in the United States, it is often because those dirty industries do their business now in developing countries instead. The frantic competitive pressures and centrifugal pulls of the global market make the need to rework the corporation into the larger social weave all the more important.

There is nothing strange or radical about the task. It is a traditionalist agenda that would restore the corporation to what it was supposed to be—a way to mobilize economic resources to meet current human needs. It would correct an omission that the framers of our guiding economic and political concepts could not have foreseen. Unless one believes that history has basically stopped, and all that remains is an expansion from an institutional status quo—that is, unless one thinks like an economist—then the kinds of government agencies and programs, corporations and the rest are going to have to change, along with changing needs.

WORKPLACE DEMOCRACY THROUGH LABOR LAW

BY ELAINE BERNARD

Few people today remember that when Congress adopted the National Labor Relations Act in 1935, its purpose was not just to provide a procedural mechanism to end industrial strife in the workplace. Rather, this monumental piece of New Deal legislation had a far more ambitious mission: to promote industrial democracy.

To extend democracy into the workplace, the NLRA instituted "free collective bargaining" between workers and employers. Unions were to be encouraged, not simply tolerated. It was understood that workers couldn't engage in meaningful collective bargaining without collective representation.

Needless to say, it has been a long time since we've heard any President or administration, much less Congress, talk about promoting industrial democracy. In fact, the very term "industrial democracy" seems like a contradiction in terms. Organized labor has long sought to restore some balance to U.S. labor law, which is currently so stacked against workers that unionization is very difficult everywhere, and almost impossible in some sectors of the economy. Supreme Court decisions rolling back union and worker rights, as well as management-inspired amendments to labor law, have tied the hands of union organizers while freeing management to penalize workers who attempt to exercise their rights.

While the battle to restore legal "fairness" to workers is important, a victory in this campaign would simply bring us back to 1935. We need instead to question the basic assumption of U.S. labor law that the workplace is naturally union-free with workers having few rights. Labor law is largely a series of barriers over which workers must climb to gain elementary rights. Each year these barriers rise higher and higher, not just for representation (through the onerous election process) but for free speech and other rights Americans take for granted outside the workplace.

Why assume that workers have no rights to participate in workplace decisions? In a democracy would it not make more sense to assume such rights and to strictly scrutinize those workers who relinquish their rights, not those who exercise them?

As power is presently distributed, workplaces are factories of authoritarianism polluting our democracy. Citizens cannot spend eight or more hours a day obeying orders and being shut out of

INSTEAD OF THE WORKPLACE BECOMING DEMOCRATIC, THE HIERARCHICAL CORPORATE WORKPLACE MODEL IS COMING TO DOMINATE THE REST OF SOCIETY.

important decisions affecting them, and then be expected to engage in robust, critical dialogue about the structure of our society. Eventually the strain of being deferential servants from nine to five diminishes our after-hours liberty, and sense of civic entitlement and responsibility.

Indeed, in the latter part of this century, instead of the workplace becoming democratic, the hierarchical corporate workplace model is coming to dominate the rest of society. Unions, as the way working people become self-organized, must play a central role both in fighting to extend democracy into the workplace and to preserve it in the public sphere.

With the United States reporting the highest levels of inequality in the advanced industrial world and the majority of U.S. workers experiencing declining real wages for 20 years, we might be tempted to think the problems of democracy in the workplace should be put on the back burner for more settled times. Maybe the labor movement should focus only on this growing economic inequality since one of its roles is to achieve decent wages and working conditions for unionists. Yet, these goals are linked. Without greater levels of democracy in the workplace, and the nurturing of power that goes with it, further organization will be difficult to achieve and inequality is unlikely to decline.

Ultimately, the labor movement builds communities—that's what unions do. By bringing together workers, who have few rights, who are isolated as individuals and often competing against each other, unions forge a community in the workplace. They help workers understand they have rights, and they provide a collective vehicle for exercising those rights. Beyond the defense and promotion of individual union members' rights, unions also provide a collective voice for workers. They provide a powerful check to the almost total power of management, and they fight for the right of workers to participate in decision-making in the workplace.

But labor movements and other communities of common interest don't just happen. They must be consciously constructed, with a lot of hard work, discussion, and engagement. Constructing democratic communities is an ongoing process; like democracy, that process can be rolled back or pushed forward.

Because we have not yet succeeded in extending democracy to the workplace, democracy and civil society themselves are threatened. The labor movement cannot be seen in isolation from the political environment, and any revitalization of unions will require an effective response to that environment. Unions must become the creators of democratic communities—in the workplace and beyond.

July/August 1999

WHAT AN ENVIRONMENTALLY SUSTAINABLE ECONOMY LOOKS LIKE

BY THAD WILLIAMSON

Greens and economic progressives are seen as uncertain, uneasy allies—and perhaps not allies at all. Think of those spotted-owl-loving, middle-class activists clashing with blue collar loggers in the Pacific Northwest. Or the clash between liberal economists who still count progress in terms of jobs created, growth generated, and increases in consumption, and environmental activists who challenge those very ways of measuring progress. "Growth" to these activists is part of the problem, not the solution.

But do green politics necessarily conflict with progressive economic goals? Or can environmental protection live and thrive in a world dedicated to eradicating poverty, nurturing equality and economic security, and the continued advancement of productivity and technology?

In a word, yes. An environmentally "sustainable" economy is one that neither depletes natural resources nor pollutes at levels that overwhelm the ability of ecosystems to absorb waste. Such an economy would almost certainly need to overlap with many of the traditional goals of economic progressives, allowing us to envision an ideal world that is both socially and ecologically sustainable. What would that world look like?

First, it would provide economic security for individuals and communities. So long as most citizens are less than six months' paychecks away from insolvency, and so long as they worry that their income may be taken away, economic expansion (i.e., growth) and job creation will, most of the time and for most people, always be a higher political priority than environmental protection.

The link between economic security and sustainability runs at a deeper level as well. In a highly inegalitarian society such as ours, where the quality of public goods like neighborhood safety and public schools varies widely, individuals and families are pressured not just to subsist, but to earn enough to live an ecology-straining middle-class lifestyle.

At the community level, if localities remain dependent on the investment decisions of private businesses for their economic health, protection of the environment will tend to take a back seat. Just look at the way poor, deindustrialized cities such as Chester, Pennsylvania, court particle-spewing trash incinerators for the modest revenue they provide.

If we want to move to a society in which acquiring more and more goods is not the highest priority for individuals, and "growth" is not the highest priority for most communities, then we need a baseline of economic security.

Second, we must create a sense of self based on something besides consumerism. Of course, economic insecurity is not the only reason Americans are driven to consume at extraordinarily high levels. As Thorstein Veblen first argued in 1899, and as Juliet Schor documented in the 1990s, consumption is often used to mark social status, particularly with regard to goods that can be made visible to one's peers, such as cars, clothes, and lipstick. As workers, most Americans are provided with little scope for individual expressiveness, but as consumers, they feel free to follow their wishes in making decisions—decisions which then form a critical part of American identities. The result is a nation of individuals shaped by a compulsion to consume goods and services, and to increase that consumption over time. By contrast, in an ecologically sustainable society, people's core satisfactions could not come from buying decisions, and they would need to have a sense of when enough is enough.

Third, producers who damage the environment must also bear the costs of their damage. As it stands, private enterprises force the public to pay the costs of their polluting and depletion of natural resources. Since the true costs of production are not reflected in the prices of goods on the market, firms benefit by shifting costs such as pollution cleanup to the public. This system gives businesses an incentive to "externalize" environmental costs off their own balance sheets if they can get away with it—and to resist attempts by governments to minimize the costs through regulation. Advocates of ecological sustainability thus argue that firms should bear the full cost of their activities. A major question, of course, is how to best accomplish that goal.

Fourth, we must also use as much environmentally friendly technology as we can in our new world. Unfortunately, over the course of this century, the U.S. government intervened in the economy to promote ecologically inefficient and destructive economic practices. While giving a pittance to the development of solar and wind power, the government sank about $100 billion of subsidies into nuclear power between 1950 and 1990. Similarly, the government lavished funds upon the Highway Trust Fund and created the interstate highway system while allowing public transit of all types to decay. To this day, over 80% of federal transportation spending supports automobile-related infrastructure, leaving less than 20% for mass transit. Such spending patterns, along with additional subsidies like tax write-offs for home mortgages, help generate suburban sprawl (and thereby exacerbate the ecological damage caused by cars). At the same time, regulators often tackle problems at the "end of the pipe" instead of seeking to change the productive processes themselves.

In any sustainable society, these sorts of choices will need to be reversed and priority given to implementing the most environmentally friendly technology possible. Environmental technology, in fact, could be the source of millions of new jobs in the next century—and jobs building high-speed rail cars would likely pay just as well as jobs making automobiles. Similarly, labor-intensive public works projects could be undertaken in support of ecological goals—to beautify cities, build bike paths, install solar panels, remove lead paint, and insulate buildings. Governments could also aggressively use their purchasing policies to help promote the development of cutting-edge environmentally sound products.

Within the current structure of power, however, the private interests that stand to lose public funds—such as the oil and car companies—thwart any shift in public spending toward more ecologically and socially rational goals and resist any laws that would mandate certain kinds of production processes. They have the money to intervene in elections and (even more importantly) shape legislation—and they are aided by the fact that few politicians are eager

to support measures that may damage companies in their districts. Just look at the way the energy lobby thoroughly discredited and defeated Vice President Al Gore's modest proposal for an energy tax in 1993. In contrast, an ecologically sustainable society would require that politics not be dominated by corporate or private interests—a very tough structural requirement rarely mentioned in the conventional policy debate about the environment.

Finally, a world where ecological and progressive economic goals are unified would be one where growth is no longer the top priority. In our corporate capitalist economy, banks and investors consider whether profits and the economy as a whole will grow before sending their capital the way of any business. In contrast, an environmentally sustainable economy would not need high rates of growth to function in a healthy manner. Growth would not be the goal of a sustainable economy, nor would the fair distribution of economic goods depend on continual growth. Instead, with every individual and community guaranteed a stake in the economy, it would not be necessary to focus so much on expanding production. Also, the gains from more efficient production would be distributed to people as reduced work-hours or more stringent environmental protection.

Still, even in a sustainable economy, economic growth *per se* need not be eliminated entirely. While one way to cut the use of resources and pollution is to cut production and shrink the economy, another is to make productive systems more efficient. We also might choose to produce those goods that cause less ecological damage. There is no inherent reason why a society that commits itself to ecologically efficient production, both in the actual production process and in the kinds of goods created, might not generate what we today call economic growth. For instance, if we decided to hire more elementary school teachers—and at the same time to consume fewer lawn care products—ecological damage would drop even as the size of the economy stayed roughly the same. The difference is that economic growth as a good in itself would not be the central aim of such an economy.

THE INSTITUTIONS OF A SUSTAINABLE ECONOMY

Ecological problems might be very easy to solve if we imagine an all-powerful state that enforces strict ecological standards on both individuals and businesses. Not only is such a vision unattractive on its own terms, it probably provides only a temporary solution to the ecological problem. Sooner or later, an ecofascist regime that tried to impose sound ecological practices without the support of its citizens would probably be overthrown, leading us back to square one: how to make the goals of democracy, economic justice, and ecological sustainability fit together.

How would that be possible? Is it possible?

At the community level, perhaps the fundamental questions to consider are: Who owns capital?, and, Who gets to make basic decisions over how production is carried out? The usual answers—small businesses, corporations, the government, or workers—would all have the incentive to pollute or use ecologically wasteful production strategies. A fifth possible solution is local community ownership. To see why, it's worth reviewing the shortcomings of the other possible answers.

Styles of regulation that allow private businesses to organize production as they see fit will always face an uphill struggle in trying to get businesses to pay for the ecological costs they generate, a hill that is especially steep in the case of nations like the United States where social democratic politics are weak. Moreover, even the success stories associated with social democratic-style environmental regulation have limitations. For example, no industrialized country has yet succeeded in constraining the growth of the automobile/highway complex, as we must to reduce greenhouse gases.

Worker-owned firms are an attractive solution, it seems, since workers may be less likely to pollute their own communities (or risk their own health in the workplace), and more subtly, because worker firms (as Douglas Booth argues) will have less incentive to grow than capitalist firms. Perhaps, but workers within a given enterprise still may have interests different from the public's. Given the reins of management, workers may come to see ecological responsibility as a threat to the bottom line, as Gar Alperovitz and Herbert Gintis have each suggested—especially if they can send the pollution from their plant downstream or to the next town.

State ownership of firms also poses problems. When government officials are not held accountable and when ecological values are subordinated to other aims, both state-owned enterprises and general government operations are capable of doing disastrous damage to the environment. Even in the most favorable circumstances, public companies may find it rational to compromise the needs of local ecosystems in the name of some larger public interest. At worst, we've seen the Energy Department contaminate desert stretches of Nevada from nuclear weapons tests carried out in the "public interest."

This brings us to a fifth possible answer to the "who should control capital?" question: local-level community ownership. "Community-owned" firms might include municipally owned enterprises, firms owned by nonprofit organizations that represent community interests (such as community development corporations), or companies whose stock can be owned only by local residents (as in Michael Shuman's concept of "community corporation.") In theory, community-owned enterprises are more likely to take full responsibility for the ecological costs of their

activity to the degree that they are made accountable to the community. If the managers of a community-owned firm chose to sacrifice ecological goals for the sake of higher production, citizens would have the opportunity, via the political process, to remove them.

Moreover, profits from a community-owned firm could be distributed to citizens as a second income, thus helping to meet the economic security requirement previously noted. And perhaps best of all, there is no threat that a community firm would move away—removing the sword hanging over towns that want tough ecological standards but not at the cost of jobs.

The most widespread form of community ownership in the United States in the 20th century are the roughly 2,000 local-level, nonprofit, public electric utilities, which offer lower rates, more public accountability, and a better (although far from perfect) environmental record than their private counterparts. But many other forms of community ownership have sprouted up in the past two decades as well. These include businesses owned and operated by community development corporations, community land trusts, community-supported agriculture operations, community credit unions, and municipal enterprises.

Community firms, then, would appear to be the best answer to the question of "who should control capital," at least within medium-size and large firms, and the recent growth of various forms of community ownership indicates this is a plausible solution. This does not mean that other forms of ownership need to be obliterated; on the contrary, community-owned firms could coexist along with small businesses, worker firms, joint public-private enterprises, and some larger scale public enterprise. The key is that the local community must have substantial control over the practices of enough enterprises to anchor the local economy and set a tone for overall production practices.

Community control of land—especially downtown land and undeveloped land—would also be important to optimizing local communities' ecological health. Patterns of land development driven by private developers have resulted in auto-dominated, sprawled out forms of urban development. Community ownership of land would make shifting to ecologically friendly, resource-saving urban designs far more plausible—and rents collected from leases to downtown businesses could also be directly distributed to residents or given to them as services to help solve the economic security problem.

A picture thus emerges of a local economy characterized by a critical mass of community ownership, along with substantial community ownership of land, allowing local level democratic politics to steer firms toward ecological goals and allowing any community dividend to be distributed to citizens (enhancing their economic security). Even if this vision could be achieved within every locality in America, would such an achievement be enough to create a sustainable society?

Hardly. We'd still need mechanisms at the state or perhaps regional level to ensure that one community does not dump on another and meets ecological standards. There would also need to be a planning mechanism to allocate enough capital to each community to guarantee local-level full employment and to help communities adjust when some industries decline due to market shifts.

Governments would also provide important public goods relevant to sustainability, including rail and public transit, the development of alternative energy sources, and oversight of needed ecological clean-ups, and coordinate the overall macroeconomy. But by essentially removing the private corporation with its disproportionate sway over the political process, and replacing it with firms directly tied to community interests, it ought to be easier to decide how to spend the public works budget, how long the standard work week should be, and so on in an ecologically rational manner. Continental or global forms of ecological governance may be appropriate on specific ecological issues such as greenhouse gas emissions. (Gar Alperovitz offers an overview along these lines involving economic institutions at the local, regional, and national levels).

This kind of system would have a far better chance of meeting the needs of a sustainable society than any industrial society that exists now (be it capitalist, social democratic, or state socialist.)

But can it be said that this proposed system is inherently sustainable? No—or, at least, not exactly. In fact, it is probably impossible to design a modern economy that could guarantee ecological sustainability while also preserving other crucial norms such as liberty, equality, and democracy. The best we can hope for is an economy that meets the logical prerequisites for a sustainable society and permits citizens to make democratic social choices about what sort of world they wish to live in.

Some citizens may chafe at any state-mandated shifts in their lifestyle and consumption habits (such as one bag of garbage per household per week) while others will believe that the trade-off is worth it. The outcome of such political struggles is uncertain, and from time to time the public no doubt would make the wrong choices from a rigorous ecological point of view. But at least such bad choices would be made in the name of the public interest, not in response to private interests or as steps needed to grease the wheels of a growth-oriented economy.

To be sure, in the long interval before a truly sustainable society is built, there will continue to be episodes in which zero-sum tradeoffs between the economy and the environment must be made. But those episodes should not blind either greens or economic progressives to the common ground both groups share and will no doubt need to share if either group is to achieve its political aims in the 21st century.

Resources: Ted Howard, "Ownership Matters," (National Center for Economic and Security Alternatives, 1999), www.ncesa. org; Mark Hertsgaard, *Earth Odyssey* (Broadway Books, 1999); Gar Alperovitz, "Sustainability and the System Problem," *PEGS Journal,* 1996.

CHAPTER 8

Policy Spotlight: Industry Subsidies and International Trade

INTRODUCTION

Standard microeconomic theory produces some clear public policy recommendations, most of which can be summarized by the phrase, "Hands off!" A prominent case is the U.S. government's farm subsidies. Hard-headed mainstream economists generally oppose subsidies, arguing that they prop up inefficient businesses, and transfer money from taxpayers to farmers for no good reason.

Most economists also sing the praises of free trade. When governments limit trade, they contend, consumers lose—and lose more than domestic industries and their workers gain—by paying higher prices for goods. Restrictions are justified only in a few exceptional circumstances, like the unusual case of a budding "infant industry" that has the potential to flourish if temporarily protected. Many mainstream economists are suspicious not only of government regulation, but of labor and community anti-sweatshop campaigns, which they view as a back-door route to trade protection.

As always, the articles in this chapter offer a different set of perspectives. Rather than criticizing subsidies in general, the authors argue that current subsidies target the wrong businesses and reward the wrong behavior. Farm organizer Benny Bunting contends it is worth subsidizing *small* farmers, because they preserve the land and rural communities in a way that corporate agribusiness does not (Bunting, article 8.1). According to Rodney Ward, the problem with post-September 11 airline subsidies is that they went to management with the requirement that firms slash costs—something the airlines achieved through ruthless downsizing and ruinous competition (Ward, article 8.2).

The remaining four articles challenge conventional economic wisdom about international trade. Arthur MacEwan maintains that "infant industry" is far from an exceptional case: all of today's industrial powerhouses, including the United States, initially sheltered their manufacturing sectors. What's more, he says, free trade strengthens business relative to workers, worsening inequality (MacEwan, article 8.3). Ellen Frank follows up with a report card on NAFTA, which she claims has cost the United States jobs but has not brought development to Mexico

(Frank, article 8.4). Frank Ackerman adds that NAFTA is turning the United States into a pollution haven: U.S. corn has undersold Mexican corn by using environmentally destructive farming practices (Ackerman, article 8.5). Dara O'Rourke has the last word, discussing the difficulties of monitoring sweatshop production in the highly fluid apparel industry. O'Rourke's observations challenge the idea that corporations will correct their own labor abuses without pressure from governments and civil society (O'Rourke, article 8.6).

DISCUSSION QUESTIONS

1) (Bunting) Should the government aid small farmers? Why or why not? Refer to the ideas in the Benny Bunting interview and in your textbook. Be as clear as possible about the principles behind your answer, and think about how those principles would apply to sectors other than farming.

2) (Ward) Rodney Ward implies that for airlines, national ownership under worker management or renewed federal government regulation would be better solutions than the federal bailout. How would standard economic theory view these suggestions? What do you think of them?

3) (Bunting) Orthodox economists tend to view industry subsidies as a bad idea, period. Bunting supports subsidies, but thinks they are currently going to the wrong people. Explain this disagreement and the ideas behind it.

4) (MacEwan) Arthur MacEwan claims that the "infant industry" argument for trade protection is much more widely applicable than standard theory would suggest. To what countries and industries would it best apply in today's world economy? Explain.

5) (MacEwan) Free trade, MacEwan argues, gives business greater power relative to labor. Why is this so? Is it a good reason for opposing free trade?

6) (Frank) The "gains from trade" model says that both the United States and Mexico will gain from free trade. Many critics of free trade say that Mexico's gain will be the U.S.'s loss. But Ellen Frank says both the United

States and Mexico lost. How can this be? Explain her argument, and whether it makes sense to you.

7) (Ackerman, MacEwan) What are pollution havens, and why does free trade run the risk of creating them? How can a rich country like the United States be a pollution haven compared to a poorer country like Mexico?

8) (O'Rourke) The anti-sweatshop movement is demanding that certain companies (such as colleges selling insignia clothing) ensure that the goods they sell are manufactured subject to certain labor standards. Explain what this movement is trying to do in terms of consumer sovereignty and solving information problems. When some economists say that the movement is about back-door trade protectionism, what do they mean? Do you agree with them?

KEY TO COLANDER

The articles in this chapter are linked to Colander's Chapter 19, "Politics and Economics: The Case of Agricultural Markets" and Chapter 21, "International Trade Policy."

Bunting and Ward speak to issues in Chapter 19. Ward's discussion of airline mergers and restructuring also touches on some topics that came up in Chapter 15, "Anti-Trust Policy and Regulation."

Ackerman, Frank, MacEwan, and O'Rourke address Chapter 19's material on trade.

March 1989

'STEWARDS OF THE LAND'

FAMILY FARMS IN CRISIS

INTERVIEW WITH FARM ACTIVIST BENNY BUNTING

Bunting: The real farm crisis is high input costs and low returns. We're not receiving adequate funds for our labor and our products. With commodity prices so low, and with so many people having to go out of farming, and with all the farm sales, equipment prices and land values were going down. So people were being foreclosed on even if they were not delinquent because they had loans that were secured by real estate, combines, tractors, whatever.

U.S. agriculture has undergone profound changes in recent decades. The inflation of the 1970s, high real interest rates in the 1980s, falling land prices, the rising value of the dollar, and confused and inconsistent government policy contributed to an untenable debt burden for small farmers and a rash of farm bankruptcies.

The long-term farm crisis deepened with the passage of Congress' Omnibus Farm Bill in 1996. The bill was designed to eliminate government intervention in the farm sector by removing subsidies over a period of seven years and lifting long-standing production controls. Supporters in Congress argued that the act would increase production, producing lower prices for consumers and, in turn, higher demand for farm products. Farmers skeptical about the promise of rising demand were assured that the government would use the WTO and free-trade deals with Latin America to promote exports. "Free-market farming," the story went, would benefit everyone.

In reality, plummeting prices did not increase demand, and brought hard times for farmers who couldn't make a fair return. Between 1996 and 1998, corn and wheat prices fell by roughly half, and by 2000, three-quarters of the country's two million farms could not clear a profit.

The hardest hit were family farmers, who had already been struggling for decades. While family farms can vary in size from just a few acres to several thousand, family farmers are defined as those who own their own land and, with their extended families, do most of the labor on it.

Benny Bunting is a founding member of the National Save the Family Farm Coalition, as well as the United Farmers' Organization, whose several thousand members have been working since 1984 to preserve family farming in the Carolinas. Marc S. Miller, a former member of the *Dollars & Sense* collective, interviewed Bunting in November 1988 about the role of the family farm in U.S. agriculture. Bunting began by describing the farm crisis of the late 1980s.

D&S: Why do farmers get so little for crops?

Bunting: Oversupply. I'm of a mind that we need supply management. At the beginning of each year the Secretary of Agriculture determines what the domestic needs are and what the export needs are, and a quota is assigned to growers. A support price is set with a profit figured in. Some commodities are supply-managed, and that's why my area seems to be a little insulated from some of the crisis. We have peanuts and tobacco. Both these are supply-managed, so the farmer is basically guaranteed a profit if weather permits him to grow a crop.

On the other hand, the consumer is guaranteed an even, fair price on that commodity. You know the price of peanuts is going to be smooth, it's not going to be on a roller coaster, which is good. That type of policy would give small farmers a fair return on their labor and investment and also guarantee food security for the nation.

Grains could be run the same way the peanut program is, but that will never happen as long as you have the Cargills, the big exporters of grain. They make their money by volume, so the lower the price per bushel, the more they can export. They fight supply management, because they want overproduction.

D&S: If Cargill can produce grain cheaper, why protect family farming?

Bunting: When you get farming into the hands of a few, short-term gain is what they're going to be after. They are not going to be stewards of the land. They're not going to be trying to save the land to pass on from generation to generation. If you look at what some of the corporate farms are doing, they want to put the maximum amount of acres they can into production right now. They don't terrace the land. They aren't going to rotate their crops to keep from depleting the soil of minerals.

The family farm gives stability to the rural areas. Some of these corporations will give donations to school systems or to parks that look big. But the individual small family farmers are paying much more into the community because the small farmer is going to buy from rural suppliers. The corporate farmers are going to try to buy straight from some large distributor outside of the area. The small supplier is going to be out of business.

D&S: Are there measures that might limit the threat to family farming from agribusiness?
Bunting: I think we need restrictions [on non-family corporate ownership of farmland], because farmers cannot compete with multinational corporations [that drive prices down]. With the low prices, family farmers have had to increase acreage. To be able to handle the increase in acreage, you have to increase chemical use. That is a short-term gain. In the long term, we are hurting the land, the productivity of the land and our own health.

D&S: What is your own farm in Oak City, N.C. like?
Bunting: We have poultry and hog houses. Our hogs and chickens are both on contract. The poultry is contracted with Perdue, and the hogs are with a local guy, C. D. Bunting. He's a relative. We also have row crops—peanuts, beans, corn. We have tobacco, but we don't raise it ourselves; my uncle tends to the tobacco. The farm is about 150 acres.

We have farmed in a way all our life. We always had 4H and FFA [Future Farmers of America] projects all during school. After I graduated high school, I went to North Carolina State for a couple of years. Then I worked for a company in Robertsonville, but I still farmed on the side. When Perdue opened up their facilities in Lewiston, I went to work over there and still did the farming. That's when I built the poultry house. We were using old, used equipment, but it was paid for. Then we built the hog facility, and I turned in my notice with Perdue.

D&S: Are you making a living at farming?
Bunting: We're surviving (laughs). My wife has had to take a job at Belks [Department Store]. In about 80% of the cases around here [eastern North Carolina], at least one member of that family has to bring in income from outside the farm.

We lost an awful lot of money farming, and we actually filed a Chapter 12 bankruptcy—farm reorganization. That plan is working and we'll survive the crisis, it looks like.

D&S: What has it been like for you to organize farmers and lobby in Raleigh and Washington?
Bunting: Very taxing, because it's taking so much time away from the farm. If it wasn't for my father, I could not go. That's just pure and simple. He's doing the work, and he's there to look after things when I leave. It's a two-man operation. We only hire part-time help at very peak times. Something always gets behind when I'm gone. But I think I've grown a lot in being more aware of the issues, and being more aware of my own destiny.

It's been an education to find out about the benefits of restructuring versus the benefits of bankruptcy. And we've been able to educate people to fight for mediation. That's something farmers would like: to work out their own problems, their own way, without court intervention.

Being able to work on the issues has been a blessing to an awful lot of people. It seems like there have been so many suicides, so much depression in the farm sector, and I think there would be much more if it were not for these organizations that gave people an outlet to work for their own destiny.

I'm really compassionate for the family farm unit. I hope I'm not just being selfish, but I think it is part of the stability of the nation. I think we need the rural areas. I hate to see small farmers moving off, especially young farmers. The average age is up around 60.

D&S: There are so many obstacles to making a living farming. Why do you do it?
Bunting: Well, I like farming. It's flexible. I like the independence. There's not as much independence now as there used to be, because I'm on contract on some of the stuff. But I like being a small businessman.

My grandfather's dead now, but last year he'd come out to farm some. My father was there—he and I do everything together. And my 10-year-old son is there working with me every day when school is out. I count that as a real advantage, the relationship that he and I have. I'll pay in lower income to have that type of relationship. To be out there and be able to look at my grandfather, my father, myself, and my son there on the land…

> "WHEN YOU GET FARMING INTO THE HANDS OF A FEW, SHORT-TERM GAIN IS WHAT THEY'RE GOING TO BE AFTER. THEY'RE NOT GOING TO BE TRYING TO SAVE THE LAND TO PASS ON FROM GENERATION TO GENERATION."

Resources: Maren Anderson, "Un-FAIR to Small Farmers," *Dollars & Sense* (September 2001); Rob Scott, "Exported to Death: The Failure of Agricultural Deregulation," *Dollars & Sense* (January 2000).

SEPTEMBER 11 AND THE RESTRUCTURING OF THE AIRLINE INDUSTRY

BY RODNEY WARD

On September 11, 2001, stunned flight attendants and pilots learned that workplaces just like theirs had been transformed into lethal missiles. Flight workers lucky enough not to be on one of the hijacked planes prepared frantically for orders to land at the nearest airport. Crews then worked to calm passengers and arrange for transportation and lodging. In some cases, school gymnasiums accommodated passengers and crew, while church buses provided rides to the nearest sizeable city.

Through the four-day grounding of the U.S. civilian airlines, airline unions' Employee Assistance Programs worked overtime to provide support for traumatized workers. Crews themselves huddled together in front of TVs, watching as the nightmare unfolded before them, worrying about their friends and future.

As the first flights began again on September 15, some crews refused to fly, not confident of airport security. Those who steeled themselves to work entered a strange new workplace. With no guidance from the airlines or the Federal Aviation Administration (FAA) on how to handle potential future hijackings, flight attendants inventoried galleys for objects they could use as defensive weapons. Shell-shocked passengers sometimes hugged flight attendants as they boarded. Many crewmembers barely contained tears, often hiding in galleys to avoid alarming passengers.

But as airline workers returned to the skies, a new danger loomed: layoffs. On September 15, Continental announced that it would cut 12,000 jobs. One by one, the other airlines followed suit: United and American announced 20,000 layoffs each; Northwest, 10,000; US Airways, 11,000. Delta forecast eliminating 13,000. As the toll topped 140,000, Washington Post writer David Montgomery quipped: "What thanks are flight attendants getting? How does this sound: You're fired."

The September 11 catastrophe hit the airline industry hard, but it also opened the door for airlines to accelerate the restructuring they already had underway. Many airlines, including giants like US Airways, were in bad shape before September 11. And the industry's agenda already included layoffs, mergers, greater restrictions on airline workers' rights, and a global deregulation of air travel. If post-9/11 politics allow the airlines to impose these changes, this will hurt not only airline workers, but also working people beyond the aviation industry.

THE EXECUTIVE RESPONSE

Within hours of the September 11 hijackings, an army of airline lobbyists descended on Congress (whose members have received $12 million in airline-industry contributions since 1998). The mission: Demand a massive taxpayer bailout for the industry (as much as $24 billion). If Congress failed to pony up the cash, the airlines would become "a major casualty of war," argued Delta CEO Leo Mullin.

While pleading their case, the airlines neglected to request any aid for the airline workers they were preparing to dump. Both houses of Congress defeated amendments, proposed by House Minority Leader Richard Gephardt (D-Mo.) and Sen. Jean Carnahan (D-Mo.), to provide relief to laid-off workers. Greg Crist, the spokesperson for House Majority Leader Dick Armey (R-Texas), rationalized his boss's opposition as "focused on getting the airline industry back on its feet and [thus] getting these people back on the job. An expanded unemployment insurance benefit won't do anything to get you back on the job." It took six more months for Congress to provide even meager aid supplements for airline workers. (Even then, the March 9, 2002 unemployment extension legislation tacked on $8 in corporate tax breaks for every $1 spent on aid to laid-off workers.)

Rather than simply neglecting workers, however, the bailout does worse—it encourages attacks on union contracts and working conditions. Office of Management and Budget regulations state that airlines getting bailout money should provide a "demonstration of concessions by the air carrier's security holders, other creditors, or employees…." Not surprisingly, it's the employees who are bearing the brunt.

With the war on Iraq, the airlines received yet another bailout of $3.2 billion, as well as commercial airlift contracts worth nearly half a billion dollars. Once again, the wartime bailout requires airlines to cut operating costs, which will certainly mean more pressure for concessions from workers.

Leaving aside tax cuts and new military contracts, Congress has handed the airlines $18.2 billion in taxpayer money since 2001: $8.2 billion in direct grants and $10 billion in loan guarantees. At the depressed prices of airline stocks, the government could have easily bought a controlling interest in the entire industry for $18.2 billion. In another place or another time, the airlines might have been nationalized under management by airline workers. But this is far from the reality in Washington, D.C., today.

DOWNSIZING STOCK PRICES, DOWNSIZING AIRLINES

September 11, of course, delivered a serious hit to the airlines' bottom line. Troubled Midway Airlines closed up shop on September 12, 2001. (The company has since resumed limited operations, aided by bailout money.) In the following weeks, airplanes flew mostly empty. As the airlines shed workers, they also mothballed planes. Today there are approximately 2,400 planes, about 11% of the world's civilian air fleet, parked in the Mojave Desert.

Airline shares plummeted when the stock markets reopened on September 17. US Airways and America West shares each lost over half their value in just one day. The rest of the airlines suffered declines as well. Recently, some airline stocks have recovered to pre-September 11 levels, but several, like US Airways, are still in the dumps.

Competitive pressure, already at a high pitch, intensified. While big carriers like United, American, and Northwest downsized, Southwest and startup carrier JetBlue refused to lay employees off and began to move into markets the industry giants had evacuated. The economic shockwaves rolled through the aviation industry globally. Sabena and Swissair collapsed. British Airways carried out massive layoffs. British and Japanese carriers sought mergers. Other carriers (including Iberia and Air India) announced capacity cuts and restructurings. So did aircraft manufacturers.

NOT ALL BAD NEWS, IF YOU'RE AN AIRLINE EXECUTIVE

Not all economic impacts on the airlines have been negative, however. The industry is extremely capital intensive, its two largest costs being airplanes and fuel. Deferrals on airplane orders, the retirement of older and less fuel-efficient planes, and a tremendous drop in global fuel prices have dramatically cut costs. Though labor costs represent a small portion of overall airline costs (flight attendants represent less than 4.5% of operating expenses at United, for example), slashing the workforce also cut airline expenses.

So far, over 300 airlines have collected over $8 billion in bailout grants. The lion's share has gone to industry giants United, American, and Delta. Also, on March 9, Congress passed a new tax break for the airlines. Airlines are now allowed to claim losses from 2001 and 2002 on their taxes over the last five years, a change that could mean $2 billion in cash for the companies.

In addition, the airlines routinely carry "business-interruption" insurance to cover losses due to weather, strikes, or other unforeseen circumstances. It's not clear how much airlines are collecting on claims stemming from the four-day shutdown of U.S. airports in September. The Baltimore Sun reported that, when asked about business-interruption insurance, US Airways spokesperson David Castelveter replied guiltily, "That's something I don't think we would publicly discuss with anyone." The insurance firm Swiss Re, however, estimated in March that September 11-related business-interruption claims (to all industries) will amount to $3.5–$7 billion. Undoubtedly, a big chunk will go to the airlines.

THE AVIATION WORLD BEFORE SEPTEMBER 11
Deregulation Degradation
The airline industry's chaotic state is not just a result of the September 11 attacks, but also the culmination of a quarter century of deregulation. Advocates had touted the 1978 Airline Deregulation Act as a way to increase competition and bring down ticket prices. Indeed, deregulation initially enabled upstart carriers to get in the air and made flying affordable for many people who had never flown before.

But that was not the whole story. Since deregulation, service to smaller, less profitable cities has suffered and pricing has become a crazy quilt of discriminatory arrangements. Travel to and from many airports has become monopolized by one or a few airlines. Nonetheless, airlines operate on very tight profit margins compared to other industries. As airline bottom lines have been squeezed, argues author Paul Stephen Dempsey, so has the margin of safety.

Deregulation resulted in a host of problems for airline workers, too. New competitive pressures caused the airline industry to lose more money in a few years than it had made in all the years prior to 1978 combined. These losses led to mergers and bankruptcies, and set the stage for leveraged buyouts. Financier Frank Lorenzo took over both Continental and Eastern, and then used Chapter 11 bankruptcy to break union contracts at both airlines.

Consolidation or death became the choices for many carriers. The competitive carnage destroyed once-great airlines such as Braniff and PanAm, and saw many others gobbled up. USAir bought PSA and Piedmont (ultimately dismantling PSA's entire West Coast operation). Delta swallowed up Western and the remains of PanAm, while Northwest took over Republic. More recently, American Airlines absorbed the venerable TWA. Not only did these mergers lead to route disruptions, but they also destroyed thousands of jobs, as overlapping sections of newly merged companies created "redundancies." The mergers also created challenges for union workforces—how to integrate seniority lists, for example. Conflicts over seniority in the American-TWA merger will likely sow internal union conflicts for years to come.

Management Mishaps

Spectacularly inspired mismanagement by airline executives actually deserves much of the blame for the state of the industry. Airline workers frequently complain that they could run the airlines better than the executives. Meanwhile, management jealously guards its decision-making prerogatives against labor input. Who's right? You be the judge.

Over a year ago, the Airline Pilots Association (ALPA) proposed to US Airways management "hedging" on fuel (purchasing options to buy fuel in the future at current prices) while prices were low. This would protect the airline against expected increases in fuel costs. Company management rejected the suggestion. After that, fuel prices skyrocketed and so did a major portion of the airline's costs. Several pilots have bitterly joked to me that the entire pilot group could work for free for a year and a half and still not make up for management's mistake.

In another case, in 2000, United Airlines stonewalled its pilots in contract negotiations to the point that pilots re-fused to volunteer for overtime. This led to 9,000 flight cancellations that summer. A key demand of the pilots was that the company hire more pilots (who wants exhausted pilots working overtime anyway?). Eventually the company gave in to the pilots' demands, but only after alienating huge numbers of passengers.

Frank Reeves of Avitas, a Virginia airline consulting firm, told the Pittsburgh Post-Gazette that the post-September 11 crisis has given management "a golden opportunity ... to write off all the bad decisions they made over the last 10 years."

And so they have. With bailout money and lucrative military contracts in hand, airline management has taken full advantage of the post-September 11 political environment. Never before has an industry been able to use *force majeure,* federal subsidies, and bankruptcy laws to roll back 50 years of workers' collective bargaining gains. But that is just what the airlines have done, and it is airline workers and taxpayers who are paying for this savage restructuring.

ARTICLE 8.3   *November 1991*

THE GOSPEL OF FREE TRADE

THE NEW EVANGELISTS

BY ARTHUR MACEWAN

In the early 1990s, the passage of the North American Free Trade Agreement marked a new epoch of U.S. economic expansion into the Americas. Today, the chimes of "free trade" are ringing out even more loudly in corporate America, as neoliberal economic policies—such as the Free Trade Area of the Americas—continue to make their way around the world.

With his article, "The Gospel of Free Trade," published in November 1991, Arthur MacEwan helped Dollars & Sense *readers to demystify the role of trade in the development of domestic economies. Drawing on the lessons of economic history, MacEwan shows that "free trade" is not the best route to economic prosperity for nations.*

Just as British corporations cheered in favor of free trade in the 19th century, the largest U.S. corporations today are pushing to reduce restraints on trade and investment. The result: downward pressure on wages and social welfare programs in both rich and poor countries, and a reduced capacity of citizens across the globe to control their own economic conditions.
—Darius Mehri

Free trade! It's the cure-all for the 1990s. With all the zeal of Christian missionaries, the U.S. government has been preaching, advocating, pushing, and coercing around the globe for "free trade."

While a Mexico-U.S.-Canada free trade pact is the immediate aim of U.S. policy, George Bush has heralded a future free trade zone from the northern coast of Canada to the southern tip of Chile. For Eastern Europe, U.S. advisers prescribe unfettered capitalism and ridicule as unworkable any move toward a "third way." Wherever any modicum of economic success appears in the Third World, free traders extol it as one more example of their program's wonders.

Free traders also praise their gospel as the proper policy at home. The path to true salvation—or economic expansion, which, in this day and age, seems to be the same thing—lies in opening our markets to foreign goods. Get rid of trade barriers, allow business to go where it wants and do what it wants. We will all get rich.

Yet the history of the United States and other advanced capitalist countries teaches us that virtually all advanced capitalist countries found economic success in protectionism, not in free trade. Likewise, heavy government intervention has characterized those cases of rapid and sustained economic growth in the Third World.

Free trade, does, however, have its uses. Highly developed nations can use free trade to extend their power and their control of the world's wealth, and business can use it as a weapon against labor. Most important, free trade can limit efforts to redistribute income more equally, undermine progressive social programs, and keep people from democratically controlling their economic lives.

A DAY IN THE PARK

At the beginning of the 19th century, Lowell, Massachusetts, became the premier site of the country's textile industry. Today, thanks to the Lowell National Historical Park, you can tour the huge mills, ride through the canals that redirected the Merrimack River's power to the mills, and learn the story of the textile workers, from the Yankee "mill girls" of the 1820s through the various waves of immigrant laborers who poured into the city over the next century.

During a day in the park, visitors get a graphic picture of the importance of 19th-century industry to the economic growth and prosperity of the United States. Lowell and the other mill towns of the era were centers of growth. They not only created a demand for Southern cotton, they also created a demand for new machinery, maintenance of old machinery, parts, dyes, skills, construction materials, construction machinery, more skills, equipment to move the raw materials and products, parts maintenance for that equipment, and still more skills. The mill towns also created markets—concentrated groups of wage earners who needed to buy products to sustain themselves. As centers of economic activity, Lowell and similar mill towns contributed to U.S. economic growth far beyond the value of the textiles they produced.

The U.S. textile industry emerged decades after the industrial revolution had spawned Britain's powerful textile industry. Nonetheless, it survived and prospered. British linens inundated markets throughout the world in the early 19th century, as the British navy nurtured free trade and kept ports open for commerce. In the United States, however, hostilities leading up to the War of 1812 and then a substantial tariff made British textiles relatively expensive. These limitations on trade allowed the Lowell mills to prosper, acting as a catalyst for other industries and helping to create the skilled work force at the center of U.S. economic expansion.

Beyond textiles, however, tariffs did not play a great role in the United States during the early 19th century. South-ern planters had considerable power, and while they were willing to make some compromises, they opposed protecting manufacturing in general because that protection forced up the price of the goods they purchased with their cotton revenues. The Civil War wiped out Southern opposition to protectionism, and from the 1860s through World War I, U.S. industry prospered behind considerable tariff barriers.

DIFFERENT COUNTRIES, SIMILAR STORIES

The story of the importance of protectionism in bringing economic growth has been repeated, with local variations, in almost all other advanced capitalist countries. During the late 19th century, Germany entered the major league of international economic powers with substantial protection and government support for its industries. Likewise, in 19th-century France and Italy, national consolidation behind protectionist barriers was a key to economic development.

Only Britain—which entered the industrial era first—might be touted as an example of successful development without tariff protection. Yet, in addition to starting first, Britain built its industry through the expansion of its empire and the British navy, hardly prime ingredients in any recipe for free trade.

Japan provides a particularly important case of successful government protection and support for industrial development. In the post-World War II era, when the Japanese established the foundations for the modern "miracle," the government rejected free trade and extensive foreign investment and instead promoted its national firms.

WHEREVER ANY MODICUM OF ECONOMIC SUCCESS IN THE THIRD WORLD APPEARS, FREE TRADERS EXTOL IT AS ONE MORE EXAMPLE OF THEIR PROGRAM'S WONDERS.

In the 1950s, for example, the government protected the country's fledgling auto firms from foreign competition. At first, quotas limited imports to $500,000 (in current dollars) each year; in the 1960s, prohibitively high tariffs replaced the quotas. Furthermore, the Japanese allowed foreign investment only insofar as it contributed to developing domestic industry. The government encouraged Japanese companies to import foreign technology, but required them to produce 90% of parts domestically within five years.

The Japanese also protected their computer industry. In the early 1970s, as the industry was developing, companies and individuals could only purchase a foreign machine if a suitable Japanese model was not available. IBM was allowed to produce within the country, but only when it licensed basic patents to Japanese firms. And IBM computers produced in Japan were treated as foreign-made machines.

Today, while Japan towers as the world's most dynamic industrial and financial power, one looks in vain for the role free trade played in its success. The Japanese government provided an effective framework, support, and protection for the country's capitalist development.

Likewise, in the Third World, capitalism has generated high rates of economic growth where government involvement, and not free trade, played the central role. South Korea is the most striking case. "Korea is an example of a country that grew very fast and yet violated the canons of conventional economic wisdom," writes Alice Amsden in *Asia's Next Giant: South Korea and Late Industrialization,* widely acclaimed as the most important recent book on the Korean economy. "In Korea, instead of the market mechanism allocating resources and guiding private entrepreneurship, the government made most of the pivotal investment decisions. Instead of firms operating in a competitive market structure, they each operated with an extraordinary degree of market control, protected from foreign competition."

> FREE TRADE IS A WEAPON IN THE HANDS OF BUSINESS WHEN IT OPPOSES ANY PROGRESSIVE SOCIAL PROGRAMS.

With Mexico, three recent years of relatively moderate growth, about 3-4% per year, have led the purveyors of free trade to claim it as one of their success stories. Yet Mexico has been opening its economy increasingly since the early 1980s, and most of the decade was an utter disaster. Even if the 1980s are written off as the cost of transition, the recent success does not compare well with what Mexico achieved in the era when its government intervened heavily in the economy and protected national industry. From 1940 to 1980, with policies of state-led economic development and extensive limits on imports, Mexican national output grew at the high rate of about 6% per year.

The recent Mexican experience does put to rest any ideas that free market policies will improve the living conditions for the masses of the people in the Third World. The Mexican government has paved the road for free trade policies by reducing or eliminating social welfare programs. In addition, between 1976 and 1990, the real minimum wage declined by 60%. Mexico's increasing orientation toward foreign trade has also destroyed the country's self-sufficiency in food, and the influx of foreign food grains has forced small farmers off the land and into the ranks of the urban unemployed.

THE USES OF FREE TRADE

While free trade is not the best economic growth or development policy, the largest and most powerful firms in many countries find it highly profitable. As Britain led the cheers for free trade in the early 19th century, when its own industry was already firmly established, so the United States—or at least many firms based in the United States—finds it a profitable policy in the late 20th century.

For U.S. firms, access to foreign markets is a high priority. Mexico may be relatively poor, but with a population of 85 million it provides a substantial market. Furthermore, Mexican labor is cheap; using modern production techniques, Mexican workers can be as productive as workers in the United States. For U.S. firms to obtain full access to the Mexican market, the United States must open its borders to Mexican goods. Also, if U.S. firms are to take full advantage of cheap foreign labor and sell the goods produced abroad to U.S. consumers, the United States must be open to imports.

On the other side of the border, wealthy Mexicans face a choice between advancing their interests through national development or advancing their interests through ties to U.S. firms and access to U.S. markets. For many years, they chose the former route. This led to some development of the Mexican economy but also—due to corruption and the massive power of the ruling party—created huge concentrations of wealth in the hands of a few small groups of firms and individuals. Eventually, these groups came into conflict with their own government over regulation and taxation. Having benefited from government largesse, they now see their fortunes in greater freedom from government control and, particularly, in greater access to foreign markets and partnerships with large foreign companies. National development is a secondary concern when more involvement with international commerce will produce greater riches quicker.

In addition, the old program of state-led development in Mexico ran into severe problems. These problems came to the surface in the 1980s with the international debt crisis. Owing huge amounts of money to foreign banks, the Mexican government was forced to respond to pressure from the International Monetary Fund, the U.S. government, and large international banks. That pressure meshed with the pressure coming from Mexico's own richest elites, and the result has been the move toward free trade and a greater opening of the Mexican economy to foreign investment.

Of course, in the United States, Mexico, and elsewhere, advocates of free trade claim that their policies are in everyone's interest. Free trade, they point out, will mean cheaper products for all. Consumers in the United States, who are mostly workers, will be richer because their wages will buy more. In both Mexico and the United States, they argue, rising trade will create more jobs. If some workers lose their jobs because cheaper imported goods are available, export industries will produce new ones.

Such arguments obscure many of the most important issues in the free trade debate. Stated, as they usually are, as universal truths, these arguments are plain silly. No one, for example, touring the Lowell National Historical Park could seriously argue that people in the United States would have been better off had there been no tariff on textiles. Yes, in 1820, they could have purchased textile goods more cheaply, but the cost would have been an industrially backward, impoverished nation. One could make the same point with the Japanese auto and computer industries, or indeed with numerous other examples from the last two centuries of capitalist development.

In the modern era, even though the United States already has a relatively developed economy with highly skilled workers, a freely open international economy does not serve the interests of U.S. workers, though it will benefit large firms. U.S. workers today are in competition with workers around the globe. Many different workers in many different places can produce the same goods and services. Thus, an international economy governed by the free trade agenda will bring down wages for U.S. workers.

The problem is not simply that of workers in a few industries—such as auto and steel—where import competition is the most obvious and immediate problem. A country's openness to the international economy affects the entire structure of earnings in that country. Free trade forces down the general level of wages across the board, even of those workers not directly affected by imports. The simple fact is that when companies can produce the same products in several different places, it is owners who gain because they can move their factories and funds around much more easily than workers can move themselves around. Capital is mobile, labor is much less mobile. Businesses, not workers, gain from having a larger territory in which to roam.

CONTROL OVER OUR ECONOMIC LIVES

But the difficulties with free trade do not end with wages. Free trade is a weapon in the hands of business when it opposes any progressive social programs. Efforts to place environmental restrictions on firms are met with the threat of moving production abroad. Higher taxes to improve the schools? Business threatens to go elsewhere. Better health and safety regulations? The same response.

Some might argue that the losses from free trade for people in the United States will be balanced by gains for most people in poor countries—lower wages in the United States, but higher wages in Mexico. Free trade, then, would bring about international equality. Not likely. In fact, as pointed out above, free trade reforms in Mexico have helped force down wages and reduce social welfare programs, processes rationalized by efforts to make Mexican goods competitive on international markets.

Gains for Mexican workers, like those for U.S. workers, depend on their power in relation to business. Free trade and the imperative of international "competitiveness" are just as much weapons in the hands of firms operating in Mexico as they are for firms operating in the United States. The great mobility of capital is business's best trump card in dealing with labor and popular demands for social change—in the United States, Mexico, and elsewhere.

None of this means that people should demand that their economies operate as fortresses, protected from all foreign economic incursions. There are great gains that can be obtained from international economic relations—when a nation manages those relations in the interests of the great majority of the people. Protectionism often simply supports narrow vested interests, corrupt officials, and wealthy industrialists. In rejecting free trade, we should move beyond traditional protectionism.

Yet, at this time, rejecting free trade is an essential first step. Free trade places all the cards in the hands of business. More than ever, free trade would subject us to the "bottom line," or at least the bottom line as calculated by those who own and run large companies.

For any economy to operate in the interest of the great majority, people's conscious choices—about the environment, income distribution, safety, and health—must command the economy. The politics of democratic decision-making must control business. In today's world, politics operates primarily on a national level. To give up control over our national economy—as does any people that accepts free trade—is to give up control over our economic lives.

Resources: "The New Gospel: North American Free Trade," *NACLA's Report on the Americas* 24(6), May 1991; Robert Pollin and Alexander Cockburn, "Capitalism and its Specters: The World, the Free Market and the Left," *The Nation*, 25 February 1991; P. Armstrong, A. Glyn, and J. Harrison, *Capitalism Since World War II*, 1984.

HOW HAS NAFTA AFFECTED TRADE AND EMPLOYMENT?

BY ELLEN FRANK

Dear Dr. Dollar:

Free-traders claim that free trade will increase U.S. exports, providing more jobs for Americans. So I would expect that NAFTA increased U.S. exports and reduced our trade deficit. I would also expect to see employment increase both in our country and in our trading partners. Has that in fact happened?

—*Lane Smith, Ronkonkoma, NY*

Since the North American Free Trade Agreement (NAFTA) between the United States, Mexico, and Canada went into effect, trade within North America has increased dramatically. Exports from the United States to Mexico have risen 150% and exports to Canada are up 66%. This much is beyond dispute.

NAFTA's effects on employment, on the other hand, are hotly debated. Clinton administration officials estimated in the late 1990s that expanded trade in North America had created over 300,000 new U.S. jobs. Economic Policy Institute (EPI) economists Robert Scott and Jesse Rothstein contend, however, that such claims amount to "trying to balance a checkbook by counting the deposits and not the withdrawals."

This is because NAFTA and other trade agreements have also increased U.S. imports from Canada and Mexico—and by quite a lot more than exports. Since 1993, America's trade deficit with its North American trading partners (exports minus imports) has ballooned from $16 billion to $82 billion annually. As Scott points out, "increases in U.S. exports create jobs in this country, but increases in imports destroy jobs because the imports displace goods that otherwise would have been made in the U.S. by domestic workers."

Employment in virtually all U.S. manufacturing industries has declined since NAFTA went into effect. Count-

ing jobs that actually left the United States plus those that would have been created if not for rising imports, EPI estimates that NAFTA caused a net loss of 440,000 U.S. jobs. In fact, during the 1990s, the overall U.S. trade deficit quadrupled, resulting in a net loss of 3 million jobs, according to EPI president Jeff Faux.

Of course, in a large and complex economy, trade is only one of many factors that affect job creation, and its influence is difficult to isolate. As trade expanded during the 1990s, for example, the United States also experienced an investment boom that created jobs faster than rising imports destroyed them; overall, the number of jobs in the United States has risen by 28 million since 1994.

Any free-trade booster worth her lobbying fees would argue that the boom itself resulted from liberalized trade. Lower trade and investment barriers, the story goes, unleash entrepreneurial talents, spurring innovation and productivity gains. Old jobs lost are offset by new jobs gained, and falling wages by cheaper prices on imported goods. Moreover, free-traders contend, any reckoning of NAFTA's impact should tote up new jobs and factories in Mexico against shuttered plants in the United States.

So what about NAFTA's effect on Mexico? In a study for the Interhemispheric Resource Center, analysts Timothy Wise and Kevin Gallagher conclude that NAFTA has given Mexico "trade without development." Since NAFTA weakened barriers to U.S. investment in Mexico, foreign investment into the country tripled and exports grew rapidly. But the development promised by free-trade advocates never materialized. Mexican employment did grow during the early years of NAFTA, but in recent years, it has declined as mobile manu-

facturers have sought even cheaper labor in Asia. Mexican manufacturing wages fell 21% during the 1990s and poverty worsened.

Wise's and Gallagher's findings echo the conclusions of Harvard development specialist Dani Rodrik. Poor countries that turn to trade as a cure for poverty find themselves ensnared in the "mercantilist fallacy": they can't all export their way to riches, since one country's exports are another's imports. Someone has to buy all this stuff. The United States, with its annual trade deficit approaching $500 billion, is the world's buyer and its manufacturing industries suffer as a result. But poor countries don't fare much better. They face increasing competition from low-wage manufacturers in other poor countries, and world markets are now saturated with cheap apparel and electronics, driving prices and wages down.

The result is one thing that almost everybody who studies trade now agrees upon. Whatever else they have wrought—more jobs, fewer jobs, more or less poverty—globalized trade and production coincide with greater inequality both within and between countries. The reasons for this are complex—globalization weakens unions, strengthens multinationals, and increases competition and insecurity all around—but the data are clear. Markets do not distribute wealth equitably.

Resources: Robert Scott and Jesse Rothstein, "NAFTA and the States: Job Destruction is Widespread," <www.epinet.org>; Jeff Faux, "Why U.S. Manufacturing Needs a 'Strategic Pause in Trade Policy,'" Testimony before the Senate Committee on Commerce, Sciences and Transportation, June 21, 2001; Timothy Wise and Kevin Gallagher, "NAFTA: A Cautionary Tale," *FPIF Global Affairs Commentary*, 2002; Dani Rodrik, *The New Global Economy and Developing Countries: Making Openness Work* (Overseas Development Council, 1999).

IS THE UNITED STATES A POLLUTION HAVEN?

BY FRANK ACKERMAN

Free trade, according to its critics, runs the risk of creating pollution havens—countries where lax environmental standards allow dirty industries to expand. Poor countries are the usual suspects; perhaps poverty drives them to desperate strategies, such as specializing in the most polluting industries.

But could the United States be a pollution haven? A look at agriculture under NAFTA, particularly the trade in corn, suggests that at least one polluting industry is thriving in the United States as a result of free trade.

In narrow economic terms, the United States is winning the corn market. U.S. corn exports to Mexico have doubled since 1994, NAFTA's first year, to more than five million tons annually. Cheap U.S. corn is undermining traditional production in Mexico; prices there have dropped 27% in just a few years, and a quarter of the corn consumed in Mexico is now grown in the United States. But in environmental terms, the U.S. victory comes at a great cost.

While the United States may not have more lax environmental *standards* than Mexico, when it comes to corn U.S. agriculture certainly uses more polluting *methods*. As it is grown in the United States, corn requires significantly more chemicals per acre than wheat or soybeans, the other two leading field crops. Runoff of excess nitrogen fertilizer causes water pollution, and has created a huge "dead zone" in the Gulf of Mexico around the mouth of the Mississippi River. Intensive application of toxic herbicides and insecticides threatens the health of farm workers, farming communities, and consumers. Genetically modified corn, which now accounts for about one-fifth of U.S. production, poses unknown long-term risks to consumers and to ecosystems.

Growing corn in very dry areas, where irrigation is required, causes more environmental problems. The United States also has a higher percentage of irrigated acreage than Mexico. While the traditional Corn Belt enjoys ample rainfall and does not need irrigation, 15% of U.S. corn acreage—almost all of it in Nebraska, Kansas, the

> IN NARROW ECONOMIC TERMS, THE UNITED STATES IS WINNING THE NORTH AMERICAN CORN MARKET, BUT IN ENVIRONMENTAL TERMS, THE VICTORY COMES AT A GREAT COST.

Texas panhandle, and eastern Colorado—is now irrigated. These areas draw water from the Ogallala aquifer, a gigantic underground reservoir, much faster than the aquifer naturally refills. If present rates of overuse continue, the Ogallala, which now contains as much fresh water as Lake Huron, will be drained down to unusable levels within a few decades, causing a crisis for the huge areas of the plains states that depend on it for water supplies. Government subsidies, in years past, helped farmers buy the equipment needed to pump water out of the Ogallala, contributing to the impending crisis.

Moreover, the corn borer, a leading insect pest that likes to eat corn plants, flourishes best in dry climates. Thus the "irrigation states," particularly Texas

and Colorado, are the hardest hit by corn borers. Corn growers in dry states have the greatest need for insecticides; they also have the greatest motivation to use genetically modified corn, which is designed to repel corn borers.

Sales to Mexico are particularly important to the United States because many countries are refusing to accept genetically modified corn. Europe no longer imports U.S. corn for this reason, and Japan and several East Asian countries may follow suit. Mexico prohibits growing genetically modified corn, but still allows it to be imported; it is one of the largest remaining markets where U.S. exports are not challenged on this issue.

Despite Mexico's ban, genetically modified corn was recently found growing in a remote rural area in the southern state of Oaxaca. As the ancestral home of corn, Mexico possesses a unique and irreplaceable genetic diversity. Although the extent of the problem is still uncertain, the unplanned and uncontrolled spread of artificially engineered plants from the United States could potentially contaminate Mexico's numerous naturally occurring corn varieties.

An even greater threat is the economic impact of cheap U.S. imports on peasant farmers and rural communities. Traditional farming practices, evolved over thousands of years, use combinations of different natural varieties of corn carefully matched to local conditions. Lose these traditions, and we will lose a living reservoir of biodiversity in the country of origin of one of the world's most important food grains.

The United States has won the North American corn market. But the cost looks increasingly unbearable when viewed through the lens of the U.S. environment, or of Mexico's biodiversity.

September/October 2001

SWEATSHOPS 101

LESSONS IN MONITORING APPAREL PRODUCTION AROUND THE WORLD

BY DARA O'ROURKE

Navy blue sweatshirts bearing a single foreign word, Michigan, and a well-known logo, the Nike swoosh, were piled high in a small room off the main factory floor. After cutting, stitching, and embroidering by the 1,100 workers outside, the sweatshirts landed in the spot-cleaning room, where six young Indonesian women prepared the garments for shipment to student stores and NikeTowns across America. The women spent hour after hour using chemical solvents to rid the sweatshirts of smudges and stains. With poor ventilation, ill-fitting respiratory protection, no gloves, and no chemical hazard training, the women sprayed solvents and aerosol cleaners containing benzene, methylene chloride, and perchloroethylene, all carcinogens, on the garments.

It used to be that the only thing people wondered when you wore a Harvard or Michigan sweatshirt was whether you had actually gone there. More and more, though, people are wondering out loud where that sweatshirt was made, and whether any workers were exploited in making it. Students, labor activists, and human-rights groups have spearheaded a movement demanding to know what really lies beneath their university logos, and whether our public universities and private colleges are profiting from global sweatshop production.

WHERE WAS THAT SWEATSHIRT MADE?

So far, few universities have been able to answer these questions. Universities generally don't even know where their products are produced, let alone whether workers were endangered to produce them. Indeed, with global outsourcing many brand name companies cannot trace the supply chains which lead to the student store, and are blissfully ignorant of conditions in these factories.

Under pressure from student activists across the country, a small group of university administrators decided it was time to find out more about the garments bearing their

schools' names and logos. As part of a collaborative research project, called the "Independent University Initiative" (IUI), funded by Harvard University, the University of Notre Dame, Ohio State University, the University of California, and the University of Michigan, I joined a team investigating where and under what conditions university garments were being made. Its report is available at web.mit.edu/dorourke/www. The team included staff from the business association Business for Social Responsibility, the nonprofit Investor Responsibility Research Center, and the accounting firm PricewaterhouseCoopers (PwC). PwC was responsible for auditing the labor conditions in each of the factories included in the study. At the request of student activists, I joined the team as an outside evaluator.

The IUI research team evaluated garment manufacturing for the top apparel companies licensing the logos of these five universities. It looked at factories subcontracted by nine companies, including adidas, Champion, and Nike. The nine alone outsource university apparel to over 180 factories in 26 countries. This may sound like a lot, but it is actually the tip of the global production iceberg. Americans bought about $2.5 billion worth of university-logo garments in 1999. Overall, however, U.S. apparel sales totaled over $180 billion. There are an estimated 80,000 factories around the world producing garments for the U.S. market. The university garment industry is important not so much for its size, but for the critical opening it provides onto the larger industry.

The research team visited factories in the top seven countries producing apparel for the nine companies: China, El Salvador, Korea, Mexico, Pakistan, Thailand, and the United States. It inspected 13 work sites in all. I personally inspected factories for the project in China and Korea, and then inspected factories in Indonesia on my own to see what things looked like outside the official process. Through this research I discovered not only exploitative and hazardous working conditions, but also an official monitoring process designed to gloss over the biggest problems of the apparel industry. PwC auditors found minor violations of labor laws and codes of conduct, but missed major labor problems including serious health and safety hazards, barriers to freedom of association, and violations of overtime and wage laws. This was a learning experience I call "Sweatshops 101."

Lesson #1
Global Outsourcing

The garment industry is extremely complicated and highly disaggregated. The industry has multiple layers of licensees, brokers, jobbers, importer-exporters, component suppliers, and subcontractors on top of subcontractors.

The University of Michigan does not manufacture any of the products bearing its name. Nor does Notre Dame nor Harvard nor any other university. These schools simply license their names to apparel makers and other companies for a percentage of the sale—generally around 7% of the retail price for each T-shirt, sweatshirt, or key chain. Until recently, the universities had little interest in even knowing who produced their goods. If they tracked this at all, it was to catch companies using their logos without paying the licensing fee.

Sometimes the companies that license university names and logos own the factories where the apparel is produced. But more often the licensees simply contract production out to factories in developing countries. Nike owns none of the hundreds of factories that produce its garments and athletic shoes.

A sweatshirt factory itself may have multiple subcontractors who produce the fabric, embroider the logo, or stitch sub-components. This global supply chain stretches from the university administration building, to the corporate office of the licensee companies, to large-scale factories in China and Mexico, to small-scale sub-contractor factories everywhere in between, and in some cases, all the way to women stitching garments in their living rooms.

Lesson #2
The Global Shell Game

The global garment industry is highly mobile, with contracts continuously shifting from subcontractor to subcontractor within and between countries. Licensees can move production between subcontractors after one year, one month, or even as little as one week.

It took the university research team three months to get from the licensee companies a list of the factories producing university-logo garments. However, because the actual factories producing university goods at any one time change so fast, by the time I had planned a trip to China and Korea to visit factories, the lists were essentially obsolete. One licensee in Korea had replaced eight of its eleven factories with new factories by the time I arrived in town. Over a four month period, the company had contracted with twenty one different factories. A range of factors—including price competition between contractors, changes in fashions (and factories capable of filling orders), fluctuations in exchange rates, and changing import quotas for different countries—is responsible for this constant state of flux.

Even after double-checking with a licensee, in almost every country the project team would arrive at the factory gates only to be told that the factories we planned to inspect were no longer producing university goods. Of course, some of this may have been the licensees playing games. Faced with inspections, some may have decided to shift production out of the chosen factory, or at least to tell us that it had been shifted.

Some of the largest, most profitable apparel firms in the world, known for their management prowess, however, simply did not know where their products were being produced. When asked how many factories Disney had around the world, company execs guessed there were 1,500 to 1,800 factories producing their garments, toys, videos, and other goods. As it turns out, they were only off by an order of magnitude. So far the company has counted over 20,000 factories around the world producing Disney-branded goods. Only recent exposés by labor, human rights, and environmental activists have convinced these companies that they need better control over their supply chains.

Lesson #3
Normal Operating Conditions

The day an inspector visits a factory is not a normal day. Any factory that has prior knowledge of an inspection is very likely to make changes on the day of the visit.

In a Nike-contracted shoe factory in Indonesia I visited in June 2000, all of the workers in the hot press section of the plant (a particularly dangerous area) were wearing brand new black dress shoes on the day of our inspection. One of the workers explained they had been given the shoes that morning and were expected to return them at the end of the shift. Managers often give workers new protective equipment—such as gloves, respirators, and even shoes—on the day of an inspection. However, as the workers have no training in how to even use this equipment, it is common to see brand-new respirators being worn below workers' noses, around their necks, or even upside down.

At one factory the university team visited in Mexico, the factory manager wanted to guarantee that the inspectors would find his factory spotless. So he locked all of the bathrooms on the day of the inspection. Workers were not allowed to use the bathrooms until the project team showed up, hours into the work day.

Licensees and subcontractors often try to subvert monitoring. They block auditors from inspecting on certain days or from visiting certain parts of a plant, claim production has moved, feign ignorance of factory locations, keep multiple sets of books on wages and hours, coach workers on responses to interviews, and threaten workers against complaining to inspectors. The university research team was unable to get around many of these obstructions.

Lesson #4
Conditions in University Factories

Factories producing university apparel often violate local laws and university codes of conduct on maximum hours of work, minimum and overtime wages, freedom of association, and health and safety protections.

In a 300-worker apparel plant in Shanghai, the university team found that many of the workers were working far in excess of maximum overtime laws. A quick review of timecards found women working over 315 hours in a month and 20 consecutive days without a day off. The legal maximum in China is only 204 hours per month, with at least one day off in seven. A sample of 25 workers showed that the average overtime worked was 101 hours, while the legal limit is 36 hours per month. One manager explained these gross violations with a shrug, saying, "Timecards are just used to make sure workers show up on time. Workers are actually paid based on a piece rate system."

The factory also had a wide range of health and safety problems, including a lack of guarding on sewing and cutting machines, high levels of cotton dust in one section of the plant, several blocked aisles and fire exits, no running water in certain toilets, no information for workers on the hazardous chemicals they were using, and a lack of protective equipment for the workers.

Living conditions for the workers who lived in a dormitory on site were also poor. The dormitory had 12 women packed into each room on six bunk beds. Each floor had four rooms (48 women) and only one bathroom. These bathrooms had only two shower heads and four toilet stalls each, and no dividers between them.

And what of workers' rights to complain or demand better conditions? The union in this factory was openly being run by the management. While 70% of workers were "members" of the union, one manager explained, "We don't have U.S.-style unions here." No workers had ever tried to take control of this group or to form an independent union.

Lesson #5
The Challenges of Monitoring

Finding a dozen factories is relatively easy compared to the job of tracking the thousands of rapidly changing factories that produce university goods each year. Systematically monitoring and evaluating their practices on wages, hours, discrimination, and health and safety issues is an even bigger challenge.

Most universities don't have the capacity to individually monitor the conditions in "their" factories, so some are joining together to create cooperative monitoring programs. The concept behind "independent monitoring" is to have a consulting firm or non-governmental organization inspect and evaluate a factory's compliance with a code of conduct. There are now two major university monitoring systems. The Fair Labor Association (FLA) now has over 157 universities as members, and the Worker Rights Consortium (WRC) has over 80 affiliated universities. (The four smaller monitoring initiatives are Social Accountability International (SA8000), the Ethical Trading Initiative, the Clean Clothes Campaign, and the Worldwide Responsible Apparel Production (WRAP) program.)

The FLA emerged from the Clinton-convened "White House Apparel Industry Partnership" in 1998. It is supported by a small group of apparel companies including Nike, Reebok, adidas, Levi-Strauss, Liz Claiborne, and Philips Van Heusen. Students and labor-rights advocates have criticized the group for being industry-dominated and for allowing companies to monitor only 10% of their factories each year, to use monitors that the companies pay directly, to control when and where monitors inspect, and to restrict the information released to the public after the audits.

The United Students Against Sweatshops (USAS) and UNITE (the largest garment-workers' union in the United States) founded the WRC in 1999 as an alternative to the FLA. The WRC promotes systems for verifying factory conditions after workers have complained or after inspections have occurred, and to create greater public disclosure of conditions. The WRC differs from the FLA in that it refuses to certify that any company meets a code of conduct. The group argues that because of the problems of monitoring, it is simply not possible to systematically monitor or certify a company's compliance. Some universities and companies have criticized the WRC as being a haphazard "gotcha" monitoring system whose governing body excludes the very companies that must be part of solving these problems.

Both groups profess to support the International Labour Organization's core labor standards, including upholding workers' rights to freedom of association and collective bargaining, and prohibiting forced labor, child labor, and discrimination in the workplace. The WRC, however, goes further in advocating that workers be paid a "living wage," and that women's rights receive particular attention. Both programs assert a strong role for local NGOs, unions, and workers. However, the two have widely varying levels of transparency and public disclosure, and very different systems of sanctions and penalties.

Lesson #6
How Not To Monitor

Corporate-sponsored monitoring systems seem almost designed to miss the most critical issues in the factories they inspect. Auditors often act as if they are on the side of management rather than the workers.

PricewaterhouseCoopers (PwC) is the largest private monitor of codes of conduct and corporate labor practices in the world. The company performed over 6,000 factory audits in the year 2000, including monitoring for Nike, Disney, Walmart, and the Gap. (PwC recently announced that they were spinning off their labor monitoring services into a firm called Global Social Compliance.) PwC monitors for many of the top university licensees, and was hired as the monitor for the university project. Like other corporate monitors, the company has been criticized for covering up problems and assuaging the public conscience about sweatshop conditions that have not really been resolved.

PwC's monitoring systems epitomize current corporate monitoring efforts. The firm sends two auditors—who are actually financial accountants with minimal training on labor issues—into each factory for eight hours. The auditors use a checklist and a standard interview form to evaluate legal compliance, wages and benefits, working hours, freedom of association and collective bargaining, child labor, forced labor, disciplinary practices, and health and safety.

On the university project, PwC auditors failed to adequately examine any major issue in the factories I saw them inspect. In factories in Korea and Indonesia, PwC auditors completely missed exposure to toxic chemicals, something which could eventually cost workers their lives from cancer. In Korea, the auditors saw no problem in managers violating overtime wage laws. In China, the auditors went so far as to recommend ways for the managers to circumvent local laws on overtime hours, essentially providing advice on how to break university codes of conduct. And the auditors in Korea simply skipped the questions on workers' right to organize in their worker interviews, explaining, "They don't have a union in this factory, so those questions aren't relevant."

The PwC auditing method is biased towards managers. Before an inspection, PwC auditors send managers a questionnaire explaining what will be inspected. They prepare managers at an opening meeting before each inspection. In the Chinese factory, they asked managers to enter wages and hours data into the PwC spreadsheet. Even the worker interviews were biased towards the managers. PwC auditors asked the managers to help them select workers to be interviewed, had the managers bring their personnel files, and then had the managers bring the workers into the office used for the interviews. The managers knew who was being interviewed, for how long, and on what issues. Workers knew this as well, and answered questions accordingly.

The final reports that PwC delivered to its clients gave a largely sanitized picture of the factories inspected. This is unsurprising, considering PwC's business interest in providing companies with "acceptable" audits.

WHERE TO BEGIN?

Universities face increasing public pressure to guarantee that workers are not being injured or exploited to produce their insignia products. They have no system, however, to track apparel production around the world, and often no idea where their production is occurring. Monitoring systems are still in their fledgling stages, so universities are starting from a difficult position, albeit one they have profited from for years.

What can universities do about this? They should do what they are best at: produce information. They should take the lead in demanding that corporations—beginning with those they do business with—open themselves up to public inspection and evaluation. Universities have done this before, such as during the anti-apartheid campaign for South Africa. By doing this on the sweatshop issue, universities could spur a critical dialogue on labor issues around the world.

To start, the universities could establish a central coordinating office to collect and compare information on factory performance for member universities' licensees. (The WRC has proposed such a model.) This new office would be responsible for keeping records on licensee compliance, for making this information available over the internet, for registering local NGOs and worker organizations to conduct independent verifications of factory conditions, and for assessing sanctions.

Such a program would allow universities to evaluate different strategies for improving conditions in different parts of the world. This would avoid the danger of locking in one code of conduct or one certification system. In place of sporadic media exposés embarrassing one company at a time, we would have an international system of disclosure and learning—benchmarking good performers, identifying and targeting the worst performers, and motivating improvement.

It is clearly not enough to expose one company at a time, nor to count on industry-paid consulting firms to monitor labor conditions. The building blocks of a new system depend on information. This fits the mission of universities. Universities should focus on information gathering and dissemination, and most importantly, on learning. If the universities learn nothing else from "Sweatshops 101," it is that they still have a lot of homework do to—and their next test will be coming soon.

> AUDITORS IN KOREA SIMPLY SKIPPED THE QUESTIONS ON WORKERS' RIGHT TO ORGANIZE IN THEIR WORKER INTERVIEWS, EXPLAINING, "THEY DON'T HAVE A UNION IN THIS FACTORY, SO THOSE QUESTIONS AREN'T RELEVANT."

CONTRIBUTORS

Frank Ackerman is Director of Research and Policy at the Global Development and Environment Institute at Tufts University, and a founder of *Dollars & Sense*.

Randy Albelda, a *Dollars & Sense* Associate, teaches economics at the University of Massachusetts-Boston.

David Bacon is a journalist and photographer covering labor, immigration, and the impact of the global economy on workers.

Dean Baker is co-director of the Center for Economic and Policy Research.

Phineas Baxandall teaches at Harvard University and is a former *Dollars & Sense* collective member.

Elaine Bernard is executive director of the Harvard Trade Union Program.

Annette Bernhardt is a senior associate at the Center on Wisconsin Strategy, University of Wisconsin-Madison.

Jeanette Bradley is program director of the Community Reinvestment Association of North Carolina.

Marc Breslow is co-chair of the Massachusetts Climate Action Network and a *Dollars & Sense* collective member.

Alan Durning is executive director of Northwest Environment Watch and a former senior researcher at the Worldwatch Institute.

Ellen Frank teaches economics at Emmanuel College in Boston and is a member of the *Dollars & Sense* collective.

Amy Gluckman is a co-editor of *Dollars & Sense* and a former charter school teacher.

Barbara Goldoftas is a freelance writer based in Cambridge, Massachusetts.

Eban Goodstein teaches economics at Lewis and Clark College and is a research associate with the Economic Policy Institute.

Robin Hahnel teaches economics at American University.

Lisa Heinzerling is a professor of law at Georgetown University Law School, specializing in environmental law.

Edward S. Herman is an economist and co-author of *The Global Media: The New Missionaries of Corporate Capitalism*.

David Kiron is co-author of *The Consumer Society*.

Jabulani Leffall is a George Washington Williams Fellow for the Independent Press Association and a former editor for both the London *Financial Times* and *Variety*.

Arthur MacEwan, a *Dollars & Sense* Associate, teaches economics at the University of Massachusetts-Boston.

Anuradha Mittal is co-director of Food First/The Institute for Food and Development Policy in Oakland, California.

Amy Offner is a co-editor of *Dollars & Sense*.

Dara O'Rourke is an assistant professor of Urban Studies and Planning at the Massachusetts Institute of Technology (MIT).

Cynthia Peters is a freelance editor and writer, and political activist.

Alejandro Reuss is former co-editor of *Dollars & Sense*.

Peter Rosset is co-director of Food First/The Institute for Food and Development Policy in Oakland, California.

Jonathan Rowe is senior fellow at Redefining Progress in San Francisco and a contributing editor at the *Washington Monthly*.

Peter Skillern is executive director of the Community Reinvestment Association of North Carolina.

Chris Tilly, a *Dollars & Sense* collective member, teaches at the University of Massachusetts-Lowell.

Heidi Vogt is a former *Dollars & Sense* intern and works for the Associated Press.

Rodney Ward is the business manager at *Dollars & Sense*, a laid-off flight attendant, and a union activist in the Association of Flight Attendants (AFA).

Thad Williamson is a graduate student at Harvard University and a member of the *Dollars & Sense* collective.